Shaping Entrepreneurial Mindsets

The **Palgrave Macmillan IESE Business Collection** is designed to provide authoritative insights and comprehensive advice on specific management topics. The books are based on rigorous research produced by IESE Business School professors, covering new concepts within traditional management areas (Strategy, Leadership, Managerial Economics) as well as emerging areas of enquiry. The collection seeks to broaden the knowledge of the business field through the ongoing release of titles, with a humanistic focus in mind.

Available titles:

MANAGING eHEALTH
Magdalene Rosenmöller, Diane Whitehouse and Petra Wilson

LEADERSHIP DEVELOPMENT IN A GLOBAL WORLD
Jordi Canals

GLOBAL TRENDS
Adrian Done

MANAGEMENT ETHICS
Domènec Melé

THE ESSENTIAL FINANCE TOOLKIT
Javier Estrada

THE FUTURE OF LEADERSHIP DEVELOPMENT
Jordi Canals

HUMAN FOUNDATIONS OF MANAGEMENT
Domènec Melé and César Gonzàlez Cantón

STRATEGY AND SUSTAINABILITY
Michael Rosenberg

SHAPING ENTREPRENEURIAL MINDSETS
Jordi Canals

Forthcoming titles:

ETHICAL FINANCE
Jan Simon

Series ISBN: 9780230292499

Shaping Entrepreneurial Mindsets

Innovation and Entrepreneurship in Leadership Development

Edited by

Jordi Canals
*Dean and Professor of Economics and Strategic Management,
IESE Business School, Spain*

First published 2015 by
PALGRAVE MACMILLAN

Palgrave Macmillan in the UK is an imprint of Macmillan Publishers Limited,
registered in England, company number 785998, of Houndmills, Basingstoke,
Hampshire RG21 6XS.

Palgrave Macmillan in the US is a division of St Martin's Press LLC,
175 Fifth Avenue, New York, NY 10010.

Palgrave Macmillan is the global academic imprint of the above companies
and has companies and representatives throughout the world.

Palgrave® and Macmillan® are registered trademarks in the United States,
the United Kingdom, Europe and other countries.

ISBN 978–1–137–51665–7

This book is printed on paper suitable for recycling and made from fully
managed and sustained forest sources. Logging, pulping and manufacturing
processes are expected to conform to the environmental regulations of the
country of origin.

A catalogue record for this book is available from the British Library.

Library of Congress Cataloging-in-Publication Data
Shaping entrepreneurial mindsets : innovation and entrepreneurship in
leadership development / [edited by] Jordi Canals.
   pages cm.—(IESE business collection)
   ISBN 978–1–137–51665–7 (hardback)
   1. Entrepreneurship.   2. Leadership.   3. Corporate culture.
   I. Canals, Jordi, editor.
   HB615.S4787 2015
   658.4'092—dc23   2015019262

Typset by MPS Limited, Chennai, India.

Contents

List of Figures, Tables and Exhibits

Exhibits

Preface and Acknowledgments

Over the past decade, leadership development in international companies has mainly focused on how companies should attract and nurture local talent to better manage their global strategy and operations in new markets. This is an uphill task, but many companies have designed and implemented good corporate policies and practices to tackle this important issue.

Nevertheless, the acceleration of global economic integration is only one of the many challenges that companies will face over the next years. The need to grow internationally will remain strong, but many emerging markets will provide companies fewer growth opportunities than in the past. As some emerging countries become more mature, new local, nimble competitors will find smart ways to successfully compete with multinational firms, both at home and abroad. Technology will also exert additional pressure on traditional competitors to lower costs, and smaller local competitors will benefit from it because they have lower legacy costs. As a result, rivalry coming from growth markets, based both on low cost and innovation, will become more intense.

In a world with more volatile and uncertain growth, corporate innovation and entrepreneurship will become more important than ever to create and sustain growth opportunities. Mid-size and large companies need to accelerate innovation and the discovery of new opportunities, quickly test them and go fast to the market. In this process, companies should develop the capabilities to behave like agile entrepreneurs.

The new business landscape and the need to generate growth opportunities inside and outside the firm to push CEOs and global HR managers to rethink leadership development and adopt a different mindset regarding innovation and growth. The battle to attract, retain and develop local talent will become more complex, both in mature and growth markets. Companies should think beyond the traditional benefits of cultural diversity and consider how to help general managers develop the capabilities to operate in different geographies and business functions, with a diverse innovation and entrepreneurial mindset, and transfer the experiences and best practices across countries.

This book deals with the challenge of how to include in global leadership development programs the need that companies have to speed up innovation and entrepreneurial initiatives to sustain corporate growth. We know a few facts about what makes innovation work and why entrepreneurship in large, established companies succeeds or fails. Unfortunately, our knowledge and expertise in helping design and implement initiatives that improve leadership development along those dimensions is still small. This book tries to provide an answer to the challenge of what companies can do to generate a more solid and deeper entrepreneurial mindset among their people, and how to do it in a consistent way with the firm's strategy. It also offers some experiences on how business schools try to tackle this challenge.

This book is structured in four parts. **Part I: Nurturing Entrepreneurial and Innovation Capabilities** provides an introductory framework to understand how to boost entrepreneurial and innovation capabilities for global leadership development and highlights an agenda for top managers in this crucial area (Chapter 1).

Part II: Entrepreneurship, Intrapreneurship and Innovation includes some chapters that deal with key topics: the impact of entrepreneurship on successful companies and society (Chapter 2); developing company capabilities and organizational design for continuous innovation (Chapter 3); creating the context for sustained corporate entrepreneurship (Chapter 4); a conceptual framework to develop innovative mindsets and capabilities in large, established firms through executive education programs (Chapter 5); and business model innovation and the role of CEOs in this process (Chapter 6).

Part III: Innovative Methodologies and Learning Processes to Foster Innovation deals with some new methodological initiatives developed at business schools to boost the innovation mindset of participants and maximize learning and development. It includes new initiatives on design thinking curricula and frameworks (Chapter 7) and the design of innovative blended courses on leadership development, combining online and face-to-face courses, and their learning potential (Chapters 8 and 9).

Finally, **Part IV: Innovation at Business Schools: Creating an Entrepreneurial Learning Context for Leadership** offers an overview on different approaches to make a business school a better context for developing entrepreneurship and innovation capabilities. Chapter 10 describes how to create a unique learning ground for developing entrepreneurs. Chapter 11 opens a new perspective on how business schools should innovate by embracing wider notions than economic value creation and introduce social value explicitly. Chapter 12 explains how MBA programs can be very good development contexts for young entrepreneurs and which elements make those contexts more impactful.

These chapters share some key attributes. The first is that their authors take the top management perspective on the issues explored and how CEOs and senior managers look at leadership development and think about growth in a more uncertain world. The second attribute is their inter-disciplinary design, involving experts from different areas and experiences.

The chapters' authors come from different academic and geographical backgrounds. They include scholars in the areas of innovation, entrepreneurship, leadership development, strategy, marketing and operations. They work at international business schools in Europe, the US and Asia. Some of them are involved in developing universities and working with companies in Africa and Latin America as well. The geographical and cross-cultural expertise of the authors is diverse and deep, which gives the work a very insightful perspective.

The title of this book was inspired by R. McGrath and I. MacMillan's (2000) pioneering book *The Entrepreneurial Mindset* (Boston, MA: Harvard Business School Press) and the widespread use of the entrepreneurial mindset concept. McGrath and MacMillan provide some unique insights on the nature and implications of this mindset. Our book offers a different, complementary perspective: how to shape that entrepreneurial and innovation mindset, based on the assumption that different methodologies and frameworks can make a positive contribution to it. Moreover, we should try different and eclectic approaches, as the authors of the different chapters do in this volume.

Most of the chapters were presented at the 2014 IESE Global Leadership Conference, held in Barcelona on 3 and 4 April 2014. Conference speakers included CEOs and board members such as Isak Andic (Mango), Patricia Francis (International Trade Center), Rosa García (Siemens), Denise Kingsmill (IAG), Bruno di Leo (IBM), Hans Ulrich Maerki (ABB), Andrea Morante (Pomellato), Francisco Reynés (Abertis), Kees Storm (AB InBev), George Yeo (Kerry Logistics); senior HR vice-presidents such as Jorge Aisa Dreyfus (HSBC), Marta de las Casas (Telefonica) and Erwin Lebon (General Electric); scholars, experts and business schools deans such as Wendy Alexander (LBS), Rolf Boscheck (IMD), Srikant Datar (Harvard Business School), Marta Elvira (IESE), John Gapper (*Financial Times*), Franz Heukamp (IESE), Pankaj Ghemawat (IESE), Pedro Nueno (IESE), Michael Pich (Insead), M. Julia Prats (IESE), Bernard Ramanantsoa (HEC Paris), Sandra Sieber (IESE), Peter Tufano (Oxford Saïd Business School), Eric Weber (IESE), Zhang Weijiong (CEIBS) and Adrian Wooldridge (*The Economist*). My IESE colleagues Carlos García-Pont, Alex Lago, Elena Liquete, Javier Muñoz and Mireia Rius, and the

Alumni and Institutional Development, did a great job organizing and planning the conference.

I am very grateful to Liz Barlow and her team at Palgrave Macmillan. They have been an important partner in the intellectual effort to open new ground in studies around leadership development from different perspectives. Liz also helped improve the outline of the book and highlighted some important topics to be covered, including the title. Tamsine O'Riordan provided the initial support for the book. Kiran Bolla and Geetha Williams helped me effectively during the editing process. I am also very grateful to Teresa Planell, Míriam Freixa and Carolina Olmo, who helped me in the book-editing process with professionalism, while managing so well the daily activities of the dean's office.

Jordi Canals
IESE Business School
April 2015

List of Contributors

Caitlin N. Bowler, Research Associate, Harvard Business School

Jordi Canals, Dean and Professor of Economics and Strategic Management, IESE Business School, University of Navarra

Bruno Cassiman, Nissan Professor of Strategic Management, IESE Business School, University of Navarra, and Herman Daems Chair of Strategy and Entrepreneurship, University of Leuven

Srikant Datar, Arthur Lowes Dickinson Professor of Accounting, Harvard Business School

Tony Dávila, Alcatel-Lucent Professor of Entrepreneurship and Accounting and Control, IESE Business School, University of Navarra

Marc Epstein, Distinguished Research Professor of Management (Retired), Rice University

Pankaj Ghemawat, Anselmo Rubiralta Professor of Global Strategy, IESE Business School, University of Navarra

Franz Heukamp, Professor of Managerial Decision Sciences, IESE Business School, University of Navarra

Susanna Kislenko, PhD Candidate, IESE Business School, University of Navarra

Pedro Nueno, Bertran Foundation Professor of Entrepreneurship, IESE Business School, University of Navarra, and President, CEIBS

M. Julia Prats, Professor of Entrepreneurship, IESE Business School, University of Navarra

Bernard Ramanantsoa, Dean and Professor of Strategy and Business Policy, HEC Paris

Joan Enric Ricart, Carl Schroeder Professor of Strategic Management, IESE Business School, University of Navarra

Peter Tufano, Peter Moores Dean and Professor of Finance, Saïd Business School, University of Oxford

Eric Weber, Professor of Accounting and Control, IESE Business School, University of Navarra

Part I
Nurturing Entrepreneurial and Innovation Capabilities

1
Leadership Competencies for Innovation and Entrepreneurship: A Top Management Perspective

Jordi Canals

Introduction

The infusion of a more dynamic, innovative and entrepreneurial spirit has become an urgent need for companies, in particular in mature economies. Some social and economic trends—like decreasing population, slowing demand and stronger global rivalry—are putting additional competitive pressure on companies. The threat of disruptive innovation—mostly associated with the digital revolution—is making companies more aware of the need to build the capacity to innovate and change. Today disruption not only comes from Silicon Valley companies. Some emerging countries' companies are not only formidable cost competitors but they are also developing and applying reverse innovation—innovative products developed in emerging markets and brought to mature markets.

Unfortunately, the increasing relevance and need for innovation and entrepreneurship in established companies are some steps ahead of the formal process of developing managerial capabilities that are needed to tackle this challenge. Innovation involves creativity and willingness to experiment, but it also needs some key competencies, like discovering, framing and assessing new opportunities, or the discipline to accelerate and launch a new project to make innovation successful and sustainable. Leadership development has made great progress over the past decade, including capabilities development to work in a more global business world (Canals, 2012). Unfortunately, the development of the innovation and entrepreneurial competencies (IEC) is still a challenge for many companies. A sustainable approach to IEC development needs to integrate those competencies into the firm's innovation strategy, and the latter should be a central part of the overall firm's strategy.

This chapter focuses on how the firm's top management should approach the process of developing leadership competencies for innovation and entrepreneurship within an established company. I do not refer here to entrepreneurial or innovation competencies in general or for start-ups, but those that can be nurtured and deployed in already existing firms. In this chapter, I focus on IEC and do not deal with innovation strategy or innovation management. The IEC development aims at turning innovators into good general managers who can lead innovative projects inside firms or improving the IEC that a general manager needs to have.

This chapter presents two frameworks. The first describes leadership competencies for innovation and entrepreneurship. It provides the building blocks for a systematic development of those leadership competencies for innovation. The second framework presents some guidelines on how top managers can help develop those competencies. In section "Leadership competencies development for innovation and entrepreneurship", I outline a framework of leadership competencies for innovation and entrepreneurship. In section "How top managers add value to innovation and entrepreneurship", the role and functions of a CEO are presented in a model that includes innovation and entrepreneurship. I introduce the CIPS framework—CIPS: Context, Ideas, People, Structure—that can help top managers—CEOs, business unit heads or global HR managers—think about the development of leadership competencies for innovation and entrepreneurship. This framework is developed in the following sections and pays special attention to the assessment of new ideas. The final section provides a summary of how a CEO can help develop leadership competencies that take innovation and entrepreneurship to a higher and more sustainable level. CEOs should work on them with the conviction that, through this process, people can become better professionals and human beings. These leadership competencies not only make an organization better and with more solid competencies but they also make individuals better by developing innovation and entrepreneurial capabilities.

Leadership competencies development for innovation and entrepreneurship

Some leadership development models include a few qualities and dimensions that are related with innovation and entrepreneurship. This is the case in frameworks explaining global leadership development (Javidan et al., 2006). Nevertheless, this integration is still work in progress.

An integrative framework requires the connection of IEC with innovation strategy. We will use some basic hypotheses on innovation and innovation strategy that are needed to clarify some concepts and provide a better frame for capability development. The first is that innovation could be good or bad, depending on how it is conceived and executed, and how it is perceived by customers. Innovation should be connected with customers' experience. Effectiveness in managing innovation is important, but focusing innovation on delivering value for customers is a question of survival.

The second is that the right type of innovation depends on each company. Any company needs some degree of innovation if it wants to avoid the risk of obsolescence. How much innovation a company needs depends on the economic cycle, the industry, consumer behaviour and the firm's positioning. Some companies may need gradual innovation; others, disruptive innovation.

The third hypothesis stems from the previous one. IEC need to be aligned with the firm's innovation strategy, which should also be integrated in the wider firm's strategy. This principle highlights the fact that innovation competencies should not be defined or considered in an isolated way. They are part of a wider system of competencies that good companies should try to develop.

There is a rich literature on the capabilities of innovators (among others, McGrath and MacMillan, 2000; Dávila, Epstein and Shelton, 2006; Teece, 2007; O'Connor, Corbett and Pirantozzi, 2009; Desouza, 2011). Most of the studies on this issue focus on the specific attributes to be expected of a good innovator or entrepreneur, like discovering opportunities and pursuing them in an effective way. In this chapter, I try to offer a wider framework, based upon the knowledge, capabilities, inter-personal skills and attitudes framework (Canals, 2012).

Leadership competencies for innovation and entrepreneurship can be grouped around three categories: observe and understand customers' behavior, develop the business idea and accelerate the new project. Each category involves a set of knowledge, capabilities, inter-personal skills and attitudes—see Table 1.1.

Observe—and learn from—customers' behavior. The first category is the drive to observe customers' behavior and discover new opportunities, where other people only see threats or uninteresting pathways. This group of attributes includes the knowledge about customers, products and markets. It also includes the capabilities to understand customers and how they use products and services; to discover new

Table 1.1 Leadership competencies for innovation and entrepreneurship

Innovation & entrepreneurial activities	Competencies			
	Knowledge	Capabilities	Skills	Attitudes
1. Discover new opportunities	Customers Products Markets	Customer behavior Analysis	Listen Observe Transform into action	Entrepreneurial mindset Experiment Passion for costumers Curiosity
2. Nurturing new business ideas	Industry analysis Business functions Business plan Risk framing	Analyze Synthesize Communicate Build consensus Worst-case scenarios Set up alliances	Engage team members Listen to critics Energize Focus	Integration Determination Humility Integrity
3. Acceleration and commercialization	Organization Build a team Market development P&L management	Manage people Customer relationship Effectiveness Execution	Network Engage Focus	Speed Resilience Perseverance

ways of serving those needs, think about needs that are not currently served, and frame a new value proposition; the skills to listen and observe; and attitudes like the entrepreneurial mindset to try new things and the passion to serve customers better or fill a gap in the product offer.

Development of the business idea. The second category of competencies relates to developing and nurturing the business idea that stems from observed opportunities. In this stage, innovators need to learn and develop more general management competencies to make the project sustainable. These competencies are made up of a portfolio of knowledge, capabilities, skills and attitudes, some of them valid for any general manager, and some of them specific to innovators and entrepreneurs. Knowledge includes the notions and models of the different business functions—finance, strategy, marketing and so on—and the concepts to analyze the business idea, to develop a credible business plan, to have a specific understanding and experience on the industry, and to assess the risk the organization or investors are assuming.

There is also a set of relevant capabilities in this area: analyze and synthesize, communicate and build consensus among the different stakeholders, set up alliances and coalitions to make the project viable, convince senior managers to get the right people on board and commit resources to the project, engage potential investors, prepare specific action plans, and carefully define worst-possible scenarios with an exit plan. Inter-personal skills include the following: engage and convince team members to come up with a solid action plan, listen to critics of the project and learn from them, keep the energy around the project intense, and be grounded to stop the project if most market signals are against it. The fourth group refers to personal attitudes: the strong determination to make the project happen must be combined and balanced with a deep sense of humility that makes everybody feel the ownership of the project and keep an open mind to consider all the dimensions of the challenge, beyond the passion to see it happen.

Acceleration of the new project. The third category of competencies is related with the stage of acceleration and commercialization of the project, once its viability has been considered and tests around its feasibility have been passed. In this third stage, a new combination of competencies is needed. Knowledge on how to organize for scale and commercialization, build up a team of professionals, lead them toward market entry and market success, understanding customer relationship and managing the P&L of the project are important attributes. On the capabilities side, organizational abilities, people leadership and customer relationships are key functions that need to be developed properly. On inter-personal skills, the ability to develop relationships with customers, distributors and suppliers, and to get ready for future growth are key ingredients in this step of acceleration. It is also very important to keep listening to market reactions to understand what attributes in the offer need to be changed or adapted because customers expect it, far beyond the personal preferences of innovators. On attitudes, speed, resilience and perseverance are of utmost necessity, since indicators of success take time before they become reliable.

The different IEC presented above highlights that innovation requires some special competencies, but sustainable innovation requires champions that are able not only to launch an innovation but also make it a strong pillar within a company. This step requires innovators with strong general management competencies. This portfolio of competencies needs to be framed into a wider context. In this respect, the model of global leadership capabilities presented elsewhere (Canals, 2012) that discusses the role of knowledge, capabilities, inter-personal skills and attitudes can be applied here. IEC introduce new dimensions that make this framework richer. More important, this framework not only looks at how innovators may come up with new ideas or discover new opportunities but also at how innovators can grow into general managers, with the capabilities to move from an idea to a business plan that is implemented and, later on, into a company ready for growth. The experience with entrepreneurship and new business ventures is that many promising ideas never see the light; after they are tested, turned into prototypes and go to market, very few of them survive the passing of time. The failure rate is very high in internal corporate venturing (ICV; Burgelman and Välikangas, 2005) and in stand-alone entrepreneurial projects. Business failure has many roots. Nevertheless, the lack of competencies to turn an idea into a project, later on into a business plan and move to a full-scale launch is a very important factor.

It is true that discovering and growing individuals with those competencies is a difficult task. Nevertheless, senior managers must make sure that there are a few of them that understand the whole process and are good enough to lead a diverse team with the wisdom and strength to make a project successful. And CEOs need to provide the firm's commitment to those champions of new projects that can rejuvenate a company and add new growth potential. These are some of the key dimensions of senior managers' contributions to making companies more innovative and entrepreneurial.

How top managers add value to innovation and entrepreneurship

A recent framework organizes the CEO's job around some major functions or tasks (Canals, 2010). A CEO should develop the firm's mission and nurture its values, have a point of view about the firm's future and how to compete (strategy), grow people and develop future leaders, make decisions on resource allocation according to the strategic priorities, and design the organization to execute effectively.

In this context, the typologies of CEOs regarding innovation fit in a natural way. Some authors propose different types of roles for CEOs who foster innovation, depending on the company, the CEOs' personal attributes or the culture of the firm. Dávila and Epstain (2014) distinguish four different roles that CEOs can adopt regarding innovation: the innovation strategist, the innovation sponsor, the innovation architect and the innovation evangelist. In terms of our framework, the strategist is the CEO thinking about strategy. The evangelist is the CEO who includes innovation in the firm's mission and values. The architect is the CEO who organizes for innovation. The sponsor is the CEO who not only supports innovation with ideas but also commits resources to it. Innovation is considered as a special set of activities that are a central part of the CEO's job.

Moreover, leadership capabilities development—including innovation—should be consistent with the firm's mission and values, should be embedded in the strategy process, and should be supported by the indispensable resources and have the backing of the CEO's commitment. Innovation strategy should be coordinated and included into the firm's strategy. More specifically, IEC need to fit well within the specific innovation strategy followed by the firm.

How can a CEO support IEC development? The CIPS framework presented here is consistent with the CEOs' functions. CEOs should help develop leadership competencies for innovation and entrepreneurship in four ways or key areas—see Table 1.2. The first is the development of the right context, with a corporate culture and values that appreciate innovation and entrepreneurial mindset—Context. The second is to stimulate new ideas and concepts—Ideas—that will help serve customers better and asses them. The third is to grow general managers who can become innovators or develop innovators who can become

Table 1.2 CEO's key areas in developing leadership competencies for innovation and entrepreneurship

Context
Ideas
People
Structure and systems

general managers—People. The fourth is to organize the firm for innovation—Structure. The CIPS framework—Context, Ideas, People and Structure—provides the building blocks that help develop leadership competencies for innovation and entrepreneurship—see Table 1.2. It can be observed that this framework has a close parallelism with the CEOs tasks framework, presented above (Canals, 2012), except that in the CIPS framework the resource allocation task is considered together with strategy. We will discuss these four dimensions in the following sections.

It is also worth noting that those four areas highlighted by the CIPS framework are fully related with the activities presented in the previous section: discover new opportunities, nurturing new business ideas and acceleration. By working on the areas highlighted by CIPS, senior managers help develop the entrepreneurial capabilities.

Context

The role of culture and values has a long tradition in management and leadership development. Its impact on corporate performance over the long run is significant. The more specific question in discussing innovation and culture is how senior managers create a culture in which people, while managing the current challenges, believe that their ideas can have a positive impact on the firm and include innovation as part of people's daily jobs (O'Reilly and Tushman, 2004). A strong cultural context that encourages innovation is the best mechanism to make innovation pervasive in an organization.

This is a very relevant challenge for several reasons. The first is that established companies are not always a welcoming place for innovation that drives change. People who have been doing things in a certain way may be reluctant to change behaviors. The second is that a company needs to operate effectively in the short term and, sometimes, this may be in contradiction with innovative behaviors whose payoff will only come in the long term. The third is that general management capabilities for short-term effectiveness are different from capabilities that encourage innovation and experimentation.

Table 1.3 Some levers of an innovative corporate culture

Focus on how to improve customers' experiences
Openness to learn new ideas
Passion for quality products and services
Give people time to experiment

There are a few important levers of corporate culture that can make innovation stronger within an established firm—see Table 1.3. The first is a strong focus on customers and customer satisfaction. It may a be a surprise to observe companies whose people are not focused on serving customers but on other tasks, like organizing or becoming more cost-conscious. Any of these activities is valid for a company as far as it serves its customer better. A firm whose activities are organized to make the customers' experience much better in one or several dimensions is also a company that will be open to innovation and experimentation, and will look for innovative solutions to customers' problems. This basic principle also highlights that innovation only makes sense if it is designed to make customers' experiences better.

In connection with this attribute, openness to new ideas is also a second lever of innovation. The willingness to serve customers is matched with the determination to find new solutions to problems and challenges that customers may have. A customer's need stimulates entrepreneurial behavior and is always a great incentive to come up with creative ideas.

A third quality of an innovative culture is to instill a sense of passion among employees about the importance of quality products aiming at excellence, with the goal of meeting current or future customers' needs. Discovering new ways of meeting and surpassing customers' expectations unleashes innovation that is aligned with serving customers better.

Innovative cultures also include top managers' commitment to allocate resources and free people's time to explore new products, technologies or processes within a company. Nevertheless, this bottom-up process to innovation should be matched and reinforced by some top-down initiatives that help consolidate the importance of innovation within the firm. In the end, top managers define corporate culture, not only with clear statements of what the firm's culture is but also by walking the talk, supporting innovative good decisions on developing people, financial backing and personal interest and commitment.

Ideas

CEOs can help develop IEC by providing a context to generate new ideas on products or services, help turn them into business projects and nurture the competencies to assess them. Ideas about new products or services, new ways to serve customers, or new approaches to make manufacturing or operations simpler are at the root of relevant innovations. The determination of an entrepreneur to pursue new ideas is important, but top managers should care about the development of leadership competencies that help develop and implement new ideas.

The generation of new ideas can follow the principles described above. New ideas with a potential for impact require a focus and passion for customers and a determination to constantly improve their experience with the firm's products or services. A good understanding of the customers' experience in using the product or service is indispensable for developing innovative ideas. This is true in all types of industries: in consumer goods, using the product in the household, as P&G or Unilever do; in industrial products, co-developing solutions for customers, as Siemens or GE do; or in software and computer services, where companies like IBM rediscover new ways of designing customized solutions working with customers as one team.

Ideas that could lead to innovation and an improvement in customers' experience can be grouped in different categories. For instance, Day (2013) presents a framework of 14 different initiatives in two basic categories: initiatives that improve the firm's business model and initiatives that improve the value proposition for customers.

A simple way to organize new ideas and business insights is the following. Innovative ideas can aim at current customers or new customers not served currently by the company—in the same or different geographical markets. In both cases, companies can focus on how to serve customers better in three ways: with the same products or services at a lower price, with new products or services that improve the overall experience at the same price, or with new products or services that improve the overall experience for which customers are willing to pay a premium price.

This category of new business ideas is useful as far as it helps senior managers think about innovation initiatives and develop the necessary competencies. There are two crucial challenges that senior managers need to face in managing innovation when discussing business ideas. The first is to make sure that there is a process for generating and managing new ideas in the context of the daily operations. The second is the challenge of valuating and assessing new ideas.

Generation of new ideas

Desouza (2011) observes that organizations are chaotic in encouraging and managing new ideas. Moreover, idea innovation could lead to lack of focus. He distinguishes among the different stages that new ideas should follow: generation, mobilization, advocacy, screening, experimentation, commercialization and escalation. Dávila, Epstein and Shelton (2006) provide a useful framework for understanding the steps that new business ideas follow: generation, selection, execution and value creation. Datar and Bowler in Chapter 8 in this book offer some useful design-thinking frameworks to generate new ideas and implement them.

There are methodologies that help generate and advance some new business ideas, like the one developed by IDEO (Kelley and Littman, 2005), the business design and innovation firm; discovery-driven planning, developed by McGrath and MacMillan (2009); or methodologies developed by start-up incubators. As Miller and Wedell-Wedellsborg (2013) point out, ideas always need to be refined; their supporters need to challenge and reframe those ideas in a way that they make some sense for customers and for the company.

The experience of some innovative companies like Nestlé or Schneider highlights some specific practices and policies that help the generation of new ideas: ask current commercial and product development teams to offer every few months some new ideas on how to serve customers better and improve their overall experience; ask manufacturing and operations teams for ways to improve productivity; make operations leaner and offer some cost advantages to be translated into more value for customers; create cross-functional teams to solve problems that have not been properly tackled before or develop new solutions for customers; or create teams to think about an extension of current products or services to new groups of customers, in current or new markets. In any of those initiatives, the opportunity to work and connect with external partners, current or future customers, or colleagues from other divisions and geographies is extremely important. Innovation is not only about having a unique idea alone but also being able to get it by observing, working with others and integrating different perspectives.

The opportunities for international companies to benefit from ideas and business concepts developed in other geographies are tremendous. Bartlett and Ghoshal (1989) observed that the transfer of learning from one hub of the organization to the rest is not only a formidable challenge but also a potential source of unique advantages. Growth in emerging markets, with their diversity of customers and consumer behavior, makes the challenge of learning transfer more important than ever, so much so that some international companies are speeding up their innovation activities by articulating the reverse innovation process, moving ideas and products developed in emerging countries to mature markets (Govindarajan and Ramamurti, 2011).

The implementation of new ideas requires that they eventually deserve the attention of top managers, to whom projects and new concepts should be eventually presented, and that teams are able to free time to spend in working on the projects. Determination to bring about new projects should go hand in hand with some resources and time to think about them.

Idea generation is a competency whose development follows the same pattern as other competencies. It includes attributes related with knowledge about products or customers, and the different business functions to analyze them; the capabilities to define a customer value proposition, including the ability to articulate and execute a business plan; the skills to work across the organization and outside of it to get the ideas necessary to complete the project; and finally, the focus to work on the project thinking about customers' experience, with a strong sense of discipline and, at the same time, keep the current operations going.

Valuation of new ideas

The generation of new business ideas to improve customers' experience while maintaining focus is an important capability in innovation strategy. Protecting those ideas to get the interest and support of top management is also indispensable. Nevertheless, assessing those ideas and making a judgment about their potential to improve customer experience and make them sustainable from a financial viewpoint deserve special attention. CEOs can make a deep contribution by shaping this process and defining criteria for decision making.

There is an important distinction to be made here. The assessment of an innovative idea, product or service is one task. The assessment of an innovation strategy is a different task. We focus here on the first, assuming that the second falls within the principles of assessing a firm's strategy.

The valuation of new ideas should use both financial criteria—like NPV (net present value) or real options—and non-financial criteria. Financial criteria outcomes depend very much on the information used by the model. In particular, there are some assumptions about costs, pricing and consumer behavior that should be elaborated in a circular way, getting more information as the firm tests the idea or product, and nurturing the process with the new set of data developed with the new iteration of experimentation.

McGrath and MacMillan (2000) have advocated the use of real options to value entrepreneurial opportunities as a useful methodology to avoid the short-term perspective of many investment analysts. They developed a principle that fits well with that method: in assessing an innovation project, its designer or sponsor should frame it in a way that its investment commitment and launch costs are minimized until the upside potential of the project becomes clearer, by testing the product or service with customers in different markets. In the end, there is always risk and uncertainty surrounding new projects.

Another group of criteria is related with how a new idea can improve customer experience, how it can be translated into premium prices or lower costs, and how it can help get access to new customers in current or new markets (Ghemawat, 1991). It is clear that most of those dimensions can be also captured by financial models. Nevertheless, the point here is different. An innovative idea is one that while helping customers improve their experience also helps the firm develop new capabilities, with potential value for the future. Innovation also shapes the firm's culture and develops reputational capital for the firm. It is true that some of those dimensions can be expressed in quantitative form and be formally included in the process of financial valuation of an idea. But the power of those ideas goes beyond finance: it introduces a special innovation boost to the culture of the firm, stimulates the process of developing new capabilities and improves the reputation of a company as an innovator.

The role of senior managers in leading the project at this stage is critical. There are some dimensions to be considered here that go beyond quantitative methodologies. The first is the determination and passion of the whole team to make the innovation feasible and the top management commitment to back it up with the necessary resources. The second is the development of critical judgment about the factors that may make the project a success or a failure, and keep working on the driving factors to tilt the project toward the success camp. In this step, it is very important to count on external voices to develop that judgment, so that the emotional closeness to a certain project does not become a major block in overcoming its weaknesses. The third is a systematic assessment of the project and its overall worth for the firm, in terms of learning, developing new capabilities and growing a reputation. Finally, the need to manage and contain risk, including the boundaries within which the project will be launched, and the assumptions under which the project will be killed if its execution and market launch does not prove successful.

As we can observe from the discussion on how to valuate innovative projects, a whole new set of capabilities is needed. The innovator or creator of an idea in the first step may be a scientist in the lab or a salesperson close to customers. But the competencies to make that idea a business project with strong potential for customers go beyond the science and creativity in designing a product. Moreover, those competencies are not the ones that a good investment analyst should develop. It requires the combination of general manager competencies with a good understanding of customer needs, a deep knowledge of the products and services discussed, and good judgment to understand that the challenge that the innovation poses goes beyond financial analysis. It needs to take a look at the impact on other dimensions of the organization beyond finance: the new capabilities that the firm can develop, the reputation that the firm grows both for external talent and customers, and the impact on the firm's culture.

CEOs and top managers should make the process of assessing and valuating innovative projects manageable, with the additional uncertainty that surrounds them. Otherwise, any intent to make an organization more effective will get bogged down by the sheer complexity of assessment. In this respect, top managers should develop an assessment system of new innovative projects that should include indicators on how customers can be better served—how value for money changes with the new idea; what firm's capabilities get developed and why and how it matters for the organization; how the decision reinforces the culture of innovation, the willingness to improve and the passion to serve customers; what opportunities it creates for the firm's people; and, finally, the reputation that innovation nourishes to become more attractive for people outside of the firm—see Table 1.4.

People

Innovation outcomes do not depend on the value of ideas in abstract, but how those ideas are turned into business insights and projects by people who are willing to take the risk to develop them. People with solid competencies also make a difference. These competences help them do things better, and individuals themselves become better human beings.

In this chapter, we do not focus on creative people who have new ideas or inventors who develop a new product. It is about how CEOs pursue leadership development and focus on innovators who can become good

Table 1.4 Qualitative criteria to assess new business ideas

New value for customers
Passion to serve customers better
New organizational capabilities
Fostering the culture of innovation and the ability to change
Development opportunities for employees
Firm's reputation

general managers to lead new projects, or general managers who work with scientists, innovators or customers to bring new ideas to the market.

For those people, IEC are not only a set of attitudes—passion, determination, persistence—in pursuit of innovation. They require new competencies that help them to conceive the idea, frame it into a project, turn it into a business plan and launch it. More important, each one of those steps requires a set of competencies regarding the information and data used to analyze the situation and the quality of judgment. The previous sections have described some basic IEC. This section focuses on some competencies that help general managers make better judgments.

The first is the competency to observe how customers behave and how they consume or use the product or service, what they expect and what can be done to improve that experience. Observing the reality and understand it well is the first step toward transforming it with new ideas. The second is the competency to look at customers' expectations or challenges through a multi-disciplinary approach: how product developers think, how manufacturing or operations experts design, or how financial specialists frame the problem. New projects always require a different set of perspectives to see the future in a more comprehensive way. In this second stage, the art of questioning and posing key questions to different people is crucial. Very often, asking "Why not?" is a very powerful resource to stimulate creative solutions.

The third competency is to come up with a product or a solution to improve customer experience and start experimenting with it. Designing prototypes to be used by a group of customers is critical here. A new venture is not an all-or-nothing proposal. It involves a gradual approach, nurturing the roots of innovation and making sure that what evolves is something that will give customers the value that they expect at a reasonable cost.

The fourth competency is to be able to frame the new product or service into a full solution, develop the business plan and design scenarios for a future launch. We have already discussed the implications in terms of capabilities that this stage in the process of launching a new venture actually requires. Moreover, the need to refine the capacity to make a judgment about complex situations with blurred data and high uncertainty about consumer behavior is indispensable. Nevertheless, developing people with those competencies is not only relevant: in the end, it is the foundation to improve the capacity of a company to become more innovative, to manage the process in a reasonable way and to eventually increase the success rate of new ventures.

In established organizations, entrepreneurs rarely emerge spontaneously. Beyond the process of nurturing and developing the required capabilities, CEOs and senior HR managers have a critical role in creating a context for developing a generation of general managers with a strong innovation drive. The experience of established companies that have a good track record of innovation and new initiatives, like Henkel or Inditex, to mention some of them, highlights three important HR practices that can help in this process. The first is to define a long-term horizon for the development of those competencies. In the same way as a scientific discovery is usually the outcome of many years of serious work, the development of a new business idea that adds value to customers takes time, and the development of the necessary competencies takes even more time.

The second is the relevance of including innovation and new ideas in any general management job description. In recruiting for general manager positions, candidates should be asked about innovative initiatives that they have developed in their previous jobs or ideas that they may have about some of the firms' customers. The third practice is to mentor general managers with an innovative profile, so that the complexities of their jobs do not bog them down. CEOs' interest and commitment to innovation and the possibility of presenting ongoing work on new ideas to them is a very powerful incentive and signal for general managers.

Structure and systems

The impact that innovation may have on a firm depends very much on how it is executed and how that firm is organized to welcome and make innovation part of its daily behavior. CEOs can have a deep impact in this respect. Innovative ideas may come from any part of a company, and people should feel that they can reach with those ideas senior managers who eventually will decide to pursue them. Day (2013) highlights that organizational configuration defines, together with the firm's culture and capabilities, the potential that a company has to innovate.

The design of an organizational structure and management systems needs to answer the following questions: what needs to be done (tasks), who does it (people in charge), which structure and specific mandate and power (with whom to work and whom to report to), how its implementation gets measured (measurement for performance) and how it gets rewarded (compensation system). In a nutshell, a good management system for innovation and entrepreneurship that helps develop the necessary competencies needs to include the following dimensions: tasks/functions, people, decision making, measurement and rewards.

We can observe that any of these functions is also a proper formal function of an effective firm. Moreover, in the same way as any strategy needs a well-functioning organization structure that helps its implementation, any innovation strategy needs a good organizational infrastructure so that it can make a lasting contribution to the firm.

Organizational design is context-dependent: what works well for a company in a certain industry may not work for other companies in the same industry, or what works for a company at a certain point in time may not work in the future. Innovation follows the same rule. The uncertainty surrounding innovation and the challenge of managing it make solutions for organizational structure even more difficult to design. In particular, the integration of innovation activities within the larger organization is particularly difficult. We have seen the sheer complexity of this challenge by observing how well-established companies are fighting to integrate their digital, online business into the mainstream organization, without good results. But the same phenomena can be observed in traditional, innovative firms: integrating innovation within an organization is complex. We can see it in the cement industry—Cemex—chemicals—BASF—pharma—Roche or Pfizer—or in automobiles in integrating the electric car—BMW or Renault.

There are some specific issues of innovation and organization structure that need to be considered. The first is how to start a new business in established firms. The options here are essentially three: to keep them separate, to integrate the new venture into the old one since the beginning, and to develop a blended model. We find that experiences can be successful under the three forms. Nevertheless, it is true that more often than not the old business may stifle the new one; protecting the new organization maybe essential for its survival. On the other hand, top management needs to make a decision about how quickly the new organization should transfer its know-how and capabilities to the old one. Top managers must make a judgment about this decision with two specific dimensions: consider a long-term horizon and look at the new project in terms of competency development—not only in terms of the financial resources that it can generate.

The second issue is whether innovation can be outsourced. The answer depends on the firm's context. For a company already innovative and good at integrating new ideas, outsourcing of some solutions, or acquiring some innovative solutions in the marketplace, could be a reasonable option. A company that lacks behind in terms of innovation needs to gradually develop internal capabilities before deciding to buy big projects in the market; the risk of not being able to absorb them and integrate them is too high. P&G says that 50 per cent of its innovations should come from open innovation and outside ideas, but a company should have a core of competent professionals being able to identify and assess those innovations and integrate them inside the firm. Otherwise, firms can buy innovation but seldom will make innovation work in the existing firm.

The third issue is the role of corporate venturing. As Burgelman and Välikangas (2005) point out, corporate venturing is becoming more common, but it is a strategy with many nuances and is complex to manage. Companies need different leadership capabilities depending on the corporate venturing cycle and the available competencies and resources that a company has. It has the advantage that the company has thought a lot about managing innovation and transferring that innovation into the existing company. Nevertheless—by being context-dependent—corporate venturing is also subject to the vagaries of the economic cycle itself. Well-known companies like Xerox or Nokia used to run big corporate venturing units, to discover how difficult it is to transfer that knowledge into products and services that truly add value to the customers' experience.

The fourth issue is the role of corporate headquarters in innovation and the relationship between headquarters (HQ) and subsidiaries. This relationship has become even more complex as subsidiaries—in particular, those in emerging markets—are developing and marketing new products or services that are good enough for consumers' experience and with cheaper prices. As we have discussed, reverse innovation is becoming an important innovation paradigm in large companies operating in emerging markets.

There are two additional dimensions in the relationship between headquarters and subsidiaries regarding innovation. The first is how to make sure that headquarters do not kill innovation in subsidiaries. The traditional way to organize innovation—introduce new products or services in advanced markets and transfer them afterwards to emerging markets—no longer works with the same intensity as before. For this reason and in order to help companies capture all the innovative capacity of their organizations, HQ not only should avoid killing innovation but also should help design a networked system that allows any part of the organization get to know and use any innovation generated somewhere else.

The second dimension is about cultural and geographical diversity at headquarters. Creativity is a capacity to generate new ideas out of existing ones or by observing customers' needs. The richer and more diverse the experience of people talking about those new ideas, the deeper the discussion can get and more successful the results. Diversity at headquarters in international companies is not only an issue of opening access to opportunities or developing a pipeline of senior managers able to lead operations in different parts of the world. It is about infusing openness to new ideas into the headquarters and the whole company. And it is also a matter of having diverse points of view at headquarters, as well as perspectives and experiences of people with a deep knowledge of other cultures.

When thinking about innovation, it is easy to conclude that creative people or the unique value of new ideas are the fundamental attributes. Smart ideas are necessary, but without a good action plan and an effective organization that encourages and supports those ideas, they will never see the light or, even if they see the light, they will not last. Effective organization structure and management systems are necessary for any company that wants to last and have an impact. It is also indispensable to make a company innovative and reap the fruits of its innovativeness. CEOs should work to design organizational arrangements that make the most out of the IEC embedded in the organization, by enabling them, absorbing them and, eventually, launching them into the marketplace.

Top managers as innovation supporters: an agenda

CEOs do not need to be the most creative people to be effective leaders in backing innovation. But they need to know how to give support to innovation and entrepreneurship, as well as to the development of IEC to make the organization more effective in introducing successfully new ideas to renew it. The CIPS model and its four key areas presented above help develop this framework.

I will summarize the discussion in the previous sections by presenting an agenda for CEOs and senior managers who want to make their companies more open to new ideas and innovation and make those new ideas work—see Table 1.5. This agenda is related with the CIPS framework presented above.

Table 1.5 A CEO's agenda

CIPS framework	Agenda
Context	Shape and renew corporate culture
Ideas	Strategy and innovation Focus on customers' experiences Long-term time horizon
People	People and leadership development
Structure	Organization design

The first item on the agenda is the culture and values of the firm to develop IEC. It is linked with the notion of Context described in the CIPS framework. Before developing a very innovative organization, CEOs should consider that innovation comes from paying attention and observing consumers, products and experiences. Learning from those observations is the first step into a more innovative culture. CEOs can have a deep impact on their companies by asking themselves what can be done to improve customers' experiences and make customers feel better with the company in the long term. They can overcome reluctant people by helping them ask themselves, when thinking about customers' experience: "Why not?" By helping people ask themselves those questions, CEOs will help not only tilt the culture of the place toward innovation but also help create an organization where people think about innovation for customers in a systemic way.

The second item is related with Ideas in the CIPS framework. CEOs should be aware that they need a strategy that involves investing in the future. Any company with a portfolio of products and services need renewal, and aspirations that challenge complacency and inertia, and that lead the company beyond its current performance, are always useful. We all become too quickly accustomed to success and enter a comfort zone that avoids experimentation and risk taking.

A good strategy should look at innovation around customers and improving customers' experience. Innovation makes no sense for a company if it is not developed with the final customer in mind. It is true that some innovations in specific industries, like pharmaceuticals or complex materials, require research whose outcome will only appear in the distant future. But even in those cases, research teams should keep in mind that their discoveries should make human life better. CEOs can render a great service to their firms by helping people at all levels develop a deeper empathy with customers: an attitude to get to know them, to discover their needs, to serve them, to observe how they use their products or service, and develop a real intent to make customer experience with the firm's products more rewarding and meaningful.

In the same way as companies should be managed for the long-term success and survival, while making sure that they do not fail in the short term, innovation should be approached with the same perspective. Innovative projects take time to mature and become successful. In this respect, framing the decision, defining the risk boundaries of the project, using real-options methods to minimize investment and expenses, and be determined to establish the red lines that the project should not cross are very important and prudent decisions-making competencies.

The third item in the CEOs' agenda is people development for inno-vation. It is linked with the concept People in the CIPS framework. This chapter has been organized around it, and the framework described in the previous sections tries to describe a way to structure this process. Innovation and entrepreneurship competencies in established organi-zations highlight the indispensable role that people play in them. The more important technology and digitalization become in our lives, the more indispensable will be people managing them, but also people with the competencies and capacity for judgment need to make sense of an increasing amount of available information. The development of those capabilities is not an easy task. Scientific discoveries that lead to innova-tive products take time and require a huge commitment. Developing, selecting, launching and managing new ideas and ventures are even more complex activities than finding some new molecules in laborato-ries. They deal with human experience, which is shaped by freedom and not pre-determined by laws.

Finally, organizational design as a CEO's task is linked with Structure and Systems. CEOs should work to make sure that their organization works well to serve costumers effectively, to accept and stimulate inno-vation and help their people perform well and grow as professionals and individuals. Organizational design is not an end in itself; in dealing with entrepreneurship, CEOs need to make sure that a certain organi-zational structure does no harm to innovation and, if possible, helps develop innovative initiatives. Managing the balance between short-term efficiency and long-term dynamic innovation is a complex challenge.

In the end, entrepreneurship and innovation is not only a must for companies to succeed in the future, and a challenge for CEOs, but also a source of great joy—not only effort—for all the people involved in it. They help not only improve customers' experience and create jobs and social progress but also help all of us involved in it develop better competencies and moral virtues to face the future.

References

Amit, R. and Zott, C. (2012) "Creating value through business model innovation" *MIT Sloan Management Review*, 53 (3): 41–49.

Bartlett, C. and Ghoshal, S. (1989) "Managing across borders" (Boston: Harvard Business School Press).

Burgelman, R. and Välikangas, L. (2005) "Managing internal corporate venturing cycles" *MIT Sloan Management Review*, 46 (4): 26–34.

Canals, J. (2010) "Building respected companies" (Cambridge: Cambridge University Press).

Canals, J. (2012) "Rethinking global leadership development: Designing new paradigms" in J. Canals (ed.) *Leadership development in a global world* (Houndmills: Palgrave MacMillan).

Dávila, A. and Epstein, M. (2014) "The innovation paradox" (San Francisco: Berrett-Koehler Publishers).

Dávila, A., Epstein, M. J. and Shelton, R. (2006) "Making innovation work" (Upper Saddle River: Wharton School Publishing).

Day, G. S. (2013) "Innovation prowess" (Philadelphia: Wharton Digital Press).

Desouza, K. C. (2011) "Intrapreneurship" (Toronto: University of Toronto Press).

Ghemawat, P. (1991) "Commitment" (New York: Free Press).

Govindarajan, V. and Ramamurti, R. (2011) "Reverse innovation, emerging markets and global strategy" *Global Strategy Journal*, 1 (3–4): 191–205.

Javidan, M., Dorfman, P., Sully de Luque, M. and House, R. J. (2006) "In the eye of the beholder: Cross-cultural lessons in leadership from project GLOBE" *Academy of Management Perspectives*, 20 (1): 67–91.

Kelley, T. and Littman, J. (2005) "The ten faces of innovation" (New York: Currency Doubleday).

McGrath, R. G. and MacMillan, I. (2000) "The entrepreneurial mindset" (Boston: Harvard Business School Press).

McGrath, R. G. and Macmillan, I. (2009) "Discovery-driven growth" (Boston: Harvard Business Review Press).

Miller, P. and Wedell-Wedellsborg, T. (2013) "Innovation as usual" (Boston: Harvard Business School Press).

O'Connor, G. C., Corbett, A. and Pierantozzi, R. (2009) "Create three distinct career paths for innovators" *Harvard Business Review*, 87 (12): 78–79.

O'Reilly, C. A. and Tushman, M. L. (2004) "The ambidexterous organization" *Harvard Business Review*, 82 (4): 74–83.

Teece, D. (2007) "Explicating dynamic capabilities: The nature and microfoundations of (sustainable) enterprise performance" *Strategic Management Journal*, 28 (13): 1319–1350.

Part II
Entrepreneurship, Intrapreneurship and Innovation

2
Entrepreneurship and Companies' Success

Pedro Nueno

Introduction

Entrepreneurship inside organizations is one of the reasons why companies survive. But let us see what entrepreneurship is about. Entrepreneurs are those who identify an opportunity (something needed, something that people will like or even will need) and are capable to transform an opportunity into business. This means developing and implementing a model that includes clarification of what is the product or service that will be created, who exactly will the customers be, how the product or service will be produced, how the customer will be benefited by the product, who will execute the different decisions, or how the project will be financed. This can be done as a startup or inside an existing company, and in this case it can be from the top or even from lower levels inside the company.

Most of the existing companies were born through an entrepreneurial process. If the need the new company addresses is big, it can allow the company to grow, even globally, until this big market is satisfied. As time goes, the company may find ways to innovate aspects of the product or service it delivers that helps maintaining the market or even further expanding it. We can think, for example, about King Gillette, launching more than a hundred years ago the simplified razor in the US. From then, through continuous innovation, the company has created and sustained a global presence. At about those times, early last century, Gabrielle Chanel (Coco) launched her fashion shop in Paris, and today she is one of the renowned world leaders. Camilo Olivetti launched his typewriters, and unfortunately the company was not innovative enough to evolve in the future. And Antonio Puig launched his startup in Barcelona in 1914 to distribute imported cosmetic products and, in this case, through continuous innovation and good management the company also acquired and sustained a relevant global presence, becoming a leader in the prestige fragrance business in 2015, with a global market share of 9 per cent (Krishna and Nueno, 2013).

The first stage of a company—as in the cases we have shown—is the entrepreneurial stage, while the sustained innovation that facilitated growth and global reach is more the result of good management. It is important to remember that both entrepreneurship and management can be done by teams. We have entrepreneurial teams like William Hewlett and David Packard who launched, and managed for many years, their company, Hewlett Packard, and complemented each other very well. But we have many cases of entrepreneurial teams, family related or not, like Maurice McDonald and Richard McDonald who launched McDonald's or Charles Rolls and Henry Royce who did it with Rolls-Royce.

The issue of entrepreneurial teams is very important. We talk and write a lot about "the entrepreneur." Sometimes people refer to the "genetics of the entrepreneur." But when we study the creation of new companies in our days, we see more and more firms created by groups of entrepreneurs. And this makes a lot of sense. A new opportunity may originate in a scientific environment: the research of one university or the analytical laboratory of a hospital. Scientists may not be capable of transforming that opportunity into business. They may even not be motivated to do it; they feel comfortable as researchers, and publishing a paper in a prestigious journal can be for them a highly valued result.

Somebody with certain knowledge of business may see how the scientific opportunity could be transformed into a company and may even help finding the necessary funds. Investors however may put pressure to grow fast and with a global reach, and somebody with a certain international marketing experience may be welcome to the startup. We may have one of the scientists as head of the R&D, and other scientist in the team as head of operations and head of sales and marketing. Probably they keep the same percentage of company shares and they are at the same level, each one in his area but well coordinated. The rapid progress of technology in many fields (biotechnology, nanotechnology, digital technology, etc.) and the need to cover quickly the market at global level (otherwise somebody else will copy and take relevant portions of the market) make speed crucial, and this can be better achieved by well-coordinated teams.

Teamwork is not an easy thing, and we have seen cases of companies failing or loosing relevance due to conflicts between the founders. To be a good team player you need values. You cannot look at your team members trying to measure all the time if they contribute as much as yourself. This requires being humble and generous. If you can show to your stakeholders (clients, investors, suppliers and employees) that you have a solid and well-integrated team, the result is very positive.

Entrepreneurship from the top

If we look at the history of most existing companies, we see the entrepreneurial stage and then more or less development. Some companies sustained a sound development over many years, but others had relevant ups and downs or periods of fast change and evolution and other periods of modest growth and continuity. Fiat was the result of an entrepreneurial movement of the Agnelli Family, but in 2006 the company was practically bankrupt. Mr. Sergio Marchione took it over and brought it to growth, profitability and globalization (acquiring Chrysler in the process). We can probably say that Marchione was an entrepreneurial CEO (Díaz, Fité and Nueno, 2006). Geely was a Chinese automobile manufacturer who was unable to export to markets like the European Union or the US because of low product quality. But its founder and major shareholder, Mr. Li Shufu, managed to acquire Volvo, becoming a global player immediately. Volvo had been acquired by Ford for over 6,000 million dollars, but it was sold again for 1,500 million dollars six years later because Ford desperately needed cash to avoid an eventual bankruptcy. The move would justify considering Li Shufu also an entrepreneurial CEO (Nueno and Shengjun, 2010).

Looking at huge acquisitions and fast turnarounds, we can see many companies around the world that transformed themselves in a very relevant way. Some not only grew globally but transformed themselves. Under the leadership of Rafael del Pino, Ferrovial went from a construction and real estate company toward a much bigger and stable infrastructure company. Key to the process was the highly leveraged acquisition of BAA (with the major airports of the UK, including Heathrow) through a hostile takeover. Successful cases like this can also be considered entrepreneurial management (Nueno and Rodríguez, 2007).

We could say that Marchione and Li Shufu saw the opportunity in the form of powerful brands like Fiat and Volvo, poorly managed for years but with high recognition, loyal customers, adequate infrastructures (manufacturing, distribution, financing and after sales service) and excellent price. In the case of Ferrovial the opportunity included the airports as indicated above, but it was combined with the fact that at the time of the transaction it was easy to borrow money from capital markets. Ferrovial took debt well above its full value. The surprising thing is that neither Marchione nor Li Shifun or Rafael del Pino had to fight with competitors looking after the opportunities they had identified.

These cases have something in common: they created a lot of value for shareholders in a short period of time. We can then consider entrepreneurial management as the capacity to protect and create a relevant value for the shareholders.

We can find cases in which we have an entrepreneur as defined early in this chapter (identified the opportunity and transformed it in one company), but also who was capable of creating a high volume of value in a relatively short period of time for the shareholders. In 2001 I presented in "Mastering Management 2.0" (Pickford, 2001) the recent launching of Alibaba by the Chinese entrepreneur Jack Ma. It took only 14 years of sustained growth to create over 20 billion dollars of value.

Intrapreneurship

We have seen that it is possible to be an entrepreneur creating a company, an entrepreneurial manager, creating fast high volume of value for the shareholders, but what if you are a manager, somewhere inside the company? Can you also be an entrepreneur?

This is a complex issue. I was once contacted by a former student. This happens quite often to IESE faculty because the relationship with our alumni is one of the values of the school. He explained to me, as his professor of entrepreneurship years ago, a new opportunity he had discovered and how to transform it into a new business unit for his company. The concept had a certain relationship with the business he was involved but it had many differences. He said that he saw a tremendous future for this new opportunity, much more than to his current business that could support a moderate growth only.

I agreed with his views and told him: "have you informed your boss about this?" His answer was: "I know him well. If I tell him about this he will say that I have enough work with my current business and that I must make an effort to improve this rather than losing time with strange ideas." "Well," I told him, "and if he tells you this (his boss was Vice President of the company), could you find a way to explain your idea to the President?" His reaction was: "I know the President; he may like the idea, but he will probably ask my direct boss to listen to me. Then my boss will see that I went over him and my future in the company will be zero." I said, "then, at least, see if you can convince your boss."

A few months later he visited me again. He had informed his boss whose reaction was indeed: "John, you have enough on your desk now. Focus. Do not waste your time." He had left the company, started a new company with his idea and things were going fantastically well, even better than he imagined before starting. Obviously his former employer had lost the opportunity to move in this direction that had a much better future than its current business. A soft move in this direction as the industry was evolving would have been possible. All the energy, creativity and enthusiasm of his executive were lost for his former employer.

We have seen how companies that were at some point global leaders in one field were not capable of successfully following the evolution of their field. Kodak was unquestionable leader in photography when this industry had chemical base. But as photography became digital, Kodak did not follow at the adequate speed. As a Harvard doctoral student, I was asked to write a case on Kodak in 1972. The CEO of Kodak mentioned to me that photography would be digital one day. Kodak had made excellent profits in photography and diversified into good business, chemicals, pharmaceuticals and others. But the company sold these businesses to try to save photography although it went bankrupt in 2013. I wonder how many people left Kodak during all those years with portions of interesting knowledge and business ideas that they could not implement inside their company.

But there are success stories also. Abengoa's Manuel Sánchez, contributed to create Telvent, an IT services unit within Abengoa, a Spanish company with sales of 2.900 million euro in 2008, of which Telvent represented 18%. Manuel Sánchez developed this business unit internationally. To gain international visibility and prestige, he listed Telvent in NASDAQ in 2004, being the first Spanish company to be listed there. His office was in Washington.

Obviously Telvent was an extraordinary example of intrapreneuship. Manuel Sánchez was clearly the intrapreneur, but Abengoa has the tremendous merit of having facilitated the process of Manuel Sánchez keeping his business unit from the rest of the company, and even putting it inside a new company with its own name. This made possible its listing and the creation of value for Abengoa.

Intrapreneurship became a fashionable topic in the eighties. Many companies created an intrapreneurship unit like an internal venture capital company. Those managers who had an idea which could be the basis of a business activity could obviously talk to their bosses about it. But if the idea did not fit their unit or their supervisors did not consider it, they had the alternative of going to the "Intrapreneurship

Office" where their project could be studied and eventually supported. Companies like Philips created this internal office.

It was somewhat politically incorrect not to report to your boss that you were exploring a potential new venture in another department of your company. And it was not well received by the boss that somebody was entering into his area of responsibility by financing innovations or diversifications, which had not been forecasted or budgeted. The result was that the structuring of intrapreneurship did not work. In a sense it was seen as a lack of trust in the chain of management, and the result is that it was not well supported by the organization. Little by little the "intrapreneurship infrastructures" were eliminated. Today, we continue to have the problem of using in the company the business ideas generated by their managers, and many continue to leave when they believe that their business idea is strong enough. Cases as Telvent and Abengoa are very unusual.

Some companies have maintained venture capital units that in many cases are used to attract entrepreneurs who have ideas that could become interesting opportunities for the company. These venture capital units can be a bridge to negotiate with these entrepreneurs a possible acquisition of their startups by the parent company.

Acquiring entrepreneurs

Large companies are supporting entrepreneurs in a different way however. It is more and more frequent that large companies acquire entrepreneurial ventures while, in some cases, reducing their R&D. Large pharmaceutical, new materials, chemicals, telecommunications and many other companies have been spending billions, each one of them in R&D with, sometimes, poor results. As a consequence, many have decided to keep a good control of startups in their fields of interest. Quite often they can save money and time and still pay very well a startup that has potential in an area of their interest. Evolution in biotechnology, nanotechnology and digitalization, amongst others, may add complications for internal R&D, while the research done by universities (often supported by governments) or public research centers can produce startups that carefully selected and guided can substitute, improve or accelerate the R&D results of companies. This is an excellent way of utilizing society's knowledge, and it is good to create mechanisms to facilitate this connection.

Will this phenomenon reduce the percentage of R&D expenditures? It may lead to a more efficient use of funds, passing part of them to acquisitions of startups that had already proven their concepts in the market. We are talking about processes which require years to have a correct evaluation, and it is still early to make conclusions. But it is undoubtedly an alternative to be seriously explored.

Successful intrapreneurship

We live in the era of information. The availability of information contributes to flatten organizations. The first management studies on organization structures had many management layers. Today, we need to go faster, we have people better prepared and the world is becoming more accessible and less different. The solution is team work. And as we already explained and it is so important that it is worth to insist on it, teamwork requires values: generosity, openness, support to others, sharing and being humble. The team succeeds rather than the individual.

In a recent "startups" competition, launched in 2015 by an important business association in Europe, 20 startups were selected as finalists for a jury to choose three winners. In these 20 promising ventures, the average of leading entrepreneurs was three, and these three had different competences in practically all cases.

Team work can be promoted in flat organizations. Availability of information (about the company, about the competition and about the industry) can be facilitated in a regular and organized way. Company structure, meetings, training and events can be organized in a way that they contribute to cross lines and facilitate team work. Some companies have made progress along these lines, and in some cases they stimulate this culture through internal presentations by successful teams and even specific prizes. It looks that this is probably the line of progress in our era.

Financing entrepreneurs and entrepreneurial teams

New ventures require financing. Sometimes they help rejuvenate a mature company. Abengoa created the successful internal venture Telvent; later sold Telvent to Schneider, thus contributing to reduce its own financial leverage. But, to be born, new ventures need funding.

Capital markets evolve all the time, but in the last decade probably they had increased the speed of change and the availability of financial instruments. Lots of venture-capital/private-equity companies have been created with a tremendous variety of specializations: by industry, by stage (start-up, second round, growth), by volume of financing needed, by length of the period of return, etc. But new instruments are also appearing: crowfunding, special bonds and business angel networks. Probably it is correct to say that in the 2010–2020 decade, lack of funding has not stopped any realistic new venture.

But, what about intrapreneurship? In the same way that the first company from Spain listed in NASDAQ was Manuel Sánchez's entrepreneurial venture Telvent, the first Chinese company to be listed in NASDAQ was Mindray, an entrepreneurial venture launched by Xu Han to produce medical diagnostic equipment. Xu Han used Mindray's listing in New York NASDAQ as a strong capitalizer for its global deployment but, above all, in the US market. Entrepreneurs like Jack Ma from Alibaba had reached valuation records in international public markets.

In 2015 many startups are getting high valuations and, in the same way that the arrival of internet to entrepreneurship created a bubble with unrealistic valuations, the fast growth of e-business in our day may also be creating a certain valuation bubble particularly if one considers the high number of similar startups being launched all over the world, all of them with global aspirations (Khanna, 2007).

Intrapreneurship can be considered a way of innovation, and practically all countries have specific financial instruments for innovation and, most importantly, beneficial tax policies. It is thus important to organize "intrapreneurship" in the correct way (from the accounting perspective, for instance) to benefit from these protective measures. In any case, an intrapreneurial venture can be organized as a new company and, through this, it can benefit from the wealth of financial instruments available.

Tools for entrepreneurs

One of the contributions of the academic world to entrepreneurship has been the development of frameworks to organize professionally the entrepreneurial process. This is particularly important in an area that generates strong emotions, requires acting fast and has many complexities.

Probably the most important framework is the so called "business plan," a kind of step-by-step comprehensive guide to start the company. Once a company is in motion, the conventional management knowledge is applicable: from good accounting through ambitious strategic planning, going through efficient operations, good management of adequately motivated people, correct addressing of customers through marketing and sales, and fitting the whole project within the correct financial scheme.

The business plan starts from a good opportunity, and it is the detailed, complete and scheduled process to transform the opportunity, which is seen as an idea, into a process that will lead to a company. The implementation of the "business plan" is called the "start up process." This is valid for all the types of entrepreneurial approaches: create a new company, transform an existing company, launch a new business unit within a company and transform an existing company through relevant mergers, acquisitions, globalization or innovation.

In my publications I like to offer some guidelines for a business plan (see Table 2.1). From the experience of reading thousands of business plans from my students (MBAs, Executive MBAs or even more senior professionals) and seeing many of them transformed into real companies, it is possible to say that twenty well-written pages allow in general to present the project with enough detail to attract investors and guide the process. Obviously, when the entrepreneurs enter the action stage

Table 2.1   A business plan: An outline

1. Executive summary
2. The business concept
   2.1. The product or service
   2.2. Specific approach to production and sales
   2.3. Fundamental differentiating factors
3. The new company in its industry
4. The product and the possibility of reinforcing it with related products or services
5. Technology (where appropriate)
   5.1. R&D plan. Technology to be developed and/or purchased. Timetable and budget
   5.2. R&D staff. Motivation and retention
   5.3. Main technology risks and how they will be managed
6. The market and the competition
7. Marketing and sales plan
8. Production plan
   8.1. Make or buy. Suppliers
   8.2. Subcontractors
9. Staff. Recruitment plan. Profiles. Motivation and retention
10. Financial plan. Cash flow budget. Profitability
11. Financing. The new company's financial needs
    11.1. Sources of finance. Capital. Debt
    11.2. Shareholders and their rights and obligations
12. Management of the new company. People responsible for each activity and management control
13. Detailed company launch plan. Main risks and how they will be managed

it is possible that they need to adjust what they put in the business plan. But in most cases, the adjustments are minor and do not change completely the project.

Obviously, most of the business plans I have read have been prepared by people with good general knowledge and experience about management. This means that all the relevant areas were covered with available frameworks, and the critical aspect of the circulation of money—raising capital, borrowing debt, investing, spending, selling and collecting—was well planned to be correctly implemented. A good idea may lose its "momentum" if the entrepreneurs spend their time and energy raising money because they did not calculate well their needs in their business plan. All my students know that a good business plan in unforgettable!

Conclusion

Entrepreneurship is and will remain very relevant for companies and society. Entrepreneurship is a way to introduce innovation in society and into existing companies, a way to identify new opportunities which satisfy the needs of people and society (health care, education, leisure, basic needs, etc.) and transform them into new companies. As a consequence, entrepreneurship creates new jobs and often better jobs.

Entrepreneurship can happen as a new venture, can start inside an existing company, can be practiced by the top management of a corporation or can even be the result of an alliance between two companies or an acquisition which increases the dynamism of the acquiring and the acquired companies.

As science makes progress, entrepreneurship can also be the vehicle to transform science into applicable knowledge and business. And in a world becoming global, entrepreneurship can be one of the best ways to cross borders and create activities that interest people regardless their geographical location. In many cases, it can help bringing economic development into the less-developed regions.

Entrepreneurship has stimulated the financial markets which have developed adequate concepts and products (venture capital, private equity, business angels, crowfunding). A higher level of financial professionalization of entrepreneurship is a guarantee of its sustainability and its long-term success.

Society has recognized the enormous contribution of entrepreneurship and is supporting it in many ways, from financial and tax incentives through education. It is well understood that there is a body of knowledge associated to entrepreneurship and that this can be taught.

It is becoming clear that better prepared entrepreneurs are more likely to succeed.

By highlighting entrepreneurship as one of our leading social priorities, and considering entrepreneurship a social contribution, we are contributing to add values to entrepreneurship and appreciate the social corporate responsibility that this effort, intensive and creative activity, represents.

Obviously, like it has always been the case, somebody's success attracts many others to follow or, worse, try to copy. This means that in our digital society, with the fast flow of information and the increase in the speed of business, there is a chance that here or there a bubble grows in some attractive area.

But entrepreneurship is highly valued, better studied, practiced more professionally every day and clearly contribute a lot to our social and economic progress.

References

Amis, D. and Stevenson, H. (2001) "Winning Angels" (London: Financial Times Prentice Hall)

Díaz, J. J., Fité, R. and Nueno, P. (2006) "Fiat Auto 2003: A New Opportunity." IESE Business School Case; 0-604-002

Khanna, T. (2007) "Billions of Entrepreneurs" (Boston: Harvard Business School Press)

Krishna, P. and Nueno, P. (2013) "Puig: The Second Century." Harvard Business School Case N9-114-022

Nueno, P. (2014) "E-mails to a Young Entrepreneur" (Barcelona: Planeta)

Nueno, P. and Rodríguez, A. (2007) "Ferrovial Takeover of BAA: Flying High" IESE Business School Case, 3-067-006

Nueno, P. and Shengjun, L. (2010) "Geely-Volvo: Road to a Cross-Country Marriage." CEIBS CC-310-029

Pickford, J. (2001) "Financial Times Mastering Management 2.0" (London: Pearson Education Limited)

Van Osnabridge, M. and Robinson, R. J. (2000) "Angel Investing" (San Francisco: Jossey-Bass)

3
Leading the Startup Corporation: The Pursuit of Breakthrough Innovation in Established Companies

Tony Davila and Marc Epstein

Introduction

One popular myth that often emerges in conversations about break-through innovation—innovation that can disrupt current industry structures and even create entire new ones—is that breakthroughs are largely the domain of small, agile startups. Established organizations have no chance of success in pursuing these sorts of game-changers—or at least so goes the myth.

Where many companies go wrong is just going after incremental innovation—the kind of everyday, incremental changes to products and processes that help an organization improve efficiency in its operations and keep a competitive edge. Of course, there is nothing wrong with incremental innovation. In fact, the ability to execute well and improve products and processes is absolutely essential to the long-term health of any organization. The danger lies in focusing excessively on what has always worked. Without taking the time to explore emerging and not-yet markets, established organizations run the very real risk of being blindsided by products and services that disrupt, transform or eliminate entirely the market in which their bread and butter is made.

Fortunately, many well-established organizations have proven and continue to prove this myth to be little other than fiction. 3M has consistently created new markets since its inception over 100 years ago. Nespresso essentially created the coffee-by-the-cup market, and is now worth several billion dollars as part of Nestle. Companies like Google and Apple continue to break new ground seemingly year after year, and the list goes on and on.

But what differentiates the companies who succeed in terms of developing breakthroughs from those who fall behind? There are many factors at play, but leadership has a huge impact—in terms of qualities portrayed by individual leaders, the ability to cultivate cultures conducive to innovation, as well as setting up and strengthening the hard foundations of an organization.

This chapter distinguishes four types of innovation, each one with different management needs. Then it explores how leadership and culture influence the willingness among people to innovate. The last section of the chapter discusses the role of incentives and management systems for supporting innovation.

Management models for innovation

As many as there are companies successful at developing and delivering innovations, there are ways to manage. In fact, managing any organization as if there were one single innovation model usually results in one type of innovation. The ways an organization chooses to innovate and the kind of innovation it produces are inextricably linked (Davila, Esptein and Shelton, 2006). The combination of innovation types and management approaches leads to four distinct models for managing innovation: continuous progress, emergent improvement, strategic bets and strategic discoveries (Figure 3.1).

Continuous progress

Many established organizations already excel at continuous progress—the type of innovation that improves current technology and business models. As long as the market and the broader competitive landscape remain largely unchanged, continuous progress is essential for an organization's success.

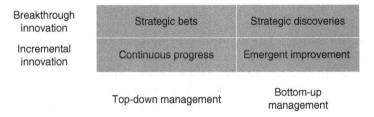

Figure 3.1   Management models for innovation

Continuous progress involves top management using strategic planning to synthesize ideas into specific objectives—incorporating improvement goals, investment decisions and new management processes and structures—for a specific time period. Achievable but demanding goals, operational budgets, non-financial performance measures and investment budgets all force people to work hard to find creative ways to meet their goals.[1]

Emergent improvement

Where continuous progress forces creativity through demanding, top-down goals, an ethos of emergent improvement encourages creativity across the organization. By making efforts to leverage the creativity of people in the larger company, leaders who see management through the lens of emergent improvement challenge the idea of top management being the only font of creativity. Making the most of the ideas emerging around the company requires both tools and structures for capturing and executing on valuable ideas.

While the most important part of incremental product and service innovation is understanding the customer better, emergent improvements can also benefit largely from tapping outside networks, stimulating them and leveraging their ideas. Part of the challenge, then, is motivating people, stimulating their curiosity and providing a means to share ideas with decision-makers.

Strategic bets

Breakthrough innovation in established companies can be driven in one of two ways. The first—strategic bets—is explicitly driven by the vision of top management. The success of these sorts of risky but potentially high-return strategies largely depends on the insight of their creator's vision—whether the future scenario on which they are betting actually plays out or not—and the ability of the organization to execute. Strategic bets underlie the kind of breakthrough innovation that organizations like Apple were capable of bringing to market with visionaries like Steve Jobs at the helm.

Leaders who leverage strategic bets are the kind of people who envision a certain future and work with creative people toward its realization. Leaders making strategic bets expect a response of "how high?" when asking employees to jump. When successful, strategic bets transform companies, industries and sometimes even society. Still, no bet is a sure thing. If the leader's vision is wrong, an organization might end up creating warehouses full of expensive, innovative and unwanted

Table 3.1 Different types of innovation require different management approaches

---

- Continuous progress involves planning and incremental goal setting; top-down demands induce people to innovate to meet targets.
- Emergent improvements result from structured processes to stimulate and capture incremental ideas throughout the organization.
- Strategic bets are breakthroughs that depend on a leader's vision and an organization's ability to execute.
- Strategic discoveries are breakthroughs that result from harnessing the collective genius of the organization and its networks.

---

paperweights. If the leader is right, but the organization as a whole fails to execute, strategic bets also result in failure.

Strategic discoveries

Now, it's pretty obvious that not every organization has a Steve Jobs. Not every leader has a crystalline vision of the future, and hardly any visionary leader is right every time. Strategic discoveries offer an alternative: the kind of breakthrough innovations that result from harnessing the insights of many people throughout an organization and its networks. Strategic discovery is about leveraging the collective talent, inspiration and vision of a variety of people with varied expertise. It is about bringing together many visionaries who are experts in their own field in the hopes of creating collective breakthrough. Rather than bet on the inspiration of a few, strategic discoveries are about elevating the collective expertise of employees throughout an organization.

The larger the number of employees an organization has, the more external networks grow. The larger the network, the more likely exceptionally gifted individuals—and exceptionally valuable breakthrough ideas—are to appear. It is just math; the law of large numbers tells us that the chance of there being someone with a great idea is significantly higher in a group of thousands than it is in a group that fits inside the walls of a board room. In the absence of a once-in-a-generation leader, strategic discoveries are the best approach for established organizations to effectively pursue breakthrough innovations (Table 3.1).

Leading the Startup Corporation: Leadership qualities

Execution comes almost naturally to many leaders and organizations; it's been their job since they joined a company. Pursuing breakthrough innovation, on the other hand, is a very different beast. Leaders must be sensitive to and aware of the natural tendency to focus all attention, energy and resources on strategies that have worked in the past. Like driving a car with your eyes permanently in the rearview mirror, such a strategy can very easily result in catastrophic consequences.

Pursuing strategic discoveries—bottom-up breakthrough innovation—requires an approach to management that leverages both the exploratory, risk-taking ethos of many a nimble startup and the resources, networks and capabilities of established organizations. To those ends, the Startup Corporation is an organizational design that established organizations can use to leverage their existing networks and resources. It is a management approach inspired by the way startup ecosystems are designed for exploration and discovery. In other words, the Startup Corporation melds the strengths of startups when it comes to developing breakthroughs with the strengths of established organizations when it comes to scaling and execution (See Figure 3.2).

Where many established companies have seen once stable markets change drastically or altogether vanish with the advent of new breakthroughs, the Startup Corporation allows for adapting management to the needs of breakthrough innovation. By devoting a portion of time, energy and resources to exploring 'not yet' markets with the gusto of

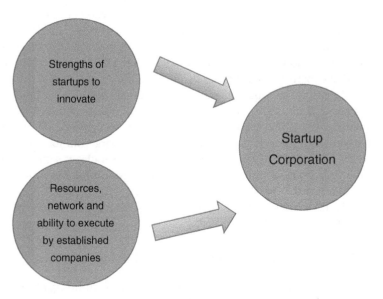

Figure 3.2   The Startup Corporation combines startup qualities with the strength of a corporation

a startup, while still allowing the larger organization to focus on the incremental innovations that make and have made it a continued success, established organizations can anticipate or even cause breakthrough developments while maintaining business in existing markets. On the opposite side of the same coin, once the Startup Corporation identifies a promising product or service, it can leverage the parent company's resources, networks and ability to execute in ways that smaller startups simply can't.

What kind of leader can command a ship whose crew is encouraged to both seek out and explore new territory, while simultaneously executing on current strategies and developing incremental innovations? One that trusts in her crew to find the best harbor and understands that breakthroughs are more effectively identified and realized together than individually. Leading the various types of innovation relies on the ability to create effective teams and motivating people, but it also requires unique abilities.

Leaders are different in many aspects, and there is no one best way to lead. Still different styles fit different strategies, and leaders who embrace breakthrough innovation have some differential aspects.

Strategic thought and action

Innovative leaders are those that point out the general direction of exploration and set the parameters for discovery, but ultimately trust in their employees to identify the specific innovations that will define the future of the organization. They believe in their people. They believe in the ability of their people to take calculated risks, pull inspiration from both internal and external sources and learn from their mistakes as quickly and inexpensively as humanly possible. While not explicitly knowing what the future holds, they are confident that the people who make up an organization will succeed in finding new opportunities for growth.

Leaders seeking breakthrough innovation must encourage people by creating space for innovation—by pushing them to think outside the constraints of current products and business models, allotting certain amounts of time for passion projects and above all making sure their ideas are heard. Of course, none of these elements should be given away without conditions. Often, guidelines are what differentiate exploration from wandering.

Sponsorship

Many potentially successful projects that ultimately failed owe their failure to a lack of resources. On the other side of the same coin, a number of projects fail because of the impression of lack of urgency an excess of resources or time can communicate. Finding the right balance—between under- and over-resourced, between long and short schedules—is essential for effective sponsorship.

One important decision leadership is often faced with is whether to implement an aggressive, offensive strategy's whose goal is winning, or a more conservative, defensive strategy whose aim is to prevent the organization from losing. There is a delicate balance when it comes to deciding what amount of resources—in terms of time, talent and capital—should be devoted to exploring new ground versus protecting ground already in the organization's possession.

Passion

When it comes to developing innovation, or simply motivating employees, anyone can present a rationally argued case, backed up with research and statistics to give it weight. Still, a lot of times that's not enough, no matter how convincing the argument. Sometimes you need some feeling. Breakthrough innovation comes from people passionate about the work that they do—and passion is infectious. When a leader is passionate, employees are more likely to see passion as a positive quality—one that can get things done, and get them places.

Passion isn't just a fluff word loosely related to success. In fact, passion is sometimes a requirement for success. At the D5 Conference in 2007, Steve Jobs talked about the importance of having passion for what you do.

> People say you have to have a lot of passion for what you're doing and it's totally true. And the reason is because it's so hard that if you don't, any rational person would give up. It's really hard. And you have to do it over a sustained period of time ... So it's a lot of hard work and it's a lot of worrying constantly and if you don't love it, you're going to fail.[2]

When it comes to leading an organization for breakthrough innovation, passion can be the difference between simply giving up after nearly inevitable failure and seeing that failure not as failure but as the completion of a successful experiment on the road to success.

Evangelization

Beyond just acknowledging and understanding the necessary risks themselves, leaders also must be able to sell their key stakeholders on that risk. Generally speaking, there are a number of vulnerabilities that successful leaders highlight to drive home the importance of constant innovation.

Not a lot of things can unite an organization behind a common cause like a common enemy. In that light, a number of organizations have successfully rallied their troops around some sort of external "villain"—usually another company competing in the same market. Painting such a villain in an unflattering light as if they were an opposing sports team or other adversary can help an organization construct a common sense of purpose.

Not every story needs a villain. Sometimes, a cautionary tale surrounding a fallen giant is enough to light a fire of innovation underneath a workforce. Playing up the catastrophic failures of once dominant players in a given industry can go a long way in terms of creating a real sense of urgency around the need to continuously work toward the development of breakthrough innovations.

Beyond external threats and tales of the once powerful giants falling from their thrones, sometimes it's enough for an organization to take a good look in the mirror. Every organization has its own flaws and weaknesses, and presenting those elements as the potential causes of future downfall can be a powerful motivator. Lou Gerstner has said, "My view is you perpetuate success by continuing to run scared, not by looking back at what made you great, but looking forward at what is going to make you un-great, so that you are constantly focusing on the challenges that keep you humble, hungry, and nimble."[3]

Of course, not all self-confidence is welcome—or a positive influence on an organization. There is a very fine line between confidence and arrogance, persistence and stubbornness. While leaders need to develop a thick skin when it comes to weathering negative feedback and maintaining enthusiasm and energy around a project, they also need to know when that sort of feedback can actually help them bring a project to fruition.

Tolerance of uncertainty, courage to take risks and long-term focus

To have a chance of successfully navigating the challenges of breakthrough innovation, leaders need to possess the kind of focus that removes unnecessary complexity. For example, Steve Jobs saw focus as meaning, "saying no to the hundred other good ideas that there are."[4] As much as leaders need to encourage exploration, that exploration needs limits, telling employees where they should *not* be focusing. A clear vision—one that sees the value and wisdom in simplicity—lowers the chances of pushing an organization to take unnecessary risks.

In the face of necessary risk, successful leaders can tolerate varying levels of uncertainty all the while maintaining focus on the long term. Like the seasoned mountaineer who can survive an unexpected snowstorm and still safely return home, innovative leaders know how to keep calm despite uncertainty.

Where the business plan is traditionally central to most strategies, working toward breakthrough innovation isn't quite that cut and dry. Take Google X, for example. Astro Teller, the director of Google X, said:

> If there's an enormous problem with the world, and we can convince ourselves that over some long but not unreasonable period of time we can make that problem go away, then we don't need a business plan. We should be focused on making the world a better place, and once we do that, the money will come back and find us.
>
> (Stone, 2013)

Sometimes, breakthroughs carry with them the serious potential to cannibalize existing businesses. In cases like these, levels of trust or mistrust in leadership can determine whether new businesses with the potential to disrupt an organizations' own current business becomes a power struggle or a banner behind which the organization can rally. Oftentimes, when people have confidence in their organization, they understand they will be treated fairly even if their role changes in the process.

The ability to cope with and manage ambiguity does not mean that leaders are necessarily relaxed. On the contrary, a great number of innovative leaders maintain impossibly high standards for themselves and others, are incredibly driven and possess a rare kind of intensity of focus. They understand that the territory into which they are venturing may be largely uncharted, that unexpected events will occur and that this is all par for the course in terms of seeking out breakthroughs.

Leading the Startup Corporation: Culture

Culture is one of the most powerful forces in organizational life. It can be the supportive environment in which developing ideas have the space and encouragement to flourish, or it can be an extinguishing force that snuffs out the sort of ideas that fall away from the party line— the kind that can occasionally lead to breakthrough innovations. At its most basic, culture "comes down to a *common way of thinking*, which drives *a common way of acting*" (Goffee and Jones, 1998: 15). Culture has everything to do with how people *think and behave* throughout an organization. Culture is constantly evolving, developed over many years of cumulated experiences. Given the power of culture when it comes to shaping the reaction of people to issues as diverse as relying on outsiders for ideas, learning from (rather than punishing) failures, taking calculated risks and going after hard but high potential challenges, a company that is risk-averse needs a powerful leader for a culture to change into one conducive to fostering strategic discoveries.

Since culture essentially reflects the values and ways of thinking shared across an organization, innovation and risk taking must be part of that culture for strategic discoveries to develop. Organizations—especially their leaders—can work to (re)shape culture in a number of ways (Table 3.2).

Employee behavior can change relatively quickly by implementing strong and consistent strategies involving most or all of these levers. Still, behavioral change in itself does not make a culture. In fact, behavioral change can translate into cultural change quite slowly. The length of time needed to effectively influence a culture depends on the change required, how deeply anchored traditional behaviors are, the size and geographic dispersion of people, and the persistence and strength of the effort to change.

The importance of recruiting talent

When it comes to pursuing breakthrough innovation, recruiting talented people is of paramount importance. In fact, most organizational problems start at recruitment. Tony Hsieh, Founder and CEO of Zappos, is so explicit about the importance of a good culture fit that at the end

Table 3.2 Mechanisms to shape cultures

- *Employee abilities* shape what individuals are able to do. Organizations can acquire skills, eliminate redundant ones and train people.
- *Innovation activities* focus on understanding current and future customers, innovative competitors (often startups), and support and circulate ideas.
- *Goals and rewards* provide the vision to take risks and a sense of fair rewards for taking them.
- *Top management behavior* models what the important aspects in the organization are, and supports particular behaviors across the organization.
- *Organizational structure* describes each individual's boss, peers, clients and suppliers, and influences individuals' organizational identity.
- *Access to time and resources* allows people to be effective. The more resource constraints, the less likely employees will display expected behavior.

of the company's extensive New Hire Training, trainees still unsure about whether or not they want to work for Zappos are offered $3,000 to leave.[5] Still, any effort to identify potential employees who mesh with a certain culture has to be weighed against the needs for the kind of diversity that innovation demands (Kelly, 2001). Companies should absolutely be explicit about deal-breaking, non-negotiable qualities, but they shouldn't be so narrow in focus as to miss opportunities to hire individuals with a broad range of life experiences, cognitive styles and overall points of view. For example, L'Oréal, the world's largest cosmetics and beauty company, developed a whole separate recruitment process for "unconventionals"—individuals with interesting profiles who might not get the attention they deserve from recruiting processes focused on filling roles with very specific criteria in the short term.

Top talent is immensely important for developing innovation. Since high-performing individuals are not always necessarily the easiest people to get along with—let alone manage—hiring and retaining top talent can also be quite challenging. Individuals with a tendency to be innovative, independently minded, goal focused and risk taking often possess individualistic and less agreeable characteristics, causing them to be perceived and behave less like team players than an average employee (Gardiner and Jackson, 2011).

While careful and specific recruiting processes are important aspects of attracting new talent, there is also much a leader can do to develop an organization's existing workforce.

Working with existing employees

An innovative culture relies on hiring talented and passionate people, but making them want to stick around is equally important. A lot of times, companies kill the initial passion employees might have by getting everyone bogged down in the minutiae of daily tasks, sometimes inadvertently playing down people's individual talents and creativity. Most employees typically spend the lion's share of their time and energy pursuing today's objectives, embedded in standardized processes, bound by the requirements of whatever the existing paradigm may be. Over time, such an emphasis on optimizing existing resources—and practices of rewarding behaviors that succeed in improving current models over creating new ones—can actually have a negative impact on the ability of employees to imagine other products, let alone new services, processes or business models.

To maintain the passion of employees to explore and discover, organizations can provide spaces for employees to come together and collaborate—allowing for the potential of cross-pollination between people and fields that may initially appear disparate. Giving employees exposure to the world outside the organization can also help employees visualize ways to break out of their everyday way of doing business.

When an organization supports interactions with networks that exist outside its own walls, it goes a long way toward ensuring employees broaden their personal and professional networks, as well as become exposed to a variety of practices and ideas. Job rotation—ensuring that managers and employees do not stay on any given job long enough for it to become stale—is another way to keep things fresh, as well as maintain employee interest and engagement. It is far more likely for innovation to occur when employee hearts and minds are authentically engaged in innovation-pursuing activities at least part of the time. While this requires employees who are both willing and able, it also requires managers to embody a style of leadership that is supportive of employee engagement and innovation efforts.

With the right teams of people in place, nurturing activities in support of innovation can largely determine whether or not an organization innovates. It is up to leadership to define the ways in which experimentation, learning, understanding customers, and tracking competition and technologies all happen.

Supporting innovative activities: Experimentation and learning

One of the most effective ways to manage risk is to systematically design experiments. For example, Tesco is also well known for trying out ideas as a pilot in a few stores, monitoring the results of the pilot, making adjustments according to what was learned and then rolling out the polished version to the broader market.

A systematic emphasis on learning from experiences—especially when that emphasis is encouraged and embodied by top leadership—supports innovation across an organization. In particular, process innovation can emerge organically from encouraging employees to ask themselves what they can learn and improve. Experimenting requires both patience and rigor. Without considering either during the course of designing experiments, working toward innovation is little more than betting on a hunch.

Appreciate employees' ideas

Ideas are worth little if they can't be captured, executed upon and ultimately brought to market. To foster an environment that encourages inquiry and exploration, a number of organizations have institutionalized something called the "astonishment report." At the end of an employee's induction period, new hires are often required to write about and discuss with their boss anything and everything that they noticed or found generally interesting or surprising since beginning to work with the company. Such an activity not only serves to show that even the ideas and contributions of new hires are valued by management and the organization at large, but gives leadership and other company long-timers an opportunity to view sometimes aging products, services and processes through a whole fresh set of eyes.

There are as many ways to leverage the ideas of internal employees as there are organizations (or employees!). Some companies work to capture employee ideas by encouraging people to congregate and exchange thoughts, often enabling them to connect dots across technologies and capabilities that might otherwise seem unrelated. Catering world-leader Sodhexo, for example, holds a fair during which all of the company's operating units have an opportunity to share internal examples of innovation and best practice.

Role models and structures

In a lot of ways, to the outside world and to employees across an organization, culture is best reflected in and embodied by the attitudes of its leadership. People around the company look to leadership for cues; leadership effectively models acceptable and encouraged behaviors to both internal and external customers. Leadership that supports a culture of strategic discoveries is reflected both in praising people that take risks and in modeling the kind of exploration necessary to push the bounds of existing markets. Top management that penalizes risk-taking, focuses disproportionately on short-term gains and shows little interest in exploring emerging and 'not yet' markets will fail to develop the kind of innovation that can disrupt current markets and create new ones.

Re-shaping the culture of an organization requires consistency and alignment. By nurturing an innovative culture, the likelihood of crowding out breakthrough innovation with the dogged pursuit of incremental innovations becomes less and less likely.

Leading the Startup Corporation: Strategy, incentives and management systems

So far, we've discussed ways in which leaders seeking breakthrough innovation can foster innovative cultures, as well as some of the characteristics that effective leaders can nurture in themselves. Innovative organizations require a management infrastructure to support both the work of the leadership team and the company culture. Beyond the soft foundations of culture and leadership, there are three fundamental hard foundations necessary for the successful pursuit of breakthrough innovation—strategy, incentives and management systems. Each of these hard foundations plays an important role in terms of ensuring that an organization has the ability to foster breakthrough innovations, as well as develop market-grabbing incremental innovations.

Strategies for breakthrough innovation

Strategies emerging from traditional business units often focus on incremental innovations—constantly looking for ways to further advance the reach and influence of existing business models. These sorts of strategic plans begin by analyzing a current industry and assume that the forces shaping existing markets won't change drastically in the immediate future. This type of assumption also takes for granted the idea that past organizational strengths will carry on into the future. The intersection of these assumptions—that industry will remain largely unchanged and that current company strengths will be suitable to remain competitive—defines the evolution of current strategies.

Companies that focus more on playing defense than offense carefully craft their strategies to further advance current business models. When it comes to resource allocation, this translates into building additional competitive advantage against existing competitors—the unspoken bet being that the industry will remain stable, and the best use of resources is to strengthen the organization's current position, gain market share and capture an incrementally higher percentage of the industry's value. Defensive attitudes toward breakthrough innovations are to essentially wait-and-see, with the expectation of having enough knowledge and resources not to lose when seismic shifts in industry take place. By investing small quantities (compared to more aggressive counterparts) in technologies, startups and networks that could lead to potentially disruptive change, defensive strategies hope to adapt quickly to the new industry structure only if and when it comes.

Companies playing aggressively still need to compete successfully in existing markets to survive. They develop a short-term strategy, but they devote additional attention and resources to exploring potential ways to upset existing markets and create new ones. Rather than put the majority of their organizational focus on operational efficiency and making incremental improvements to current products, processes and services, aggressive companies design two distinct strategies simultaneously—one for the current value proposition and another to explore growth opportunities. The two ultimately share the common goal of increasing growth, but they vastly differ in their methods. While the first pays particular attention to industry analysis matched against the capabilities of the organization in the traditional sense, the second focuses on exploration and creating an environment conducive to strategic discoveries.

Aggressive strategies make a portion of resources available to creative people in the organization, allowing them to better explore radical ideas and the myriad ways an organization might be able to capitalize on them. Of course, this sort of play-to-win strategy doesn't involve unfocused, unfettered spending in areas where promise is unlikely. On the contrary, it involves making educated guesses, experimenting and setting rough limits on exploration. For example, Swiss pharmaceutical company Novartis limits exploration to small, carefully defined groups of patients. Focusing on smaller but numerous exploration fields, they believe, will lead to more effective therapies and fewer side-effects (Capell, 2009).

While leadership won't always be able to predict from where new discoveries will emerge, they can certainly use their weight to focus exploration. As important as overall organizational strategy is to effectively and efficiently seeking out breakthroughs, motivating employees to execute and perform within such a strategy is hugely important to the successful pursuit of innovation.

Incentives for breakthrough innovation

Incentives play a central role in innovation. While some have argued for limiting economic incentives because they kill creativity and narrow employee's proverbial field of vision,[6] others charge economic incentives with being the reason for the successes of many high-growth startups (Lerner, 2012). Finding a meaningful balance and determining what is most effective for growth within your own organization can help leaders push employees toward more and better innovation. Often, innovation is driven by an internal drive to create and does not happen because of some sort of economic incentive. Still, people need to trust that they will be fairly rewarded if their efforts and ideas end up being successfully implemented.

Extrinsic motivation has everything to do with providing some type of payout for pursuing and achieving a certain objective. It's the sort of motivation which is tied to commissions and bonuses and which drives salespeople and managers to hit their numbers. While salespeople may enjoy selling and managers may appreciate the pace and environment of corporate life in and of itself, the prospect of receiving additional compensation for meeting objectives can motivate employees to find new and creative ways of achieving goals.

But breakthrough innovation is different. People don't generally take the kinds of risks of failure that are necessary to pursue breakthrough innovation just because they might get a little extra something if they succeed. People work long hours chasing breakthrough innovation because they are passionate about an idea and want to make an impact—to change the way we live, work or conduct business in a meaningful way. It is this sort of intrinsic motivation that makes any individual want to pursue an objective for its own sake.

Even if passion is the main reason for breakthrough innovation, a flat salary is often the wrong incentive structure as startups have already proven. For incentives to remain in the background and let passion do its work, people need to see their compensation as fair. Oftentimes, it means receiving a large payoff if the effort succeeds. A flat salary can easily be seen as unfair for a group that developed a breakthrough innovation and deter other people from taking risks. The organization will be perceived as failing to share in the value created with those that put in the effort, shared their skills and took risks.

Amazon founder Jeff Bezos has said, "You don't choose your passions; your passions choose you."[7] When natural passion motivates people, odds of success aren't necessarily better, but failure is much more likely to be seen as a temporary setback than a definitive end. As Winston Churchill once described success as "moving from failure to failure without losing enthusiasm," solid advice for identifying areas of exploration and seeking out breakthroughs is to pursue passion and the money will come (Kawasaki, 2010).

When it comes to encouraging passionate exploration, vision and values—known collectively as belief systems (Simons, 1995)—create context and inspire employees to use their efforts and creativity to pursue worthwhile goals. Design departments of a number of fashion firms, for example, are especially deliberate when it comes to shaping the environment in which designers work. In the hopes of providing a consistent source of design inspiration for employees, these types of organizations often sponsor trips to places related to themes of a particular collection, develop picture collages on the theme, equip their spaces with books and archives for knowledge building, and host networking events to seed the theme in potential markets.

Strategic discoveries often require leaders and employees across an organization to devote many hours beyond those present in a regular working day. Even outside of work, an innovator's brain is almost constantly churning and tweaking the next big idea. Developing meaningful breakthroughs requires the social skills to create internal support and access resources and external networks to experiment with the model.

While breakthrough innovation usually comes from passionate people doggedly pursuing an idea for reasons largely unrelated to compensation, any organization serious about developing breakthroughs has to provide both a compelling vision and fair rewards if productive passion is to thrive. The perception of what constitutes a fair reward varies across companies, professions, geographies and cultures. As much as company strategy and balanced incentive packages surrounding breakthrough innovation vary across organizations industries, so do management systems.

Management systems for breakthrough innovation

Beyond strategy and incentives, management systems and processes create the underlying structure needed to support the development of breakthrough innovation. As companies grow, they need to determine best practices for structuring functions like exchanging information, coordination and resource allocation. For instance, if your people need to explore ideas beyond the limits of the current business model, they need the resources to do so, but shouldn't be given so many resources or such long timelines that the sense of urgency needed to go beyond toying around with an idea is lost. Companies like 3M and Google give many of their employees a proportion of work time to explore ideas not necessarily related to their day-to-day duties.

Management systems and company culture reinforce each other by stimulating exploration efforts in the hopes of transforming them into valuable innovations. Policies that support exploration efforts include communicating strategic boundaries, allocating resources for exploration and holding events that bring together diverse groups of people to reinforce ties to external networks.

Accounting and tax software company Intuit has formalized connections with external networks by constantly interacting with customers and inviting promising startup companies to its headquarters—to both learn about them and nurture possible partnerships (Johnson, 2011). Founder Scott Cook decided that customer input was important to Intuit's innovation, and could be leveraged to build content. Still, he understood that ideas about the ways to most effectively involve external input would need to arise from within the company itself. By providing a challenge, setting boundaries and letting people experiment within them, he protected experimentation from being routinized by the everyday operations of the organization while managing risk at the same time (Cook, 2008).

Systems and processes like these help to bring much needed structure to the early stages of new ideas. The way an organization's management systems are ultimately designed can influence whether ideas come into the light too soon—ending up killed outright or transformed into incremental innovations by short-term strategies—or have enough breathing space to be meaningfully developed before being presented to the rest of the company. For example, Steve Jobs prolonged the secrecy of many Apple breakthrough projects almost until they were released to the public. This attitude of secrecy was not only directed toward the world outside the organization, but it existed within the walls of the company in the form of off-limits areas, silos, secrecy and the threat of being fired for leaking sensitive information (Lashinsky, 2012).

Management systems can further structure the flow of ideas through establishing effective selection processes. For example, idea fairs can help organizations select the best ideas according to the wisdom of the internal company crowd. Seeing which ideas presented to employees receive the most support in the form of votes can help determine which projects receive additional resources. Gillette, for example, used innovation fairs where business units across the organization got a chance to display their most promising concepts—everything from demoing new product ideas to methods for the legal department to highlight ethical standards (Emmons, Hanna and Thompson, 2012). Of course, leaders can always influence this sort of process by choosing ideas they see as promising alongside those "voted up" in a more democratic fashion.

Alternatively, organizations can set processes and management systems to flow ideas up to top management, allowing leadership to determine which projects should receive additional funding. For example, companies like Infosys, the Indian software giant, hold management meetings under what they call "the 30/30 rule," where "30% of the participants in a strategy discussion should be younger than age 30, because they are creative and not wedded to the past." Infosys also invites clients to meetings where they are given the opportunity to challenge internal assumptions and offer their own perspective on ideas that could have an impact on further growing the company. Beyond soliciting input from youth and customers, Infosys hosts events like strategy graffiti walls or jam sessions around strategic questions. While these sorts of semi-structured processes have led Infosys to identify important incremental innovations, they have also resulted in the development of important breakthrough ideas in fields like healthcare and education (Govindarajan and Timble, 2011).

Lastly, to execute on potentially breakthrough ideas, an organization needs to leverage the existing networks, resources and proverbial muscle of the company. Integrating new efforts into an existing organizational framework relies on developing efficient and effective systems and processes. Managing breakthrough activities—from exploring emerging ideas through their integration into the existing organization—requires an overall view of the health of projects in the pipeline. Measurement and information systems can provide the information necessary for this sort of monitoring (Davila, Esptein and Shelton, 2006).

Conclusion

The factors that influence whether or not an established organization develops breakthrough innovations are myriad and complex. Still, if companies like Google, Apple, 3M and others are any indication, established organizations are more than capable of developing breakthroughs. In fact, compared to startups, once a breakthrough idea is identified, the networks, the resources and the ability to scale and execute that are the strong suits of established companies distinct advantages to those firms.

From a leadership perspective, fostering leadership qualities like passion and comfort with ambiguity, working toward creating a space for innovative cultures to flourish and ensuring the hard foundations of strategy, incentives and management systems are all well established can go a long way toward laying the groundwork for breakthrough innovations. While incremental innovations are undeniably important for the immediate, short-term success of any organization, it is essential for established organizations to devote at least some portion of time and resources to exploring the "not yet". Sure, there are risks inherent in experimenting with processes, products and business models never before seen. But the risks of not doing so are far greater.

Notes

This chapter is based on the ideas developed in the book Davila, T. and M. J. Epstein (2014) "The Innovation Paradox. Why Good Business Kill Breakthroughs and How They Can Change" (San Francisco: Berrett-Koehler Publishers).

1. Excellent management books exist on tools for continuous improvement. For example, Simons, R. (1999) "Performance Measurement and Control Systems for Implementing Strategy" (Upper Saddle River, NJ: Prentice Hall).

2. Israelson, A. (2007) "Transcript–Bill Gates and Steve Jobs at D5" *All Things D* 31 May 2007, Available at: http://allthingsd.com/20070531/d5-gates-jobs-transcript/ (Accessed 5 February 2015).
3. Lou Gerstner, quoted in T. Davila and M. J. Epstein (2014), "The innovation paradox" (San Francisco: Berrett-Koehler Publishers).
4. Gallo, C. (2011) "Steve Jobs: Get Rid of the Crappy Stuff" *Forbes Magazine* Available at: http://www.forbes.com/sites/carminegallo/2011/05/16/steve-jobs-get-rid-of-the-crappy-stuff/ (Accessed 5 February 2015).
5. Zappos.com (1999) Available at: http://www.zapposinsights.com/about/faqs (Accessed 5 February 2015).
6. This discussion dates back to the concept of hygiene factors: Herzberg, F. (1966) "Work and the Nature of Man" (Oxford: World Publishing). See also Jensen, M. C. (2000) "Theory of the Firm: Governance, Residual Claims, and Organizational Forms" (Cambridge: Harvard University Press). Also, Kohn, A. (1993) "Why Incentive Plans Cannot Work" *Harvard Business Review*, September–October.
7. Walker, R. (2004) "Jeff Bezos, Amazon.com, Because Optimism is Essential" *Rob Walker, Inc* Available at: http://www.inc.com/magazine/20040401/25bezos.html (Accessed 5 February 2015).

References

Capell, K. (2009) "Novartis Radically Remaking its Drug Business" *Businessweek*, June 22: 30–35
Cook, S. (2008) "The Contribution Revolution: Letting Volunteers Build Your Business" *Harvard Business Review* 86 (10): 60–69
Davila, T. and Epstein, M. J. (2014) "The Innovation Paradox. Why Good Business Kill Breakthroughs and How They Can Change" (San Francisco: Berrett-Koehler Publishers)
Davila, T., Epstein, M. J. and Shelton, R. (2006) "Making Innovation Work: How to Manage It, Measure It, and Profit from It" (Upper Saddle River, NJ: Prentice Hall)
Emmons, G., Hanna, J. and Thompson, R. (2012) "Five Ways to Make Your Company More Innovative" Research Ideas, *Harvard Business School Working Knowledge*, 23 May.
Gardiner, E. and Jackson, C. J. (2011) "Workplace Mavericks: How Personality and Risk-Taking Propensity Predicts Maverickism" *British Journal of Psychology* 103(4): 497–519
Goffee, R. and Jones, G. (1998) "The Character of a Corporation: How your Company's Culture Can Make or Break Your Business" (London: Harper Collins Business)
Govindarajan, V. and Timble, C. (2011) "The CEO's Role in Business Model Reinvention" *Harvard Business Review*, 109–114
Jensen, M. C. (2000) "Theory of the Firm: Governance, Residual Claims, and Organizational Forms" (Cambridge, MA: Harvard University Press)
Johnson, S. (2011) "On the Inside, Looking Out" *CFO:* 21–24
Herzberg, F. (1966) "Work and the Nature of Man" (Oxford: World Publishing)
Kawasaki, G. (2010) "Ten Commandments from an Entrepreneurial 'Evangelist' " *Knowledge at Wharton.*

Kelly, T. (2001) "The Art of Innovation: Lessons in Creativity from IDEO, America's Leading Design Firm" (New York: Random House)

Kohn, A. (1993) "Why Incentive Plans Cannot Work" *Harvard Business Review*, September–October.

Lashinsky, A. (2012) "The Secrets Apple Keeps" *Fortune* (165): 85–94.

Lerner, J. (2012) "The Architecture of Innovation: The Economics of Creative Organizations" (Boston, MA: Harvard Business Review Press)

Simons, R. (1995) "Levers of Control: How Managers Use Innovative Control Systems to Drive Strategic Renewal" (Boston, MA: Harvard Business School Press)

Simons, R. (1999) "Performance Measurement and Control Systems for Implementing Strategy" (Upper Saddle River, NJ: Prentice Hall)

Stone, B. (2013) "Inside the Moonshot Factory: Google X's Silicon Valley Nerd Heaven—America's Last great Corporate Research Lab" *Bloomberg Business Week*, 22 May.

4
Empowering Growth from Within: Cultivating Conditions for Intrapreneurship to Thrive

M. Julia Prats and Susanna Kislenko

Introduction

Product and service expansion opportunities that are connected to an organization's core work have a greater chance of success than those ideas that are unrelated to its main activities (Sykes, 1986; Sorrentino and Williams, 1995; Thornhill and Amit, 2001). To paraphrase this idea in the wisdom of Seth Godin, it is Blockbuster that should have invented Netflix and, by the same line of reasoning, Polaroid should have been the one to bring Instagram to market. But they didn't. Not only did Blockbuster and Polaroid not capitalize on their inherent wisdom with an eye to the future, they lost to their competitors that were innovating and encouraging internal (or corporate) entrepreneurship, which led to them both having to eventually close up shop all together. It did not need to be that way.

In a world of increasingly global markets and a fluidity of technical and business talent, where competitive barriers are blurred and threats come from unexpected directions, more and more companies are looking for new and innovative ways to grow. The leaders of these forward-thinking organizations understand that leadership embodies a foremost responsibility for creative action. Furthermore, they possess knowledge of the fact that the managerial function of leadership is "not just passive, adaptive behavior; it means taking action to make the desired results come to pass" (Drucker, 1954). For entrepreneurs in particular, this behavior is closely linked to innovation, and in the discussion of entrepreneurship within organizations, there are particular ways of organizing to promote innovation from within. This chapter will explore the importance of corporate entrepreneurship, also known as intrapreneurship, and propose that the best leaders prime their people for intrapreneurship through first, creating the organizational context for this activity to happen, and second, providing them with the right tools and foundation to freely pursue new opportunities on behalf of the organization.

Innovation and the intrapreneur

Prior to diving into the layers of intrapreneurship, it is important to refine our understanding of entrepreneurship itself. In the early 20th century, Schumpeter argued that an entrepreneur is someone who creates something new by reassembling what is already known; he defined the entrepreneur as the creator of the future, a person obsessed with working on the limits of the known to create a new reality (Schumpeter, 1934). We define entrepreneurship as a process by which a person (or a team) identifies an opportunity—a future, desirable and viable situation—and transforms it into reality, even in cases where the necessary resources are not all readily available (Stevenson and Jarillo, 1991).

For decades, an entrepreneur was identified as a single individual or a team who started a company from scratch. However, as some authors have largely argued (from Schumpeter, 1934, to Davila and Epstein, 2014), for most of the 20th century, innovation was the natural territory of large organizations. It was also Schumpeter who was the first to link innovation to the entrepreneur. Schumpeter clearly separated the *invention* from the innovation, invention being viewed as the means of creation of a new production function by trying new ways of doing business. In his view, the difference was in the action of experimenting. The entrepreneur was willing to try and find new ways of producing and bringing these new inventions to market, and this is what made them unique. This perfectly applies to the individual inside of an established organization.

Though it is not the purpose of this chapter to compile a history of corporate entrepreneurship,[1] it is useful to recognize that the idea of putting science and creativity at the core of organizations for the purpose of increasing productivity goes back as far as 1841, when it was mentioned by German economist Friederick List in his book *The National System of Political Economy* (List and Colwell, 1856). However, the figure of the internal entrepreneur or intrapreneur (Pinchot, 1985) and the systematic study of her/his activity go back only about 40 years. Though this is a relatively new concept, a number of theories on corporate entrepreneurship do agree on the importance of internal facilitation of intrapreneurship and on its influence on corporate performance and innovation (Hornsby, Naffziger et al., 1993; Morris and Kuratko, 2002).

Intrapreneurship is indeed important for the field of general management because it addresses entrepreneurship at the level of the firm (Miller, 1983) depending upon, yet going beyond, the entrepreneurial behaviors of the individuals that compose it. Corporate entrepreneurship has been studied through its consequences (Guth and Ginsberg, 1990), by way of the prism of individual behaviors (Burgelman, 1983), through the effect of specific processes as enhancers or deterrents (Rosenbloom, 1994; Gilbert, 2005) and by investigating how companies organize for these activities (Kanter, 1985; Wolcott and Lippitz, 2007). Intrapreneurship can also be described as formal or informal activities aimed at creating new businesses in established companies through product and process innovations and market developments (Zahra, 1991). Following this line of reasoning, entrepreneurship witnessed within existing firms is often referred to as corporate entrepreneurship or intrapreneurship. For the purpose of this chapter, we will use the two terms interchangeably.

The intimate relationship between innovation and intrapreneurship is well explored both in literature and in practice. Indeed, innovation has been identified as critical for economic growth (Lerner and Stern, 2012) and as a key ingredient of corporate entrepreneurship (Morris, Kuratko et al., 2011), where one can take an idea or invention and create something new of value for the organization. Innovation, however, is often mistakenly seen as a singular concept, and we do not believe this to be the case. Innovation is a complex phenomenon that takes different forms and shapes. As far back as the 1930s, Joseph A. Schumpeter defined innovation as the setting up of new production functions (Schumpeter, 1939). This definition cited five specific cases leading to a new production function, which are: (1) the introduction of a new product, (2) the introduction of a new method of production, (3) the opening of a new market, (4) the conquest of a new source of supply of materials and (5) the carrying out of a new organization of any industry (Schumpeter, 1936). Furthermore, together with more traditional innovations such as product/service innovation and process innovation, several studies report the increasing importance of systemic innovations such as those that are witnessed in both business and governance models.

If we agree that a critical objective of launching new initiatives inside established firms is to increase the probability of sustaining profitable growth over time, then it is of value to consider that it has been reported that business model innovators may increase their margins by up to five points in five years compared with product innovators.[2] From a managerial point of view, what matters is the magnitude of change that a given innovation will bring to the organization: from a mere improvement in efficiency to evolving the way an entire sector works or from changing a given function to redefining the value system of the firm. Although the process of implementing each one differs, all types of innovation require a certain context within which to flourish.

The context for innovation

Large, established corporations and new, maturing firms alike are confronted with the challenge of maintaining their growth, if not their very existence, by enabling the full potential of the unique resource combinations that they have assembled. Underlying any kind of growth strategy that the firm chooses to pursue, leadership plays a key role. It is well documented that sustainable growth increases the chances of attracting and retaining talent by expanding opportunities for employees, providing greater challenge for managers and satisfying their desires for higher salaries and prestige (Baum, Locke et al., 2001). The possibility of consistently delivering superior value to customers through innovation increases employee loyalty by providing individuals with an opportunity to cultivate pride and satisfaction in their work (Heskett et al., 1994). The best employees use their talent and motivation to raise their own productivity with a particular kind of urgency that further fuels their motivation, producing even greater results for the organization. These are the types of individuals that firms should go after and work hard to retain.

Although all firms routinely say that "people are our greatest asset" and fight for hiring and retaining the best talent, in truth, few practice what they preach. In fact, a review of managerial practices often reflects a mechanistic approach where people are still viewed only as a means for the ends of production. Visionary boards and CEOs surrounded by traditional-thinking corporate managers often make innovation virtually impossible; it can be compared to attempting to drive a sports car on a racetrack without an engine or trying to run with your hands tied behind your back. Conversely, creative and forward-thinking employees whose projects are constantly being shut down or mired in red tape will either leave the company or, worse, just give up and fall back into their risk-free daily patterns. Alignment and shared values are critical, and all employees need to have a crystal-clear picture as to how and where they fit into the intrapreneurial process and why it is mission-critical to innovate from within for the individuals in question, the organization and its stakeholders at large.

There are number of ways to both move the company forward and inspire intrapreneurship from within. These strategies include acquisitions, forging new partnerships, setting up internal incubators, investing in autonomous units or launching internal ventures. Although each expansion option covers the objective of greater growth in its own way, many of the strategies also require distinct organizational structures and thus a supportive implementation process. Launching internal ventures overall brings with it specific steps that involve identifying an opportunity, gathering a team, developing the appropriate business model and knowing how to maximize the firm's assets. This kind of evolution requires the appropriate kind of both leadership and management and, as outlined in Table 4.1, each option also carries its own respective opportunities and risks.

Previous literature has identified two types of barriers to launching initiatives inside firms: structural and behavioral (Wolcott and Lippitz, 2010). Structurally, firms are designed to be efficient in planning, operations and control, and this affects how one designs the systems, processes and routines within an organization, as well as how resources are allocated (Bower, 1970; Rosenbloom, 1994; Gilbert, 2005). In fact, management systems reward the short term, putting the primary focus on today's markets and pushing activities based on increasing the price of company shares. Moreover, financing models based on mature businesses are applied to new projects, often leading to an untimely and unnecessary death (Christensen, 1997). New initiatives require a different way of both thinking and acting; the intrapreneur requires a specific organizational context to bring forth and grow new projects and initiatives.

Following this view, it is worth reviewing the organizational context that facilitates the undertaking of intrepreneurial activity,[3] and the development of intrapreneurs. Academic studies provide us with long lists of conditions to favor the development of internal ventures (Burgelman, 1982; Burgelman, 1983; Miller and Camp, 1985; Sykes, 1986; Guth and Ginsberg, 1990; Zahra, 1991; Garud and Ven, 1992; Block and MacMillan, 1993; Greene, Brush et al., 1999; Morris and Kuratko, 2002; Sathe, 2003; Wolcott and Lippitz, 2010; Morris, Kuratko et al., 2011). We must note, however, that current research does not yet allow for the delineation of specific conditions that facilitate internal entrepreneurship, but this will likely be possible in the future when intrapreneurship comes into its own as a field of study. The existing research employs distinct variables that, at present, preclude the construction of a cohesive body of knowledge.

Table 4.1 Organizing innovation—selected cases

Model	Acquisitions	Partnerships	Internal incubators	Autonomous units	Entrepreneurial organizations
Cases	ISS, Mittal Steel, Microsoft, Cisco	Valeo, AstraZeneca, Novartis,	Telefonica-Wayra, Xerox XTV, Shell	Dow Chemical, RR Donnelly, Pitney Bowes	3M, Apple, IKEA, Intuit
Features	Appropriate for highly uncertain environments. Need excess cash or debt capacity.	Adaptation to specific development needs	Portfolio investment mentality Radar	New venture unit most common model Reward for creativity	Innovation part of DNA Part of everyone's daily activity
Strengths	Can choose "winning horses" Choose companies that have fit with strategy.	Benefits of flexibility. Permits pooling of the resources/ capabilities of more than one firm.	Developed opportunities—Allows for control.	Isolate new unit from tyranny of established business Relatively easy to set up	Continuous innovation Tolerance for failures
Limitations	Costly: typically high premiums have to be paid Reduces capability development in new areas	Risk of cultural clash Learning restrictions	Substantial resource requirements Portfolio management experience	Sustainability Reintegration	Difficult to replicate Large number of small ideas

However, through a synthesis of the existing studies and our own experience, we find common and sometimes neglected elements that are at the core of the entrepreneurial process, rooted in the creation of environments that allow for experimentation. Innovative work calls for an environment that allows for trial and error, experimenting and learning. This is to say that firm policies and processes must be designed to stimulate individuals to freely innovate, to contribute to the firm with new initiatives. Managers must manage the experimentation process and this is usually at odds with short-term efficiency; it is also far from mechanistic jobs that follow pre-established rules.

The aim of experimentation is to generate the relevant information required to attain a goal, the path to which is unknown, in a quick and cost-effective manner (Thomke, 2003). Experimentation is a low-risk way to learn, as it allows the entrepreneur to proceed with greater knowledge in choosing whether to accelerate the process or abandon it altogether in favor of a new one. When treading new ground, this activity is essential and is part of the toolkit that all entrepreneurs must know how to manage. In an ideal experiment, managers separate an independent variable (the "cause") and a dependent variable (the "effect") and then manipulate the former to observe changes in the latter. The manipulation, followed by careful observation and analysis, then gives rise to learning about relationships between cause and effect, which ideally can be applied to or tested in other settings. The result is iteration: innovators make progress through iterative experimentation that is guided by some insight as to where a solution may lie. Experimentation matters because it fuels the discovery and creation of knowledge, thereby leading to the development and improvement of products, processes, systems and organizations. As few resources have been committed in the early stages, decision-making is still flexible and other approaches can be quickly experimented with. Good entrepreneurs learn through frequent experimentation.

Within large organizations, however, experimentation is often both expensive in terms of the time involved and the labor expended, even as it has been essential to innovation. It is important to note that experimentation encompasses both success and failure; it is an iterative process of understanding what works and what doesn't. Both results are equally important for learning. Given that both common sense and a large body of empirical data support this idea, it is surprising that still many consider previous errors to be the spur of learning. The roots of this myopia are to be found in different traits common in old-style-mechanistic organizations: a culture that punishes disclosure of negative issues, lack of trust, unwillingness to face complex problems, resistance to change, and so on. Cannon and Edmondson (2005) provide an interesting analysis of these technical and social barriers to the activities—identifying failure, analyzing failure and deliberate experimentation—that lead to learning from the experience. In a nutshell, experiments that result in failure are not failed experiments, though they are frequently categorized as such. For the quintessential intrapreneur, such experiences would be opportunities to grow and to further put their ideas to the test.

However, there are not many organizations designed for accepting and properly managing this reality. It is not easy—especially when one is under the pressure of competition and must demonstrate results, and even less so when operating under a vision that places productivity and utility ahead of everything else. It is further difficult when mistakes cost the entrepreneur and the firm money, time and reputation. In many ways, it is the eternally false dichotomy between efficiency and the need to explore new paths to secure the future. It is false because the idea is not to oppose efficiency to creativity but rather to provide creative solutions that solve problems at all levels in an incrementally efficient manner. The real challenge is to organizationally set up space for innovation, for experimentation, when the firm has mainly—when not only—been designed to exploit its current assets.

The solution has come in different forms and shapes. The so-called ambidextrous organization (O' Reilly and Tushman, 2004) that manages a dual structure to allow for productivity on the one hand and innovation and experimentation on the other is one of them. It is a good yet daring solution. To establish the processes of exploring and exploiting at the same time is quite a challenge for many organizations. It entails dealing not only with different procedures but also with all types of managers and distinct mindsets at the same time.[4] Still, experience shows that setting up this structure is indeed a good initial step for management teams to grasp what an exploration setting entails, not only organizationally but also in the time needed to change and develop new personal capabilities. They quickly learn that successful experimentation happens in small units, flatter structures, organic forms of control and a culture of trial and error allowing for failure as something natural to the process, as well as understanding that experimentation itself is part of the managers' job. Management teams realize that the atmosphere needed to foster this type of work in human beings is not a passive "yes-person" environment, where obedience to the status quo overrides the spirit of imagination and personal freedom to explore. It is a place where the leadership consciously cultivates and encourages safe spaces for employees to both be expressive and try out ideas they may have for improvement and evolution of the firm and its activities. It turns out that if this way of working fits better with people's aspirations and after experimenting with it, there is no turning back. Sustaining this bet over time has allowed larger traditional companies evolve toward more nimble and progressive companies.

Although it may appear as an impossible reality, there are a number of firms that embody many of the outlined principles that help create a very good internal context. One such case is Pentagram, the international design firm, which was founded in the 1960s by three designers and has been recognized by *Financial Times* as "the Rolls Royce of Design" (Prats and Jordan, 2006). Since then, the firm has grown to have 17 partners and more than 150 employees with offices in London, Berlin, New York and Austin. Its wide-ranging portfolio includes the design of singular architecture (for both institutional and private clients), industrial design, brand development, web design, museums and exhibitions.

From the beginning, Pentagram's partners defined the organization as being focused on the professionals. In contrast to other organizations that have claimed the same, Pentagram's statement has proven true to their words. While the objective from the beginning was to deliver the best work for their clients, there were also fundamental questions that were key in setting Pentagram up for success. These included: What environment do we need to allow for free creation? How do we do that without compromising the economic performance of a company which has to compete with others that are founded on the principle of shareholder value maximization? How can we design a company that attracts the best talent in order to continue to attract quality clients, which in turn helps our professionals grow? How do we make it sustainable over time? They responded to these questions by creating an organization that significantly differs from the type of business enterprise to which we are accustomed.

Pentagram's business mission informs us of its singularity: "Pentagram is an organization of designers, where humor, humanity and a passion for the craft play as important a role as profit." Each designer is responsible for his or her team's revenue and expenses. Every job is important, independent of the client's status: "Everything matters. Dedication to cultural institutions is no more important than dedication to large companies or restaurants: it all contributes to a more advanced society." Projects are decided by a qualified majority of votes, although they are executed by a responsible partner. There is no formal leadership and each partner receives both the same level of compensation and equity shares, regardless of seniority or ability to generate revenue or profit. In the words of one of the partners: "Generosity means that we respect each other's work, share ideas and are willing to give each other the [financial] freedom we need." The firm is hired by renowned brands for the most exclusive jobs and that also corresponds with their economic performance. The environment of collegiality, equality and collaboration at Pentagram is primarily possible due to the unique structure of this informally organic organization, which allows for deep mutual knowledge sharing, common sense of belonging and a unification on the long-term vision of the partners involved.

Although emulating Pentagram's organizational structure in an exact way may not always be possible or appropriate, some large firms have understood the principals behind its success and are emulating many of its key features, including smaller groups that are self-regulated and thus incentivized by achieving impactful projects more than by money or status.

The case of Pentagram, along with many others, confirms that there must be alignment between the type of work that the organization focuses on, encouragement of innovation through experimentation and the policies, processes and the rewards that support them. Managers cannot put employees under a mechanistic organization and expect them to be heroes by jumping over the system to bring new ideas to market. Any attempt at launching a growth strategy based on new initiatives must carefully and consciously design such an environment to increase the chances of success.

Intrapreneurship as behavior: developing key capabilities

Any entrepreneurial activity presupposes knowledge and commitment. It is an activity that comes up against elements of ambiguity, uncertainty and complexity that appear in varying degrees when working on something new and without a proven process. Thus, if the performance of a task requires the development of a set of competencies,[5] the creation of new solutions (in the entire range, from incremental to radical) requires knowledge of what is possible, but above all it depends on a desire and a readiness to enter into unfamiliar territory. It necessarily involves eagerness to experiment and the capacity to learn from the process. Entrepreneurship also requires learning from mistakes and not getting discouraged, as well as starting over again and again. It thus requires an abundance of extra effort for which the entrepreneur must be prepared.

We believe that both entrepreneurship and intrapreneurship are not the result of personal traits—that is, something innate that belongs to a few lucky individuals. Rather, it is the result of behavior, actions that can be observed, repeated and measured (Stevenson and Jarillo, 1991). This perspective does not answer the question of *who* an entrepreneur is but rather what an entrepreneur *does*. This approach allows us to gauge a much broader reality, one that allows the view that entrepreneurship is within anyone's reach, in keeping with their abilities. This perfectly applies to internal ventures. As such, we propose that intrapreneurship is actually a more complete way of understanding human labor and, consequently, it is a path of personal development both in individual and in social dimensions. We believe intrapreneurship[6] should be understood as a behavior that characterizes all employees and managers who offer their strongest personal talents toward the common good in a proactive way, in order to develop new opportunities. This is with strong opposition to the "administrator," managers that play the necessary role of making process more efficient but lack the capabilities for promoting new projects. This leads us to recall each individual's responsibility for developing the necessary skills for carrying out this work in a professional manner.

Internal entrepreneurs must develop a set of capabilities to be successful in launching new initiatives. In general, previous research has classified them into three levels: business related, interpersonal and personal capabilities (Prats and Agulles, 2009). However, recent research has shown that being successful in launching new initiatives (outside or inside the firm) goes far beyond the prototypical characteristics that entrepreneurs are often portrayed as having.

Prats and Sosna (2015)[7] show that what sets apart successful entrepreneurs from those that have not been successful are a few specific characteristics. A longitudinal study of more than a hundred high-growth European firms and internal projects in eleven firm-units in medium-sized companies and fourteen units in large European corporations was conducted. The findings of the study shed light on the turbulent growth path that these firms endured. In fact, during the period of study, all of the organizations (or internal projects) experienced what would be defined as a "near death experience" at least once.[8] The factor that ensured the project's ultimate survival came down to one very specific personal characteristic of the entrepreneur at the helm of the organization: the ability to deal with a crisis. The crisis in question could have been triggered by a number of factors such as a client not paying on time, a technological glitch or even a venture capital firm deciding to sell at the wrong time. Specifically, for internal ventures, crisis was also triggered by sudden organizational or leadership changes, power struggles above the intrapreneur's job, being perceived as a threat and lack of access to key internal resources among others. In any of these or similar cases, it was likely that the leaders themselves possessed the common capabilities often attributed to entrepreneurs, including a level of comfort with risk, energy and creativity. Although these attributes may serve the entrepreneur well at the start of the venture, it was a deeper subset of capabilities that was imperative in navigating through unanticipated and challenging situations. We identified differential competencies at three distinct levels:

- *Business competencies and industry knowledge*: These are the skills and knowledge that enable an intrapreneur to exploit opportunities. When confronting unsettled contexts, an intrapreneur is more likely to succeed if he or she has a clearer understanding of industry evolution, the influence of institutional arrangements, the effects of globalization, techniques for developing markets, cash management and financing opportunities and specifics of a similar nature. The intrapreneur and her team must be experts in the industry in order to shift the offering toward the right place, aligned with the client's value proposition and taking into account the current firm's offering. These competencies come from experience supported by the appropriate academic knowledge—business schools scholars have spent the past decades systematizing knowledge and techniques to do precisely this.
- *Interpersonal competencies*: Among the different managerial competences that are important in this realm, two in particular stood out as being critical in the fight for survival.
  - Communication—Intrapreneurs are masters at creating prudent transparency with the right information to the right people. The most successful intrapreneurs visualize their projects so clearly that they are able to describe them in such a way that persuades others to join them in pursuit of that vision. Successful intrapreneurs adapt their language and message to communicate their project to different groups, including investors, other departments involved, partners and employees.
  - Negotiation—Finding creative solutions from among the negotiable alternatives and favorable agreements that benefit all sides. Good intrapreneurs are in favor of win-wins. Standing firm on the non-negotiables, without damaging the relationship. Building

good working relationships with customers, suppliers, investors and the board so as to be able to continue to negotiate in the future is critical. At the interpersonal level, more than at the business level, the best way a person can learn to both communicate and negotiate is through practice.

- *Personal competencies*: The need for sound self-leadership is critical to success during such difficult times. These competencies directly affect their team-building capabilities, more specifically their credibility and the willingness to cooperate in tough situations. Personal competencies are crucial for the exercise of judgment and for learning, both of which are essential for managing crisis.

  - Tenacity/discipline—Enduring periods of sustained intense effort and showing great energy. Successful intrapreneurs persevere in their undertaking or project, illustrating determination to succeed. They also wait patiently for results and are independent enough to change or to stay in the same business, even in an adverse environment.

  - Emotional balance—Managing uncertainty and ambiguity and not being overwhelmed or discouraged by difficulties is a critical component of success for entrepreneurs and leaders of all sorts, especially when they come from within. Assessing risk and objectively identifying its sources, as well as reacting well to both are closely related to acting with integrity and ethically in adverse situations.

  - Integrity—Sincerity and transparency of opinions and objectives are important, as it means acknowledging one's own mistakes and not blaming others in the process. This also involves standing by commitments that one has made, as well as using confidential information with proper care.

  - Self-awareness and humility—Self-knowledge, confidence and a capacity for self-criticism are important for all entrepreneurs. The best intrapreneurs are eager to learn and gain experience and know when to accept criticism, as well as to seek advice. Personal and professional track record plays a key role in this process. Surviving a crisis usually requires asking for help and, at times, calling in personal favors. Reciprocity requires a consistent track record.

Many of the personal competencies are acquired and strengthened through habit. They are an exhibit of the individual's inherent character, especially those in the sphere of integrity and humility. Although many times entrepreneurs are not portrayed as such, our experience in dealing with exceptional entrepreneurs tell us that these characteristics are indispensable because they overlap between the personal sphere and the interpersonal sphere and, through personal relationships, affect the business in a major way. It is interesting to note that authors as diverse as Pérez López (1991), Scook and Khurana (2004), Gintis and Khurana (2008) all agree that character is founded on certain habits and that these habits are vitally important to any person who assumes a position of leadership. Accordingly, the same authors contend that business should be taught as a discipline, which not only provides the necessary intellectual tools and technical skills but also builds character. A person needs habits of character, such as perseverance, diligence and determination, even to acquire strict business skills and to use them at the right time and in the appropriate manner. The only way to acquire such habits is by acting in a way that is consistent with them. Bhide (1999) characterizes it as an ongoing process of "guesswork, analysis and action." Character is built on one's own and other people's successes and failures—based on habits—grow stronger with each repetition.

For an intrapreneurial initiative to succeed, there must be people who achieve excellence in business, interpersonal and personal competencies—by both mobilizing their own competencies and those of their team and combining personal experience with systematic learning. The driving force, however, comes from the habits of character that enable an intrapreneur to make the right decisions in matters that are beyond his or her knowledge. Good intrapreneurs need more than economic, technical or intellectual resources—although they must have these, too, or at least to be able to summon them when required. Even the resources of their own temperament are not enough. Above all, they need to cultivate the habits of character that allow for gathering the right people around them, navigating the complex web of relationships, power balances and interests that every social structure contains, as well as guiding action and forming the basis of all they do as architects of the future (Prats and Agulles, 2009).

Finally, we want to point out that there is practical evidence of a mechanism that has proven very useful in dealing with the difficulties that an entrepreneur faces inside large corporations. Organizations need to look at the processes that are required to bring ideas forward and how they can encourage employees to regularly take risks. To facilitate this, a mentor can help an intrapreneur to understand the culture of the firm and work their way through the politics of the organization. Thus, the mentor should ideally be someone who knows the organizational structure well, as well as its various resources. Often this proves to be a winning combination: a talented entrepreneur with the right amount of energy and a few great ideas, as well as a mentor who will support the intrapreneur within the company structure. It is important to remember that an idea for a new-growth business rarely emerges fully formed from an innovative employee's head. No matter how well articulated a concept or insight might be, it must be shaped and modified, often significantly, and thus the individual will need support and a sufficiently sturdy safety net.

A good example of this mechanism can be found on the successful launching of Wayra, one of the largest corporate accelerators in the world (Prats and De Ros, 2013). Wayra, an operation 100% owned by Telefónica,[9] was launched in 2011 to host entrepreneurs from all over the world and to serve as a radar for the dynamic and complex industry in the telecom and communications space. The initiative was led by Gonzalo Martin-Villa, an IESE MBA alumnus with a team that he personally assembled for the venture. José María Alvarez-Pallete, Telefonica's CEO, served as sponsor of the project. In 2013, Wayra had launched twelve academies in ten different companies with more than 270 entrepreneurial projects being incubated and more than 22,000 projects reviewed. Other well-documented examples of the same activity have been found in firms such as Dow Chemical and R.R. Donnelly, among others. The achievements and the rapid pace of activity in each were possible due to the winning combination of an intrapreneur with the specific competencies described and a sponsor who had the formal and moral authority to successfully sort out all the regular obstacles that entrepreneurs regularly face inside big corporations.

Mental models: a threat to intrapreneurship

Setting the right context for experimentation and hiring for personal capabilities is just the beginning. Inside of established corporations, there are other obstacles related to the organization's cultural, structural and political traits that make it difficult to develop new initiatives. Competition for power, power abuse, misalignment between individuals and groups, among groups or with the organization as a whole are all possible points of tension. In addition, different forms of political manoeuvring may lead to different forms of information distortion, such as incompleteness, bias, censorship, and so on. Authors with distinct viewpoints agree on advocating for organizations with fluid communication, flat structures, higher participation of all members and the like (Senge, 1990; Brown and Duguid, 2001; Nonaka, Krigh et al., 2006). Paradoxically, however, organizations with a fluid, flat structure are not immune to these problems either, especially when they become larger, because their potential loss of clear reference points may lead to anarchy.

Although there are different ways of transforming a company into an entrepreneurial organization,[10] the executive team must be aware that all elements of an organization are interconnected and interdependent, and thus a change in one area usually means a domino effect in another. Each one of the elements that make up an organization—product/service offering, processes, policies, people, business model and partners—must be transformed in a systematic way.[11]

This type of evolution is complex in itself and makes the implementation very challenging. However, previous research shows that on top of all these there is a bigger enemy to fight, which is a prerequisite for being successful in implementing any of the other components. This is the existence and effects of mental models, closely related to the organization's ability to learn and adapt (Foster and Kaplan, 2001).

A key issue to take into account is that as soon as the company begins to grow, learning becomes essential for survival. Learning requires the existence of certain mental maps that are organized around relatively stable points of reference. Prominent scholars have highlighted the importance of mapping for organizations and individuals to learn, and also to be able to manage eventual changes (Argyris and Schon, 1978; Hedberg, 1981). Indeed, mental models help managers in problem solving, as well, particularly the complex problems that corporate decision-makers face. Mental models are images, representations or schemes[12] of how we perceive and understand the world around us. Like all models, mental models are abstractions of reality. The model is less complex than the real world. Without recourse to mental models, our cognitive system would be too overloaded with data to function successfully. The great virtue of mental models is their ability to simplify complex situations and distribute decision-making so that thousands of people in a company can make decisions day in and day out without having to coordinate each of them with everyone else in the organization (Johnson-Laird, 1983).

However, as useful as mental models are for a while, they clearly have a dark side, as John Akers[13] discovered. No matter how well constructed, all models are wrong in some context or time. Moreover, as the context evolves, the mental models that were once successful become outdated. When faced with discontinuous conditions, the mental factors that people generally favor, based on experience, expertise, knowledge and learning, become liabilities. The very mental models that are at the heart of managerial strengths may also surface as managerial weaknesses in an age of discontinuity. Oversimplification can lead to systematic errors of judgment, logic and forecasting, and blind loyalty to a flawed model can be costly. If a mental model becomes outmoded—in the sense that it no longer provides an accurate simplification or rendering of reality—then any conclusions or predictions derived from it will be distorted as well.

Therefore, refreshing the mental model of organizational leaders is a chief requirement of strategic management. There is, however, often aversion on the part of managers to change models because there is no guarantee that the new models will be more effective than the ones they are replacing. Consequently, if the existing models seem to be working, managers are reluctant to abandon them. Moreover, the leaders who created the existing mental models often have a vested interest in protecting them. They are unlikely to abandon them unless a change in leadership of the organization ushers in a new, more appropriate mental model. Studies show that decision-makers seek data that confirms existing mental models, rather than that which would contradict it. There is a natural human bias toward confirmation (Kahneman, 2011).

This has important effects on firm performance. Research shows that mental models have an impact on four primary areas of conventional "corporate architecture": decision-making, resource allocation, action and information systems. It is thus important to have internal mechanisms in place to be able to change these models. Without such mechanisms, it is next to impossible to bring fresh ideas into fruition and thus drive the organization forward. Learning is one way of characterizing the process of changing mental models and, as Peter Senge reminds us, "the most powerful learning comes from direct experience" (Senge, 1990). In essence, leaders may be aware of the effects and set up the training programs and organizational mechanisms that support this type of learning.

Conclusion

In numerous ways, entrepreneurship is a starting point for society building—not only through conventional (profit-oriented) companies but also with the work of other kinds of organizations, including non-profits, social enterprises and even within public institutions. These words are a call to all entrepreneurs—whether working independently or on internal projects for large companies—to reflect on the ultimate goal of their initiatives. If entrepreneurship is meant to be an instrument for solving humanity's pressing problems, then value creation—as something that extends beyond the purely economic domain and affects various groups (employees, shareholders, consumers and society as a whole)—should be seen as its primary objective. This requires a bold and magnanimous approach, more imaginative solutions and an extraordinary effort to ensure cooperation from everyone. In other words, hard work can only be sustained over time if the ideals that inspire it are founded on the entrepreneur's own values.

Being an entrepreneur within an organization, an intrapreneur in the truest sense, can be more difficult than being an entrepreneur of your own initiative. The reason for this is that prior to experimenting with and implementing a new project, the intrapreneur must spend a great deal of energy and resources just to 'jump through the hoops' of existing organizational infrastructure. In some cases, this work alone will drain the individual looking to drive change and leave them exhausted in the phase of creation of something truly groundbreaking that could greatly benefit the organization at every level.

With this at the forefront, the key element to keep in mind is that in order to drive success through entrepreneurship, it is necessary to both recruit and train people who are committed to developing the business itself as well as their interpersonal and personal abilities, and then to encourage such individuals to cultivate positive character habits and virtues. If creativity, personal initiative and entrepreneurship itself are based on the development of personal competencies, a special context is necessary for developing them. Ultimately, the objective is not to hire people based on their credentials (as these are the easiest to improve and expand), but rather on their personal capabilities. Once you have the right people, place them in a supportive environment and provide training on the various facets of developing new opportunities, remembering that intrapreneurship is a process that *can*, in fact, be learned and improved with time.

Notes

1. For a comprehensive review of corporate entrepreneurship, please see Wolcott, R. C. and J. Lippitz (2010).
2. For more on this topic, see IBM (2006) *Expanding the Innovation Horizons: The Global CEO Study*, p.14. IBM Global Business Services.
3. Previous studies have identified key elements affecting entrepreneurial activity. Some researchers have suggested the relevance of the industry in which the entrepreneur wants to start the company (Bates, 1995), the institutional context (Baumol, 1993; Gompers and Lerner, 1999; Busenitz, Gomez et al.,

2000; Steier and Greenwood, 2000) and the general state of the economy (Lin, Picot et al., 2000). Based on the findings of these studies, we can conclude that entrepreneurial activity requires a complex ecosystem in which entrepreneurs, financiers, government and its institutions, as well as large companies themselves each have a specific role to play (Gompers and Lerner, 2001).

4. Sometimes organizations can find a leader or manager who can do both, but mostly that is not the case. In large organizations, individuals often have trouble performing when there are uncertainties. A person can be very good at doing their job, getting even better with time, but may not be as good at exploring. With this in mind, organizations need to hire a different type of person for the kind of thinking that requires playing outside the box and thinking beyond the status quo. It is important to note that often these individuals do not comfortably fit the accepted culture of doing things efficiently.

5. We understand competencies as a set of abilities, capacities, attitudes and ways of approaching reality which lead to a given behavior.

6. As well as entrepreneurship.

7. Data for this research project came from three main sources. First, since 2005, we have had access to the CEOs of 62 European technology companies from 20 countries. Second, we also conducted a cross-sectional study where we studied the characteristics, behaviors and strategies of CEOs and senior managers (growth leaders) of eleven firm-units in medium-sized companies and fourteen units in large European corporations who had succeeded in generating and sustaining organic growth far above the average growth rates of their respective industry segments over extended time periods. For reasons of data triangulation, we also interviewed coworkers of the growth leaders along the same dimensions. Examples from our European sample are General Electric, Samsung, OTIS Elevator, UBS, Continental and Microsoft, among others.

8. A near-death experience can be triggered by any major "building block" of the new project (e.g. top management team, technology, investors, clients, etc.)—the borders between internal and external elements are often blurred. Furthermore, we see that even if all the elements seem to be promising individually, a missing "fit" (e.g. misfit between the top-management team and the entrepreneur) can lead a firm into a downward spiral compromising its very survival.

9. Telefónica is a global leader in the telecommunication space. It operates in 21 countries. It had consolidated revenues of 50,377 million euros in 2014.

10. For an example of such a transformation, see "IBM's decades of Transformation; Turnaround to growth" L. Applegate, R. Austin, E. Collins, Harvard Business School case, 2005.

11. See "Innovation in PwC: transforming the organization", with Pedro Alberto Gómez y Alfonso Gironza, E-163-E, IESE Business School, 2013, for a good example of entrepreneurial transformation.

12. In the field of psychology *schema* (pl. schemata) refers to patterns or thought structures that represent some aspect of the world. People use schemata, built up over time from experience, to organize knowledge as a means to understand what they perceive in the present. Schemata include stereotypes, social roles, worldview and archetypes. Schemata are critical to effective

cognition and decision-making. Without schemata or mental models, effective decisions would be impossible as the data and information used would be incoherent to the decision-maker. On the other hand, when a schema or mental model does not fit reality, but the decision-maker believes it does, the results can be disastrous.
13. IBM's former CEO.

References

Argyris, C. and D. A. Schon (1978) *Organizational Learning: A Theory of Action Perspective.* Reading, MA: Addison-Wesley.

Bates, T. (1995) "Self-Employment Entry Across Industry Groups" *Journal of Business Venturing,* 10(2): 143–156.

Baum, J. R., E. A. Locke and K. G. Smith (2001) "A Multidimensional Model of Venture Growth" *Academy of Management Journal,* 44(2): 292–303.

Baumol, J. (1993) *Entrepreneurship, Management and the Structure of Payoffs.* Cambridge, MA: MIT Press.

Bhide, A. (1999) "Developing Start-up Strategies" In W. A. Sahlman, H. Stevenson and M. J. Roberts (Eds.), *The Entrepreneurial Venture,* 2nd ed.: 121–137. Boston MA: Harvard Business School Press.

Block, Z. and I. C. MacMillan (1993) *Corporate Venturing: Creating New Business within the Firm.* Boston, MA: Harvard Business School Press.

Bower, J. L. (1970) *Managing the Resource Allocation Process.* Boston: Harvard Business School Press.

Brown, J. S. and P. Duguid (2001) "Knowledge and Organization: A Social-Practice Perspective" *Organization Science,* 12(2): 198–213.

Burgelman, R. A. (1982) "Corporate Venture Creation and Strategic Management: Insights from a Process Study" *Management Science,* 29(12): 1349–1364.

Burgelman, R. A. (1983) "A Process Model of Internal Corporate Venturing in Diversified Major Firm" *Administrative Science Quarterly,* 28(2): 223–244.

Busenitz, L. W., C. Gomez and J. W. Spencer (2000) "Country Institutional Profiles: Unlocking Entrepreneurial Phenomena" *Academy of Management Journal,* 43(5): 994–1003.

Cannon, M. D. and A. C. Edmondson (2005) "Failing to Learn and Learning to Fail (Intelligently): How Great Organizations Put Failure to Work to Innovate and Improve" *Long Range Planning,* 38(3): 299–319.

Christensen, C. M. (1997) *The Innovator's Dilemma.* Boston: Harvard Business School Press.

Drucker, P. (1954) *The Practive of Management.* New York: Harper & Row.

Foster, R. and S. Kaplan (2001) *Creative Destruction: Why Companies that Are Built to Last Underperform the Market and How to Successfully Transform Them.* New York: Currency.

Garud, R. and A. V. d. Ven (1992) "An Empirical Evaluation of the Internal Corporate Venturing Process" *Strategic Management Journal,* 13(S1): 93–109.

Gilbert, C. G. (2005) "Unbundling the Structure of Inertia: Resource versus Routine Rigidity" *Academy of Management Journal,* 48(5): 741–763.

Gintis, H. and R. Khurana (2008) "Corporate Honesty and Business Education: A Behavioral Model" In P. J. Zak (Ed.), *Moral Markets: The Critical Role of Values in the Economy*: 300–328. Princeton NJ: Princeton University Press.

Gompers, P. A. and J. Lerner (1999) *The Venture Capital Cycle*. Cambridge, MA: MIT Press.

Gompers, P. A. and J. Lerner (2001) *The Money of Invention*. Boston: Harvard Business School Press.

Greene, P. G., C. G. Brush and M. M. Hart (1999) "The Corporate Venture Champion: A Resource-Based Approach to Role and Process" *Entrepreneruship in Theory and Practice*, 23: 103–122.

Guth, W. D. and A. Ginsberg (1990) "Corporate Entrepreneurship" *Strategic Management Journal*, 11(Summer): 5–15.

Hedberg, B. (1981) "How Organizations Learn and Unlearn" In P. C. Nystrom and W. H. Starbuck (Eds.), *Adapting Organizations to Their Environment*: Vol. 1, 3–27. New York: Oxford University Press.

Heskett, J. L., T. O. Jones, G. W. Loveman, W. E. Sasser and L. A. Schlesinger (1994) "Putting the Service-Profit Chain to Work" *Harvard Business Review*, Reprint 94204.

Hornsby, J. S., D. W. Naffziger, D. F. Kuratko and R. V. Montagno (1993) "An Integrative Model of the Corporate Entrepreneurship Proces" *Entrepreneruship in Theory and Practice*, 17(2): 29–37.

Kahneman, D. (2011) *Thinking, Fast and Slow*. New York: Farrar, Straus and Giroux.

Kanter, R. M. (1985) "Supporting Innovation and Venture Development in Established Companies" *Journal of Business Venturing*, 1(1): 47–60.

Lerner, J. and S. Stern (Eds.) (2012) *The Rate & Direction of Inventive Activity Revisited*. Chicago: The University of Chicago Press.

Lin, Z., G. Picot and J. Compton (2000) "The Entry and Exit Dynamics of Self-Employment in Canada" *Small Business Economics*, 15(2): 105–125.

List, F. and S. Colwell (1856) *National System of Political Economy*. Philadelphia: J.B. Lippincott & Co.

Miller, A. and B. Camp (1986) "Exploring Determinants of Success in Corporate Ventures" *Journal of Business Venturing*, 1(1): 87–105.

Miller, D. (1983) "The Correlates of Entrepreneurship in Three Types of Firms" *Management Science*, 29(7): 770–791.

Morris, M. H. and D. F. Kuratko (2002) *Corporate Entrepreneurship*. Orlando Florida: Harcourt College Publishers.

Morris, M. H., D. F. Kuratko and J. G. Covin (2011) *Corporate Entrepreneurship and Innovation: Entrepreneurial Development within Organizations*. South-Western: Cengage Learning.

Nonaka, I., G. v. Krigh and S. Voelpel (2006) "Organizational Knowledge Creation Theory: Evolutionary Paths and Future Advances" *Organization Studies*, 27(8): 1179–1208.

O'Reilly, C. A. and M. L. Tushman (2004) "The Ambidextrous Organization" *Harvard Business Review*, 82(4): 74–83.

Pérez López, J. A. (1991) *Teoria de la Acción Humana en las Organizaciones*. Madrid: Rialp.

Pinchot, G. (1985) *Intrapreneuring: Why You Don't Have to Leave the Corporation to Become and Entrepreneur*. New York: Harper and Row.

Prats, M. J. and M. d. M. De Ros (2013) "Intrapreneurship in Telefonica: Wayra a Company Faster than the Wind E-162-E" *IESE Business School*. Barcelona.

Prats, M. J. and M. Jordan (2006) "Pentagram: The Craft of Design E-88-E" *IESE Business School*. Barcelona.

Prats, M. J. and R. Agulles (2009) "Beyong Business Instinct" *IESE Insight*, Vol. Second Quarter: 50–57: IESE Business School.

Rosenbloom, D. and C. M. Christensen (1994) "Technological Discontinuities, Organizational Capabilities, and Strategic Commitments" *Industrial and Corporate Change*, 3(3): 655–685.

Sathe, V. (2003) *Corporate Entrepreneurship. Top Managers and New Business Creation.* Cambridge, UK: Cambridge University Press.

Scook, S. and R. Khurana (2004) "Developing 'Leaders of Character from West Point' " In R. Gandossy and J. Sonnenfeld (Eds.), *Leadership and Governance from the Inside Out*: 213–233. New York: Wiley.

Schumpeter, J. A. (1934) *The Theory of Economic Development.* Cambridge, MA: Harvard University Press.

Schumpeter, J. A. (1939) *Business Cycles: A Theoretical, Historical, and Statistical Analysis of the Capitalist Process.* New York and London: McGraw-Hill.

Senge, P. M. (1990) *The Fith Discipline: The Art and Practice of the Learning Organization.* New York: Doubleday/Currency.

Sorrentino, M. and M. L. Williams (1995) "Relatedness and Corporate Venturing: Does it Really Matter?" *Journal of Business Venturing*, 10(1): 59–73.

Steier, L. and R. Greenwood (2000) "Entrepreneurship and the Evolution of Angel Financial Networks" *Organization Studies*, 21(1): 163–192.

Stevenson, H. H. and J. C. Jarillo (1991) "A New Entrepreneurial Paradigm" In P. R. L. A. Etzioni (Ed.), *Socioeconomics: Toward a New Synthesis*: 185–208. New York: ME Sharpe, Inc.

Sykes, H. B. (1986) "The Anatomy of a Corporate Venturing Program: Factors Influencing Success" *Journal of Business Venturing*, 1(3): 275–293.

Thomke, S. H. (2003) *Experimentation Matters.* Boston: Harvard Business School Press.

Thornhill, S. and R. Amit (2001) "A Dynamic Perspective of Internal fit in Corporate Venturing" *Journal of Business Venturing*, 16(1): 25–50.

Wolcott, R. C. and J. Lippitz (2010) *Growth from Within: Mastering Corporate Entrepreneurship and Innovation.* New York: McGraw Hill.

Wolcott, R. C. and M. J. Lippitz (2007) "The Four Models of Corporate Entrepreneurship" *MITSloan Management Review*, 49(1): 75–82.

Zahra, S. A. (1991) "Predictors and Financial Outcomes of Corporate Entrepreneurship: An Exploratoy Study" *Journal of Business Venturing*, 6(4): 259–285.

5
Developing an Innovation Mindset

Bruno Cassiman

Introduction

When asked about the most important change in the environment affecting their job, CEOs mention the increase in uncertainty and the need for constant change. But what is really driving this "uncertainty"? And more importantly, what consequences does this uncertainty have for the role of the CEO and the executive team?

In this chapter we argue that the drivers of uncertainty are affecting the innovation eco-system and, as a result, how innovation and profitable growth are generated. CEOs and their leadership teams need to reflect more carefully on how these changes affect their job, the skills they need and the people they should hire and promote in order to leave their companies to a generation equipped to thrive in this changed environment.

As we will argue, innovation leaders have to change their mindset. To operate as *solution seekers* rather than *problem solvers* they will need to be more comfortable connecting a diverse set of innovation actors, experimenting with different potential solutions, and organizing and structuring temporary project teams to create and capture the value from their innovation efforts.

In what follows, we first discuss the key drivers of the increased uncertainty in the environment. Next, we show that these drivers are simultaneously affecting the innovation process at different levels of the eco-system through important complementarities at the level of knowledge development, asset accumulation and the organization of the value system. Profiting from innovation in this environment is complicated because of these important interconnections. Finally, we conclude with some suggestions about how these changes require a different innovation mindset by business leaders and how they need to rethink how they connect with different players, experiment with different options and organize with diverse and temporary structures in this changing environment. These changes in the environment have clear implications for the development of the innovation mindset of business leaders, and we conclude by discussing an executive program at IESE Business School developed to instill precisely these changes.

Increasing uncertainty

In a recent article Prof. Fabrizio Ferraro and I highlighted four changes in the environment of CEOs that are driving this increase in uncertainty: globalization, digitization, communitization and politicization (Ferraro and Cassiman, 2014). None of these trends should come as a surprise to business leaders. However, the critical question is how these trends should affect the mindset of current and future business leaders and how they affect innovation and entrepreneurship in the economy as drivers of growth.

As the world is globalizing, differences in the business environment get accentuated. Our colleague Prof. Pankaj Ghemawat has argued that these differences should be leveraged in creating a competitive advantage (Ghemawat, 2011). Different countries have heterogeneous populations and, hence, a diversity of user needs that companies can explore. Moreover, differences in resource endowments between countries exist, leading to different relative prices. These differences lead to opportunities of adaptation, aggregation or arbitrage across countries and regions based on these differences.

Digitization drives the entry of alternative business models into a previously more stable environment. Think of how Airbnb is revolutionizing the rental space for apartments and hotels, or, how Uber is affecting the taxi business in different cities and locations. Products such as newspapers, music and movies become digitized, and different threats to their historical business models arise.

Technology has also allowed companies to become closer to their customer communities. In early experimentation, Ducati's former CEO Federico Minoli presented the designs for a new motorcycle, the hypermotard, to the tribe of Ducatisti in the hope that they would comment and propose adjustments to increase the attractiveness of the design to the community. At the same time these communities can self-organize, providing feedback about company products and behavior even without the company's involvement.

In an additional step, the community might even take charge of the product such as is the case in the open source software. Or, take for example the Icelandic company EVE that produces a computer game with more than a hundred thousand online followers. The community can propose and write extensions to the game. Moreover, these gamers have created a board themselves to interact with the company on important strategic decisions affecting the game.

This leads to our final key driver of uncertainty: politicization. Many other actors interact with the company in addition to customers, shareholders and employees. For example, regulators and governments affect the freedom with which an innovation can attract customers. Think of Twitter, Facebook and Google in Turkey or China. But we do not have to go to emerging markets to see this effect. Airbnb was fined heavily by the Catalan government for listing unregistered rooms, and the cars of Uber-drivers were confiscated in Brussels for operating without a taxi license. Companies and in particular larger multinationals have to grapple with their roles as not only actors in business but also actors in the political arena in order to deal with these issues. Moreover, different communities are pressuring companies to take their social responsibilities seriously and companies are responding. For example, Unilever's CEO Paul Polman has been very vocal in expressing the idea that "businesses can't be bystanders."

These four trends—globalization, digitization, communitization and politicization—fundamentally alter the environment of companies as to how they should think about strategy, about creating value and about capturing value through innovation. At the same time these drivers affect the overall business environment, and innovators will need to deal with these drivers of uncertainty in the environment as they critically affect the innovation process.

In what follows we discuss how the innovation eco-system and the innovation processes are changing and how companies are responding. In the final section we discuss how this affects the skills needed to thrive in such an environment.

The changing innovation eco-system

To sustain growth, companies are encouraged to be more innovative. Innovation is consistently ranked as one of the top three strategic priorities of business leaders. But what does it really mean to be more innovative? Where the locus of innovation more than a decade ago was the firm and often the R&D department of the firm, the environment has changed considerably and innovation can surge from many different places.

In the first place the actors themselves are changing. Who will be your competitor within 5 years? Who will be your client? What will the final customers look like? Who will be your suppliers? And who will provide complementary products and services to your offering?

Did traditional mobile handset manufacturers ever imagine that Apple or Google would become their competitors in less than a decade? Did they anticipate that the number of mobile subscriptions in emerging markets would outstrip those of developed economies? Or did they envision that apps would drive the demand for smartphones, battery power and memory, or that smartphones would displace digital cameras? Understanding the actors and the dynamics of your eco-system is a first step in positioning for innovation.

Moreover, globalization is affecting who is playing the game and in which region or country. Different local companies are being set up in emerging markets, tailoring to the local tastes. Some of these companies are internationalizing with a focus on other emerging markets where they might have a competitive advantage in understanding the specific emerging market customer needs. As growth for the time being seems to be generated by these markets, understanding how to deal with these new actors in different countries and regions becomes more important.

Digitization and communitization affects who is driving innovation. Digitization allows firms to easily experiment with new business models. Moreover, new digital technologies allow innovation communities and customers to connect more easily. These innovation communities are often intrinsically motivated by the fact of contributing to the innovation process. As a result, innovation can now be sourced from the crowd. Customer communities interact with the firms about the specifications of the product, offer opinions and aggregate ideas. And in some cases the crowd even selects the specifications or designs of the product by "liking" their preferred option.

The globalization of the firm's innovation environment also implies that different organizations affect innovation leading to an increasing politicization of the innovation process. Regulators in the case of Airbnb or Uber affect the reach of an innovation. NGOs or other government agencies can influence the visibility or reach of innovative ideas. For example, DARPA, the US defense agency, crowd-sourced the next marine off-road vehicle at much lower cost and much faster than any traditional defense contractor could develop it. Similarly, NASA has been posting problems to the crowd that their scientists have not been able to solve for decades. In one case, an algorithm to predict important solar events was improved by a retired radio-signal enthusiast. NASA had been spending millions of dollars on the project to develop an algorithm that could predict two hours in advance with a 50% probability of correct prediction. The crowd-sourced algorithm predicted 8 hours in advance with 85% probability of correct prediction and cost $30,000 in prize money for the winning submission.

Profiting from innovation

While most companies have innovation as a top strategic priority, they are also unhappy about the current returns to their innovation investments. Clearly, resources need to be invested into innovation. Unfortunately, resources alone are not enough.

To illustrate how these changes taking place in the innovation eco-system affect innovation returns, take the example of Apple's iPhone.

Who actually profits from this innovation? Clearly, final consumers that value the ease of use of a smartphone and are willing to pay a substantial premium over alternatives for the iPhone's seamless integration benefit from the iPhone. Apple itself obviously benefits from this innovation as its returns and increase in market value since the launch of iPhone in 2007 indicate. Early calculations show that about 65% of the revenues of the iPhone sale price accrued to Apple. But different suppliers such as Samsung and Siemens have done well to ride Apple's coat tails in the wake of the iPhone introduction. At the same time imitators such as Samsung (again), Nokia (at some point) and several new players have benefited from Apple's introduction of the iPhone and the expansion of the smartphone market such as Huawei and Lenovo. Finally, complementors such as app-developers and accessory designers have done well following Apple iPhone's lead as they offer clear opportunities to improve the iPhone's value proposition.

How should one think about innovation in such a context? What are the incentives to innovate? and how do firms capture returns to innovation in this context?

Complementarities in the innovation process

As the innovation eco-system has changed, appropriating returns to innovation, that is, profiting from innovation, has become more difficult. In what follows I argue that complementarities in the innovation process have become more important and are more difficult to manage.

This is why profiting from innovation is so difficult and why companies struggle with the returns to innovation.

Complementarities in knowledge

First, as some of my own research has indicated, internal knowledge sources and external knowledge sources are complementary (see Cassiman, 2009). As a result, firms that are active on the external knowledge market, while simultaneously developing their own knowledge internally, tend to be more successful. These firms are able to integrate different knowledge sources into more innovative products and services. However, managing the interface between internal and external knowledge is not trivial and has been the subject of many alliance and R&D contracting studies.

In the current environment technology has become available to crowd-source. Important knowledge pieces are distributed globally. Karim Lakhani and Lars Bo Jeppesen describe the case of Innocentive (Lakhani and Jeppesen, 2007). This online site originally set up by Eli Lilly broadcasts problems to the crowd and seeks solvers for these problems. Companies such as P&G, Boeing, DuPont or even NASA post these problems that their own scientist and R&D people have not been able to solve. On average a posted problem generates about 200 serious investigations and receives about 10 solutions. In 30% of the cases a satisfactory solution is generated to a problem that could not be solved internally by the company. Interestingly, solutions tend to come from very different geographical regions compared to where they are posed. Solvers mainly reside in China, India and Russia. Moreover, successful solutions tend to come from different disciplinary areas compared to where they arose.

Not only the source of solutions matters but also how the solvers are organized seems to matter. In a series of follow-up articles, Karim Lakhani and Kevin Boudreau argue that firms need to learn how to deal with different ways of sourcing (Boudreau and Lakhani, 2013). These problems can be organized cooperatively or competitively: competing teams generate greater variance in the potential solutions to the problems posed, but cooperating teams develop more robust solutions as they incorporate the improvements from other teams during different iterations. The actual circumstance and kind of problem will dictate how the contest should be organized. Moreover, internal versus external idea generation and internal versus external idea selection present different alternatives: crowds can help to develop solutions or can help select the winning idea (King and Lakhani, 2013).

A critical change in the innovation process is that within the company, innovators are not necessarily the problem solvers from before. Given the opportunities outside the organization, innovators have to become "solution seekers" and put the right people internally and externally together to come to a solution. This requires different skills for leading innovation compared to the traditional R&D and engineering roles for innovation.

Complementary assets

But it does not end at the technology-sourcing stage. Actually, capturing returns from innovation in the eco-system has become more complicated. Recent data from the Community Innovation Survey shows that Intellectual property rights such as patents seem less effective than alternative means of appropriation such as secrecy, lead time and the complexity of reverse engineering (Cassiman, 2009). So how should firms capture the returns to innovation?

David Teece already argued that the actual inventor often did not capture the returns to his or her innovation. GE and not EMI, the inventor of the CT-scanner, captured the returns to the CT-scanner because a critical part in profiting from the innovation was building up an adequate sales and service organization around the invention (Teece, 1986). Teece argues that other complementary assets under the control of the innovator in addition to knowledge are critical to capture returns to an innovation when intellectual property rights are weak.

Continuing with the example of Apple's iPhone we know that Apple's brand (ranked as most valuable brand by Interbrand), Apple's retail stores and iTunes, and its design capability are all critical elements allowing Apple to capture returns to its innovations. Customers camp out in front of the Apple stores when the next model of iPhone is about to be released. They might be willing to pay slightly more for an Apple iPhone compared to a Samsung Galaxy even though both are considered equivalent from a technical perspective. App developers share 30% of their revenue with Apple for the opportunity to feature on the iTunes app-store. The fact that you have all your music and apps neatly organized in the iTunes stores and can transfer this seamlessly to other devices favors dishing out the extra money for the iPhone.

Moreover, probably less well known is that Apple is involved in the design of the equipment used to manufacture its products. Partnering with its suppliers on the equipment design allows Apple to control the supply chain and appropriate some of the potential margins. At the same time it allows Apple to know exactly what happens in the supply chain. The importance of this control has become more critical with the politicization of the environment as the incidents with Foxconn have shown.

As a result of controlling these *other* complementary assets—in addition to dominating the technology—Apple is able to appropriate more of the value it creates with its innovations, providing it with a higher incentive to actually invest in innovation in the first place.

Other companies have understood this as well. Google bought Motorola Mobile in order to control some critical patents related to the Android operating system, and Facebook splashed out on Instagram. This site was building a community of friends where they posted their pictures and commented on them. Facebook was faced with a potential competitor as the site was becoming a separate social networking site. Control over critical complementary assets allow the firms to appropriate the returns to their inventions, and companies would do well to understand the structure of their eco-system to spot these assets timely or face the risk of acquiring them at a premium and reducing the return to their innovations.

Complementarities in value system

The complementarities in the innovation process are not only linked to knowledge and assets of a particular company—the innovator, but often times there are important complementarities in the value system that need to reckoned with in order to profit from innovation.

Barco has a leading global market share in digital cinema systems for movie theatres. Since the late 1990s Barco had been working on the technology for digital projection based on technology licensed from TI. Only two other players, NEC and Christies, were developing similar systems based on this digital light-processing technology. Most players in the value system agreed that digital cinema was an innovation that could create tremendous value for the movie business. In particular, digital transmission of movies would eliminate the very costly transport and shipping of movie reals and allow worldwide releases of movies on the same day. The industry calculated that on a yearly basis about $1.5 billion could be saved on distribution alone, not to mention all the advantages of digital filming, editing and special effects development. Nevertheless, it took until 2009 for this innovation to take hold in the movie business.

Movie theatres were not at all excited about replacing their analog equipment. The movie theatre business had very slim margins, and the new equipment was expensive and not supposed to last as long as their analog projectors. It wasn't until the virtual print-fee was instituted in the US that movie theatres started to replace their analog machines. Movie producers and equipment manufacturers created a fund that paid a fee-per-viewing of a movie in digital format. The fund would buy the digital projection equipment with these proceeds and lease the equipment to the movie theatres. As a result, it was not the technological innovation of digital projection that revolutionized the movie business but rather a financial innovation instituted by the studios and equipment manufacturers that finally made the industry and the movie theatres convert to digital projection.

The Michelin run-flat tire did not take off as an innovation that was inspired by safety and comfort for the final user. The tire itself—the technology—ran to expectation, but the service centers needed to install different equipment for repair and servicing these tires. Unfortunately, Michelin was unable to convince service centers in the country to invest in this equipment and provide customers ease of servicing. As a result, an innovation that could potentially revolutionize the tire business has failed to deliver.

Electric vehicles face a similar issue in their value system. To reduce the "range anxiety" of drivers about how far they can go with their vehicle, easy access to "fueling" stations needs to be provided. An important part of the Tesla strategy and part of the basis of their success in California has exactly been to provide easy (and free) re-fueling opportunities for their customers.

As these examples indicate, innovation requires buy-in, development and adoption of complementary innovations in the value system. Ron Adner terms this the need to use a "wide lens" when developing innovations as businesses should look beyond their immediate innovation opportunities to make sure that all the players in the value system are on board with the innovation (Adner, 2012).

Imitating and innovating

The most successful companies are actually good imitators as well as innovators. Listen to your customers, listen to your suppliers, listen to your competitors and be agile to adapt these ideas, leading to innovation success.

Sam Walton was notorious for listening to the customer ("the boss"– note that Rosa Garcia at Siemens has implemented a similar "who is the boss" attitude[1]) and checking what the competitors were up to. As a result he spotted the opportunity of developing supercenters in which discount stores combine food items. Supermarkets were adding hard goods to their product selection. As a result they were able to draw traffic through the food items and redirect it towards the goods that were the stronghold of Walmart discount stores. Walmart took the format on and perfected it by experimenting in Arkansas with different sizes and layouts before coming up with the supercenter format.

Similarly, Steve Jobs was a master at detecting customer wants and utilizing elements that had been around in the environment to satisfy these wants. Apple did not launch the first mp3 player, nor did they launch the first smartphone, but Apple was clearly able to spot the opportunity and appropriate most of the value from these opportunities through their expertise in integration and design.

Today a company like Rocket Internet spots successful business models in different markets (mainly the US) and transports them to Europe—a pure arbitrage play were it not for the fact that they experiment with the business model across different markets in Europe and attempt to adapt it to the local market needs, imitating and innovating simultaneously.

Successful innovators spot what lives in the eco-system. They are able to make the right connections between different players and experiment with different options in order to reduce some of the uncertainties. At the same time they understand how to capture value from these initiatives by organizing their knowledge and assets accordingly.

Leading innovation

The innovation environment has changed substantially. Globalization, digitization, communitization and politicization each have their impact on how innovation is achieved by companies today. Moreover, complementarities exist in knowledge sources, assets and within the overall value system. So how does this affect the people leading innovation? And what would need to change in current management education in order to deliver managers with the right skills and mindset for thriving in this changing environment?

We propose three critical elements that need to be addressed by management and management education when considering innovation in this changing environment:

- Connecting
- Experimenting
- Organizing

Connecting. As innovation is changing from a game of problem solving to a game of solution seeking, managers need to become more resourceful in connecting with other people that can provide (partial) solutions to the problem at hand. These connections can be across knowledge sources, across functions, across assets within the own organization or, more often today, across organizational boundaries. Tapping different sources and connecting them to create value will become an important skill. As often times managers will not have the formal authority to make these connections, informal networks will become critical in getting things done. However, creating this value will not be sufficient. These managers will need to understand the interaction between creating value and capturing part of this value as a return to innovation. This means that managers will need to be comfortable with diversity along different dimensions such as culture, age, gender and backgrounds. Harnessing the power of diversity will generate a premium, but only if one understands how to build these connections for creating and capturing value through formal and informal connections.

Experimenting. As there is no "one-size-fits-all" and solutions might be elusive, managers will need to be more comfortable experimenting in order to come up with solutions for their problems. Gone are the days that we can experiment in the lab. As innovation is not only linked to technology and knowledge, experimenting needs to happen in the field. Managers will need to feel comfortable running these field experiments, and one critical aspect of experimentation is dealing with failure. One can learn from failure. Setting up experiments that will yield useful knowledge regardless of success or failure will be important. As a result, a more scientific mindset will help managers deal with this challenge. Digitization has brought the cost down for experimentation, and Google and Facebook have been known to set up different experiments within their online environments. As discussed, communities of customers ("followers") and innovators can be leveraged to generate new ideas or to evaluate and select ideas.

Organizing. As opportunities for innovation can arise at any point in the eco-system, managers will need to increase their agility in organizing for innovation. More temporary structures will become the norm. Project teams will be assembled and disassembled as the need occurs. Probably, this will become the most critical skill in the process of innovating. How do we balance the innovation opportunities that arise in the eco-system with an efficient and effective operation of the company and scaling up activities? This will require managers that feel comfortable living with ambiguity: connecting and experimenting to learn about future opportunities while running the current business successfully. This means that the organization will be in constant movement, giving managers the sense that change is the norm rather than the exception. Michael Tushman talks about managers with "ambidexterity" in exploring opportunities while exploiting the current business activities. However, given the changes in the eco-system of innovation this "ambidexterity" will need to extend across organizational boundaries through connecting with unusual partners for particular projects. As Zhang Ruimin, the CEO of Haier, says, "We are no longer the ones directing things. We are the glue binding everything together ... we have to come up with myriad ways of managing resources" (Kleiner, 2014).

These important changes in the environment also require business schools and companies to rethink how they achieve impact by training business leaders for this changing environment. Not only top management but management at any level involved in innovation will need to adapt to this new environment as innovation is not tied to a particular function within the organization. Innovation becomes a mindset.

A case on developing innovation management capabilities

At IESE we have worked with one particular company in developing this change from within. In 2005 we started to develop a program on innovation for R&D-managers. An important objective was to connect the R&D function better to the innovation function of a technology-driven company. The program dealt with strategy, marketing, operations and processes, and entrepreneurship. However, all these subjects were tied to how the changing innovation environment was affecting these areas and how R&D managers needed to understand and integrate these changes into their daily business in the R&D function, that is, how they needed to connect better inside and outside the organization, how they needed to experiment more beyond the R&D function and how they needed to organize these innovation projects differently.

The program culminated in a workshop on key issues discussed during a week-long program that were relevant to move the company forward. In this workshop teams self-selected into projects related to their interest, and these projects would deal with connecting, experimenting and organizing better for innovation. At the end of the workshop a preliminary "pitch" was made to senior management. At the same time the project pitch provided a forum for interaction between senior leadership and the R&D function on innovation-related issues to reinforce the change in the innovation mindset.

The program achieved several critical learning objectives. First, participants realized that innovation is the result of important coordination efforts across different players. Often times, there will be little formal authority to move innovation projects forward, and several of the tools discussed and work-shopped during the program were geared toward learning to lead innovation through persuasion rather than through using formal authority.

Second, innovation is the result of recombination of diverse knowledge pieces. This requires diversity along different dimensions. Through the interaction of participants with different backgrounds—cultural as well as functional—and the use of adequate teaching materials and workshops, participants became more comfortable interacting in these more diverse innovation environments.

Finally, given the increased uncertainty in the environment and opportunity for experimentation, participants developed tolerance for failure and an ability to redirect innovation projects that is critical in the changing innovation environment. Failing often but fast leads to a more productive innovation pipeline. Moreover, asking forgiveness might be a better approach than asking permission for all possible innovation opportunities that present themselves.

Between 2006 and 2013 IESE faculty ran several editions of the program, training R&D managers in dealing with this changing innovation environment. Since then we have run similar programs for innovation leaders in different companies. However, one issue kept being raised during discussions between innovation leaders and senior management of this organization: innovation requires a change in mindset not only of innovation leaders but of the whole organization from the CEO down. In particular, an innovation mindset requires a tolerance for failure.

In March 2012, IESE was approached by a member of the executive committee of the same organization to discuss a program for their leadership team (top 150 executives, executive committee and their direct reports).

The recently named new CEO of the company had coined the name "happy underachievers" for his employees and was determined to bring out the best of his people by being more demanding on growth and innovation achievements. Business was growing but employees were not inspired.

A new strategy for the company was officially launched across the company in late 2013. There were four pillars to the company strategy. First, the CEO wanted the organization to outperform its peers through a good selection of core and growth businesses in the portfolio, through innovation and customer focus while leveraging their strong brands. Second, he wanted to globalize the company. Growth would mainly come from the emerging markets. Third, the company needed to simplify its operating structures in order to scale growth more efficiently. And finally, he needed to inspire his management teams, increasing accountability and excitement in the ranks of management.

Globalizing the organization, simplifying its structures and inspiring the management teams were a tall order for this business where the majority family owner was the custodian of the company values that permeated the organization. Moreover, the organization had historically operated with a strong hierarchy. Empowering management at all levels to make decisions while creating and enforcing clear accountability for ones actions required an important change in mindset.

Several ingredients went into developing a program for the top leadership team with a focus on innovation and entrepreneurship.

A new strategy was being developed by the company and the different groups within the company, but a coherent understanding of the strategy was needed to inspire senior managers. Aligning the leadership team was therefore a critical aspect of the program in order to develop a common mindset.

But clearly, given the changing environment and the current challenges, alignment would not be sufficient. Each senior manager needed to internalize the new strategy and understand what this meant for their role as a leader in the organization. This also meant sometimes challenging the CEO and executive team, something that was the exception rather than the norm in the current organization.

IESE faculty immersed themselves in the organization to understand the issues and the strategy of the organization. Direction came from the CEO. The program should engage participants to discuss the direction of the organization, creating a dialogue and trust between members of the leadership team. Differences in opinion should be openly expressed and would hopefully lead to productive opportunities to move the organization forward based on this trust created.

We developed a program for the leadership team. Given the size of the team, the program was run several times over two years to cover the whole leadership team. The different editions of the program were held in different locations representative for the company while reinforcing the idea of a globalizing organization in need for connecting.

IESE faculty proposed to write several cases on specific issues that the company was dealing with and that were tied into the new strategy of the company. These issues needed to be sufficiently concrete and controversial to generate discussion within the leadership team. The cases were discussed by a faculty member together with the "case protago-nist" and a member of the executive committee. The case protagonist explained the team's critical problems and how their mindset changed during the development of the actual case. The member of the executive committee provided the broader context for the case and how the case fit within the change of mindset that the executive committee wanted to achieve for the leadership team and the organization.

Each of these cases nicely connected to the different challenges innovation leaders faced in today's environment: connecting, experimenting and organizing. More importantly, the dialogue ensured coherence across the organization and the building of trust between the different members of the leadership team toward a mindset of innovation and growth in the future.

During a second day of the program, the CEO launched a challenge to the leadership team participating in each of the programs. He urged each participant to carefully contemplate what these changes in the organization and the strategy implied for their role as a leader in the organization: "what will you do differently tomorrow and what do you need in order to do so?" was the question.

Teams of executives debated this challenge, structuring their thoughts and focusing on one particular element that the team wanted to have a conversation on with the executive committee. These conclusions were presented in a plenary session where the executive committee did interact with the particular team on their proposed changes. These team discussions provided a way to structure the dialogue and create trust and understanding between the leadership team and the executive committee.

The key objective of this program was to align the senior management team on the new strategy and change their mindset. To the leadership team it became clear that without such a change in mindset the new strat-egy could not be successfully implemented at all levels. Through in-depth discussions of real strategic situations of the company, business leaders developed a sense of the coherence between different changes taking place in the organization because of the implementation of the new strategy. This mutual understanding enhanced their own decision-making process in making it consistent with the overall objectives of the organization.

Moreover, a second critical objective, also related to the other program, was to provide senior leaders in the organization tools to effectively move decisions and projects forward in an environment where cooperation and persuasion had become more important relative to the historical "command-and-control" environment that the organization was used to.

Together, the programs for the senior managers and the innova-tion managers have exposed more than 350 managers of the same organization to this changing innovation environment and the need for adjusting one's mindset. If business schools want to impact the direction of organizations, it will require affecting the mindset of a significant number of the executives leading these organizations.

Conclusion

Given the changing environment where innovation is taking place, business schools and companies need to rethink how they develop programs to reflect these changes in the environment. In this chapter we have argued that management programs need to reflect these changes as well in order to expose all levels of management of an organization to the need to change their mindset and engage in new ways of connecting, experimenting and organizing to create and capture value from innovation.

Note

1. Rosa Garcia, Siemens, CEO South Europe, during the Panel on "The CEO's innovation drivers in boosting corporate grow" on "The IESE Global Leadership Conference: Innovation and Entrepreneurship for Global Leadership Development," April 3, 2014.

References

Adner, R. (2012) "The Wide Lens: A New Strategy for Innovation" (New York: Penguin/Portfolio).

Boudreau, K. and Lakhani, K. (2013) "Using the Crowd and an Innovation Partner" *Harvard Business Review* 91(4): 61–69.

Cassiman, B. (2009) "Complementarities in Innovation Strategy and the Link to Science", *Els Opuscles del CREI* 23 Universitat Pompeu Fabra.

Ferraro, F. and Cassiman, B. (2014) "Three Trends That Will Change How You Manage" *IESE Insight Magazine* 23: 23–30.

Ghemawat, P. (2011) "World 3.0: Global Prosperity and How to Achieve It" (Boston: Harvard Business School Publishing).

King, A. and Lakhani, K. (2013) "Using Open Innovation to Identify the Best Ideas" *MIT Sloan Management Review* 55(1): 42–48.

Kleiner, A. (2014) "The Thought Leader Interview: Zhang Ruimin" *Strategy+ Business* 77: 1–7.

Lakhani, K. and Jeppesen, L. B. (2007) "Getting Unusual Suspects to Solve R&D Puzzles" *Harvard Business Review* 85(5): 30–32.

Teece, D. (1986) "Profiting from Innovation" *Research Policy* 15: 285–305.

6
The CEO as a Business Model Innovator

Joan Enric Ricart

Introduction

The tasks of the CEO are experiencing fast changes and so are the necessary competencies to deal with them. The world is changing fast, perhaps something that has always been true in general but of course different in the specifics. Technology, demographics, globalization, regulatory and politics are key drivers of change, and change comes with opportunities. In particular we claim that there are many opportunities for business model innovation.

As business model innovation evolves as a response to today's changes, CEO should develop competences to compete on business model. Therefore, it is relevant to meditate about what new or different competencies are required to the CEOs of today, so that they can better face the complex challenges their companies need to deal with.

As we develop this idea of competing on business model, we will uncover some competences that CEOs will need to develop. In particular we will focus on three of them: strategic thinking, system design and system thinking. These three competences transform the CEO in a business model innovator able to craft the novel business models that leverage change opportunities to create competitive advantage.

However, it is important that we do not forget that beyond changes, there are also stable factors in the leadership role of a CEO. As a consequence the focus on differential competencies cannot hide the essence of what leadership is and therefore should be developed. We need to develop the CEOs of today without forgetting we are developing first of all CEOs that need to be effective today but also drive well toward a future that it is clearly uncertain and where perhaps new drivers of change will require new competencies ... Let us make sure we get the essentials so we can move from today into the future.

In this chapter we will focus first on the role of a CEO and the essential elements of her tasks, so that later on we can discuss how these essential tasks are evolving today and how important in particular is the involvement of CEOs in business model innovation. We will then develop some ideas of what a business model is, what business model innovation is and why it is more important today for a CEO. With this background we will focus on three important CEO capabilities, and we will conclude with some final reflections on the CEO role today.

The role of the CEO

There has always been a great interest in what CEOs do (Mintzberg, 1973; Kotter, 1982; Drucker, 2004) and the impact they may have in organizations (Finkelstein and Hambrick, 1996; Barlett and Ghoshal, 2000) or how to develop some specific competencies (Mitzberg, 2004; Bower, 2008). I have been interviewing some colleagues and more than 200 managers with general management responsibilities as it is reflected on our publications (Ricart, Llopis and Pastoriza, 2007; Llopis and Ricart, 2013). With this background and our own experience of years of teaching and helping general managers, in Andreu and Ricart (2014), we developed a framework to identify the priorities associated with any general management position.

By combining academic sources with empirical observations, we propose to split general management's responsibilities into four basic areas—areas that are different from one another yet constitute a system where the whole is greater than the sum of its parts. The key is to approach each of these responsibilities contextually in order to achieve a balanced and effective fit for the four fundamental areas. The major challenge comes in making decisions and implementing them without losing sight of any of them (See Figure 6.1).

The actions of general management fall within the broad scope of a company's institutional configuration. This includes the company's ownership, corporate governance system, as well as stakeholders. Senior management never acts alone; neither has it enjoyed absolute freedom of action. The institutional configuration always imposes limits. As such, management invariably finds itself having to explain or justify to third parties. These could include the shareholders, the board, the parent company in the case of a multinational subsidiary or government regulators. The degree of freedom of action it enjoys in any given

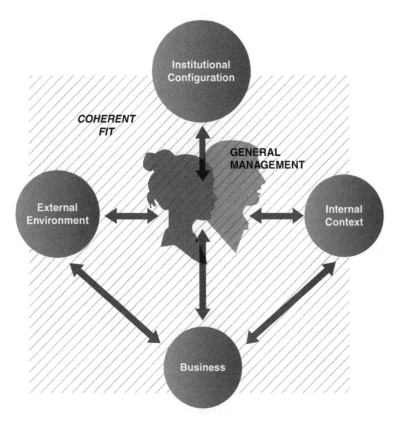

Figure 6.1   The four areas of a CEO's responsibility
Source: Andreu and Ricart, 2014.

scenario (what we generically term "governance") will vary substantially from one case to another.

The decisions taken by the top management and their implementation are, of course, also conditioned by the external environment in which the company operates. A critical task for general management is to decide on the company's role or external mission (which consists of defining the clients' real needs) within such a competitive environment. Again, the degree of freedom can vary enormously from one context to another. Perhaps the company has little chance of making its presence felt in an industry dominated by more powerful or better equipped rivals; still, it may have resources and capabilities that can be leveraged to its advantage. Whatever the case may be, designing the company's external mission in a way that is both realistic and in accordance with the nature of the external environment is an essential general management responsibility.

Management decisions are also shaped by the company's internal context, which consists of its human talent, business culture, resources and knowledge. Managers must find a way of fitting the company's internal mission into this framework, which consists of respecting human dignity and helping workers to develop, both personally and professionally.

The business model sets out how value will be created and captured for the different stakeholders involved. As such, it can be viewed as an interactive and dynamic extension of the value chain. Given its nature, the business model is a vital link between the company's strategy and its organization. A company's history, the choices it makes and the consequences of their implementation all contribute to its business model configuration. The responsibility of general management is to establish a business model that follows the company's external and internal missions within an institutional configuration, turning the business strategy into reality through its daily operations.

Managing a system in a balanced way is never easy. Maybe that is why established knowledge and practice in business and strategic management tend to group tasks into one of the four previously mentioned areas of responsibility. And though it is true that each task has a particular impact, it is important not to overlook the risk that addressing a challenge in one area may have unintended consequences on another, interdependent area (see Figure 6.2). Regrettably, one of the challenges for general management is the need to manage a complex, interconnected system, while most of the conceptual models available tend to divide the system into its constituent parts rather than dealing with them as a whole.

There is a great deal of literature on governance (including the involved stakeholders) that can be useful for defining an organization's governing model. We prefer to use the term *governing* rather than governance in order to reflect its continuous character within the system's process of adaptation.

There is also an abundance of literature on how to approach *strategizing*. Generally defined as the choice of the aspired future and the means of achieving it, this task involves developing a strategy in accordance with the external environment, simultaneously taking into account the internal context, the business reality and the demands of the company's institutional configuration.

Existing literature on organizational development comes in handy for the third task: *organizing*. To approach this challenge, one must bear in

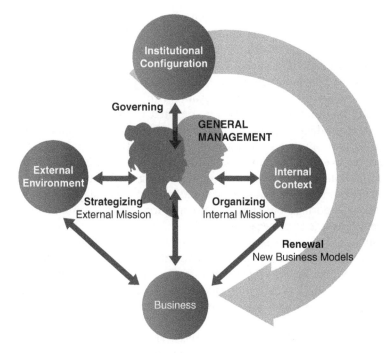

Figure 6.2   The key tasks of a CEO
Source: Andreu and Ricart, 2014.

mind that the organizational choices must of course take into account people, but also by the company's strategy, governance and business.

Finally, there is also a growing body of literature on innovation in business models, which we place under the broad term *renewal*. The resurgence of this fundamental task has a lot to do with the changes—primarily, though not exclusively, technological—taking place across the business landscape. These changes open up new opportunities for business model innovation, include new ways of creating and capturing value, and encompass strategic, organizational and more purely business innovations—innovations that often end up transforming the way we manage a business.

Business model innovation

The "business model" is one of the most widely used terms in both academic and business literature on strategy. Years after the technology bubble burst, leading to the development of many new Internet-based business models, the term continues to be used, given top priority in the agenda of senior executives worldwide. Various IBM Global Business Services studies (IBM Global CEO Study 2006, 2008, 2010 and 2012)[1] illustrate a growing interest in this topic among CEOs. In particular, the 2006 study—"Expanding the Innovation Horizon"—reveals that almost a third of innovation efforts were devoted to business models, compared to products/markets or operations. But, even more importantly, it shows that companies who focused their innovation in business models had, on average, operating margin growth over 5% higher than their competitors (calculated as compound annual growth rate in the last five years). The same indicator for companies that innovated in products/markets is positive but close to zero, and for companies innovating in operations it is even negative.

Similarly, there has been a large number of academic papers, including special issues of *Long Range Planning* (2010) and a recent special issue in *Strategic Entrepreneurship Journal* (2015), or *Universia Business Review* (2010) (in Spanish). Everyone talks about it, but what exactly is a business model and why is it so clearly in the spotlight at the moment?

A business model explains *the underlying logic of a business unit*, understood as *how it creates and captures value*. Let us first consider a few terms about this generic definition of the business model on which we find a broad consensus. First, the analysis unit refers to *business unit* (or, simply, "the business"). This term refers to a unit that covers specific needs for a group of customers in a given geographical area, and that usually faces an identifiable set of competitive bids. The business unit is therefore identified by external factors (i.e., types of customers, their needs, markets, competitors, etc.). But this unit is normally expressed as a set of activities with which to articulate the value proposition for identified customers. When it defines a business unit, a company identifies the idiosyncratic factors in which it wishes to compete to serve those needs (or to exploit that opportunity), i.e., the factors of its value proposition. To meet the goal or the business opportunity associated with the proposal, the company "designs" its business model. Stated differently, it outlines the basic guidelines to follow in order to create value and try to capture enough of the same. Thus, *business models identify the approach for creating and capturing value to exploit business opportunity*, and this approach is therefore *the logic behind the business model*.[2]

The business model is nothing new. Any firm, in its inception, has to design business models to exploit the opportunities identified in the environment. Consequently, the history of the business world is full of inventions and innovations in business models. Sometimes they are the result of *technological changes*, like those ushered in by the Industrial Revolution. These allowed leveraging incredible economies of scale. Another example is the development of the commercial radio business model, which offered a free service that was financed through advertising. Innovations sometimes stem from other types of changes, such as the identification of poorly or scarcely covered needs. For example, quick parcel services initially competed with the postal service, which was intended as a public service and did not properly cover some business needs. Similarly, when U-haul rentals started in the US there were very few services of this type. In short, as Peter Drucker (2004) noted, "Changes offer opportunities and entrepreneurs design business models, sometimes from scratch, to exploit them more effectively than available alternatives or substitutes."

While it is an "old" concept, the business model concept is fashionable today and probably for good reasons. One of these reasons is a definite acceleration in the presence of new business models or different ways to compete (create and capture value) popping up in many different fields. We were used to seeing innovation in these models associated with new companies, new business activities not previously in existence, new technologies, etc. This triggered a host of imitators and therefore also competition between companies which were "similar" in their underlying approaches. But today we are witnessing *an increasing variety of simultaneous competition with different business models in multiple sectors*. There is more room for innovation and, even more importantly, the relevant competition relies less on imitation and more on replacement or, stated otherwise, in the use of disparate business models to address the same needs (i.e. the business unit).

As an example, consider when Dell entered the personal computer manufacturing world. The business model established by the leaders of that time, such as IBM, Compaq and HP, was based on the manufacturing of computers for stock and the sale of those computers through intermediaries (value-added resellers), who provided customer service, customized PCs and coordinated installation and service. In contrast, Dell designed a business model based on special order manufacturing and direct sales. Clients contacted Dell explaining their needs, and Dell manufactured the computer (or computers) according to their specifications only once the order was confirmed. This different way of covering the same need has driven the sector to intense competition, and with companies working under different business models.

Behind this increasing variability there are obviously important changes in our competitive environment, changes that probably occur more rapidly than in the past. Without attempting to be exhaustive, it may be worth to consider some cases.

First, there are significant *technological changes*, and many but not all of them are associated with Internet. So, for example, a different way to sell emerges, very useful for niche markets through eBay-style auctions. Currently, both individuals and companies, whatever their size, can try to sell their products through brick and mortar stores or through direct online sales or intermediaries such as eBay or Amazon, to name a few. And if we take a look at social networks or online advertising, we can see how technology significantly multiplies our options for business model design.

But the world is not made up only of technology. A second type of change that we highlight is *demographic*, opening new opportunities or revealing areas that previously were harder to cover and can now be taken care of (perhaps, again, thanks to technology). For example, new family dynamics involve a significant increase in convenience foods, which, in turn, also implies major changes in the entire food chain. These are coupled with the increased demand for traceability, greater pricing pressure, greater appeal of natural products, and so on.

And in this vein, a third change force is *regulation*—or *deregulation*—or the role of governments in many sectors. This increasing role consists of consumer protection, development support, at times adopting protectionist measures, etc. For example, some sectors, such as the airline industry, have transformed significantly since their progressive deregulation has allowed huge innovations in business models (scarcely influenced by technology, by the way). And this is the case in many other industries.

Globalization is another driver of change for many industries. It involves talking about emerging economies where significant business opportunities normally hinge on having innovative business models, either to expand into these markets (e.g. strategies for the base of the pyramid) or to leverage cost advantages of moving some operations to these countries (offshoring).

In short, the combination of these factors—and probably other unidentified factors—entails a tremendous innovation potential in business models. Entrepreneurs and established companies try to exploit this potential to take advantage of emerging opportunities, which generate a more diverse competitive environment, where the design of these models is very important for managers and entrepreneurs. Therefore, the focus on business models—their variability, design, deployment, development, management, etc—is more relevant today than at any other stage in business history. *Competing in the 21st century is to compete in business models.*

A company's business model should be the core element of its business strategy. Let us consider the newspaper industry, for example. Change is everywhere: the emergence of the Internet, the ubiquity of social networks, wikis, blogs and other tools are breaking into this industry, as well as the foray of new models such as free press and new players who control advertising (which has moved from physical to electronic media). These changes are forcing us to rethink our business models in order to adapt them to new circumstances, to make them sustainable to compete with new players, even when they are our own customers and consumers, to take advantage of new technology opportunities, etc. There are no clear answers, but we do know that the industry must reconfigure its activities, find new value propositions and change the underlying logic of our business, seeking to exploit existing skills and develop new ones. It must rethink its business model.

And this is the case in a growing number of industries. For example, how to create, package, distribute and enjoy music is in a state of flux. Free downloads and Apple's business model, with its iTunes and iPods, smartphones, etc., have had great impact. But artists are also driving change, some of them willing to sell online and allow free downloads of their songs. The role of large companies as packagers becomes jeopardized. Multiple players with very different approaches are seeking the business models that will allow them to create and capture value in this complex environment.

Many other industries are changing drastically as well, such the automobile, airlines, manufacturing and distribution of clothing, food, telecommunications, television, etc. Surely there is no industry where great business model innovation opportunities have not occurred, are occurring or are soon to occur. This is the world we live in.

In this context, there is ample room for innovation, and people may be thinking how to do things differently and gain the value that, until now, someone else was able to create, or how to find a way to approach neglected or inadequately covered needs.

Business model interaction

Some companies can find themselves at times in a "blue ocean"[3]—some large or small under-served area—but usually value creation sources will attract new competitors and participants interested in capturing a share of the value. Incentives attract innovation, and thus, ultimately new or established business models end up interacting with other participants who want a slice of the pie.

Therefore, studying or analyzing business models in isolation is not only trivial but even irrelevant (Casadesus-Masanell and Ricart, 2011). There is no doubt that the alignment between elements of a business, consistent decision-making or other similar issues are important factors in the strength of a business model. But what matters "when the rubber meets the road"—as they say—is the business model's ability to survive and thrive in an environment of interaction[4] with other models. The interaction between the different models is not trivial. By taking into account the many interdependencies in a dynamic context, we often get mixed results that arguably do not interact.

With players interacting in networks, externalities and installed bases and size provide tremendous advantages but at the same time open the door to innovative competitive weapons; one can identify situations where the best business model in isolation is unable to break into the advantages of established players, where competitors entering with radically different and novel business models end up complementing more than substituting established players. Therefore, competition rules are, or may be, different in a world full of externalities, installed bases, complements and platforms.

Interactions occur not only between competitors. As indicated previously, a new principle to consider is that *other non-competitive interactions may be key to understanding a business model*. BOP businesses or those related to social entrepreneurship usually affect their target environment by interacting with it and transforming it. We can therefore not think about these kinds of businesses—known as "inclusive"—without considering their interaction with the environment, often involving nonstandard players such as NGOs, government agencies and other relevant partners.

Interactions are also relevant within corporations themselves, opening up new ways of understanding and conceptualizing corporate strategy through the creation of business units that are not only robust for interactions abroad but also leverage interactions between corporation activities to create and capture more value, that is, to design and deploy better business models (Casadesus-Masanell, Ricart and Tarziján, 2015).

Ultimately, business models should be understood in a context of dynamic interaction, where relying on the past is essential. Purely static analysis of the interdependencies between business models is not enough. The dynamics need to be explicitly considered.

In this complex, interactive, dynamic and systemic context, the key question is how we can help managers plan and design their strategies. And the answer is "with better tools to do core tasks": focus on business model design and innovation.

Companies must define their competitive strategy for each of their businesses in a context that we have seen is complex, dynamic and increasingly interrelated. The basic approach to business strategy is its model, design, development and management. It is, in short, the business model in action. Do we have the right tools to support this design and planning task?

To better deal with dynamism and interactivity, we should have a more operational definition of the business model.[5] We have defined a *"business model* as *the underlying logic of a business unit,* understood as *how the unit creates and captures value."* We can deepen this concept by defining a business model as "the set of choices a company makes and their consequences." Strategy defines choices which may be policies, assets (physical, where we invest) or governance structures for these policies and assets. But every choice has consequences, and these, in turn, can be classified as flexible or rigid, depending on their persistence when the effect causing them is no longer in place. The interesting thing is that choices and their aftermath create certain dynamism and ultimately end up closing the loop: choices generate consequences and these support the choices themselves (so that the cycle is closed). These cycles can be positive, and we call them "virtuous," or harmful, and we call them "vicious." Through this dynamic representation we are able to capture the underlying logic of the business unit.

Within the set of cycles (hopefully virtuous) generated in a business model, the most interesting one is the cycle that ends up explaining in basic terms the creation and capture of value for the company. It can do so through readiness to pay, cost, price and volume. This basic virtuous cycle defined by the business unit we call *"value loop."*[6] Obviously, for this cycle to flow properly and allow us to capture value, we will need many other choices and their consequences to feed the underlying *value loop* system. But most times it encapsulates the essence of the business and adequately describes the logic of the company, that is, its business model.

In fact, a model understood under this definition is extremely complex, as there are too many choices, too many consequences and too many cycles or loops. An analyst observes the complex reality and tries to understand, simplify and model it. To do this, he makes the choices that seem pivotal and have key consequences. Then, with the available knowledge, he looks for the necessary explanations to interpret how choices and consequences are connected, and the reason for each connection, ultimately illustrating the dynamics of this business. The rational part of each connection is what we call "theories." Thus, the business model representation is a simplified version of reality that contains basic choices, key consequences and fundamental theories behind the company's dynamic logic. Using aggregation and decomposition techniques, the analyst arrives at a sufficient representation to explain the mechanism we call "business model."

The representation of this model has two additional advantages that are worth highlighting. First, it connects perfectly with the strategy. It is a contingent plan of choices that determine the future we want to create for this business. These choices and their impact, dynamics and collective history make up the business model. This is the portrayal of the strategy at a given time. Or, stated differently, strategy is really the contingent and dynamic choice of the company's business model (or business unit).[7]

Second, this representation of business models allows incorporating into the analysis the interaction with relevant participants that may affect the creation and capture of value. This can be done properly, since the interdependence between business models involves sharing consequences or the choice of one affecting the consequences of the other, and vice versa. Thus, the representation itself allows taking into account others' choices and consequences or virtuous cycles that reinforce or contradict each other, providing a language that support not only the business model dynamics but its dynamic interaction with other interdependent models.

In fact, this interaction analysis highlights a fundamental aspect of business model design: the interdependence with other models is endogenous, that is, part of the business model design is not independent. This endogeneity is a key variable in the design of a business model.

In addition, this dynamic view of business model as choices and consequences allows to incorporate in the design or renewal of business model consequences to all key stakeholders. Therefore, the business model provides a central concept and a tool to manage the complex system associated to the general management tasks.

In short, defining a business model as "choices and consequences" (and understanding its dynamics and interaction thanks to the underlying theories) allows us to represent business models as sets of value loops. We can then create roadmaps for design and development and in the management of these models. This form of representation has four main advantages:

- It explains the underlying dynamic and allows us to understand the value creation and capture mechanism that we are designing or managing.
- The analyst is forced to think of how to connect choices and consequences and these in turn to subsequent choices, and she must therefore be precise in the underlying theories used, encouraging testing and the search for evidence of the underlying logic, thus greatly improving the understanding of the represented design and its operation.
- The interaction can be introduced intuitively and preserve the richness of this interaction in real-life situations. Obviously, the interaction analysis is complex because reality is complex, but it is within reach with maps that businesses add at the value loop level.
- By adding consequences in all dimensions of a task, we can create a map to understand not just strategy but the impact of key business model design choices on fundamental stakeholders and therefore help in the design perspective of the general management task as described before.

CEO's competences for business model innovation

As indicated above, senior executives should manage a complex open system that integrates elements of the external and internal context with the institutional configuration and the business model. Their task is managing the process of constant change in the complex system. We have also seen that today there are many drivers that open opportunities for business model change, innovation or renewal. Therefore, the business model gains status in the task of the senior manager because it offers more opportunities for innovation, for creative solutions to better respond and influence the different contextual forces that identify its essential task. This centrality is very important and it is reflected in the increasing interest in this area, not only academically but also in the managerial world. Business model innovation is now almost synonymous of the perhaps more important task in general management daily activity.

We have also highlighted the difficulty of developing this task because the business model is a central part of the complex system the

CEO designs, manages and develops. At the same time we have seen that there are important changes in the external and internal context of firms that while increasing the uncertainty and therefore the complexity are at the same source of potential novelty in the business model design. Therefore, the development of tools and concept that helps CEOs better confront this type of decision are important and useful for them, and also help identify the capabilities CEOs need to deal with entrepreneurship and innovation, in particular business model innovation.

It is important to highlight that business model innovation is quite different from other types of innovation. Most of the literature in innovation focuses on product or process innovation. Business model innovation is different, even if sometimes it may emerge due to product or process innovation. It is possible to design novel business models even without "classical" product or process innovation. Business model innovation derives fundamentally from management innovations affecting governance, policies or asset investments in a different, many time disruptive, ways of creating and capturing value. While the CEO may have influence on innovation and entrepreneurship in general in the firm, business model innovation or renewal is one of his/her central responsibility.

According to Teece (2009), there are three fundamental dynamic capabilities for a company: (1) *sensing* or the detection of opportunities, (2) *seizing* or the exploitation of such opportunities, and (3) *managing threats/transforming*, or the continuous reinvention and adjustment of business. The business model is one of the fundamental elements of the *seizing* capacity, since it determines how the company wants to capture this business opportunity. From these dynamic capabilities we can derive some competencies that CEOs should have and develop to respond to the challenges we have identified.

First, CEOs should develop competences in strategic thinking. Organizations need to sense opportunities in an effective way. Therefore, organizations need processes to perform this sensing capability. CEOs will not be able to lead well such organizational processes if they had not developed competences as entrepreneurs, as creators of the future, as strategic thinkers.

The CEO is responsible for the future of the organization and thus in need of strategic thinking. But as the future gets more uncertain and the choice opportunities more relevant, the need for strategic thinking increases in importance. But it also changes in nature. Strategy is not just a question of finding a unique positioning or owning idiosyncratic resources. The future needs to be invented and this requires an entrepreneurial perspective. Therefore, the CEO as strategic thinker should be an entrepreneur, should be creative, should understand well the complex environment and develop a creative strategy that reflects itself in an innovative business model.

Of course one can claim that this is too big of a task for just an individual. It is true that as organizations grow this task of sensing the future is increasingly a collective task. However, strategic thinking is the ability to understand strategically the environment, the resources and capabilities of the firm, the fundamental choices being made. The whole team can contribute to the thinking, to the sensing of opportunities, to the development of ideas, ... but still this process needs leadership and requires, today more than ever, the competence of strategic thinking.

Second, CEOs need competences in design thinking. Organizations need to develop capabilities to seize the opportunities. Seizing requires novel forms of design. Seizing requires new strategies based on arbitration, experimentation of new business models and the construction of complex organizations. To lead these types of processes in organizations CEOs need to develop competences in design thinking.

Probably the most established "business model representation" is the "value chain" concept introduced by Porter (1985). Porter realized that companies should design their value chain idiosyncratically to gain differential positioning and thus competitive advantage. From this moment, the value chain went from being extremely useful to becoming a ball and chain, and variations on this theme began to emerge. Even Porter decided to replace the value chain concept with the activity system to make his concept more flexible (Porter, 1996). Despite its many offshoots, the field of strategy converges toward the consensus that the value chain and its variations must give way to a broader, more systemic concept such as the business model.

Amit and Zott (2010)[8] start with the activity system as the central focus of activities and add two important aspects for reflection for the design of the system's basic parameters. First, some design elements of the activity system are established: (1) the content, which identifies *what* activities should be carried out; (2) the structure, which determines *how* activities are connected and their relative importance, and (3) the ownership, which identifies *who* must perform each activity. Second, they identify four design themes or coherent settings for activity systems, summarized in the acronym NICE: *novelty*, for novel systems; *lock-in*, designed to capture third parties; *complementarities*, for those exploiting the complementarities between these activities, and *efficiency*, for those emphasizing transaction cost reduction. The set of tools developed by these authors is tremendously useful for designing business models, especially in the context of the Internet (where transaction is the core element) and in the initial stages of the entrepreneurial process.

Given the relevance of business model design the set of tools that can be helpful for this task keep growing as the business model canvas of Osterwalder and Pigneur (2010) or the business model navigator Gassmann et al. (2014). However, to be able to use all these tools and concepts, CEOs need to develop their competences in design thinking. Business can be designed, should be designed, and the competence of design thinking is fundamental to do so (Martin, 2009).

Novel business models are complex and therefore their design may require a lot of experimentation. CEO as designers, as architects of business models, should also have the ability to design creative experiments to learn about the complex interactions of business model with relative cheap trials. The fundamental issue is fast learning at low cost, so the innovative design can evolve faster than the alternatives and without losing the right focus. Design thinking is a difficult competence to develop as well as a real novel one for CEOs.

It is also important to realize that design thinking as applied to business model innovation integrates "Strategizing" and "Organizing," therefore connecting what sometimes we refer as strategy formulation and implementation (or execution). The focus on business model thinking and innovation forces a search for a design that can be realized, so implemented. The elements of design involve assets, policies and governance choices, configuring at the same time a strategy path and organizational development. In terms of competences we consider that design thinking will integrate the design of organizational architectures consistent and reinforcing the logic of value creation and capture.

Third, CEOs need competences in system thinking. Organizations need to develop capabilities in renewal and transformation. To exercise this capability, organizations need to develop processes for continual learning, for understanding the impact on stakeholders. They need to manage the present while preparing the organization for a different future. To lead this process of "system change," CEOs need to develop competences on system thinking.

Business models innovation does not occur in isolation but in a complex interaction with external and internal factors making it an overall system. Understanding the evolution of systems is very difficult and still more their design. As commented one way to deal with this complexity is smart experimentation. System thinking is a key competence to drive such experimentation.

It is important to emphasize the systemic nature of the general management function per se and the oft-ignored notion of managerial responsibility in the design and renewal of such system. Therefore, a CEO's vision requires pulling multiple dimensions together: functional areas must be consistent with the corporate strategy; professional and personal development of the company's human talent must also be made to fit, without neglecting their duties derived from their specific roles within the organization, which set the tone for the organization's design and structure.

As such, it is essential for CEOs to see and manage the firm as a whole, made up of interdependent, highly dynamic elements. Such a vision often clashes with the traditional strategic analysis and design tools, which, while perhaps useful on an individual basis, tend to result in a chaotic amalgam of techniques and procedures that largely function independently of one another.

One can of course claim that system thinking has been a traditional CEO's competence and to some degree this is true. However, system thinking is gaining relevance in our networked economy. Systems are a key part of a general management task, but it is particularly relevant when we see the CEO as a business model innovator.

Conclusions

The CEO's task has always been complex, but the realities of the 21st century are not making things easier. At the same time the increasing change and complexity open opportunities for competent CEOs to have greater impact, create more value and develop better organizations. Opportunities also go with responsibilities; a very important one is to develop the necessary competences to do this task better.

We have conceptualized the CEO's task as managing an open and complex system that connects the institutional configuration, the external environment, the internal context and the business model. In this chapter we have focused on business model innovation or renewal as one particular element of the CEO task extremely important today. Then we have worked the details of business model innovation and interaction from the perspective of the top management decision-making. In this way we have been able to identify some competences the CEO needs to develop is he/she wants to be a business model innovator.

All this highlights the importance to develop in CEOs the essential integrative competences of strategic thinking, to articulate a future to the organization and to sense opportunities in an uncertain world;

design thinking to structure the set of business activities, governance structures or managerial capabilities to really create novel and innovative business models; and system thinking to be able to manage the transitions that are the day-to-day realities in a fast changing world of today where transformation is the only constant in organizations. The question that we need to ask ourselves is if our universities and curricula are ready for this challenge.

Notes

1. Every two years IBM Global Business Services publishes a Global CEO Study featuring results of a survey of a thousand or so CEOs on five continents. These studies are available on the Web. The 2012 study, for example, is available at http://www-05.ibm.com/services/es/ceo/ceostudy2012/
2. This definition as well as most of the section that follows is derived from Ricart (2012).
3. "Blue oceans" are previously unexplored competitive areas where competition is negligible for a period. The concept has been popularized by Kim and Mauborgne (2005).
4. We specify "interaction" and not "competition" because "interaction" is a broader concept that includes all stakeholders, including competitors.
5. This approach is documented in Casadesus-Masanell and Ricart (2010). More detail can be found in a chapter of *Handbook of Research in Competitive Strategy* edited by G. B. Dagnino (Edward Elgar, 2012). It is also explained in the *Universia Business Review* issue cited above.
6. A value loop expresses the essence of value creation and value capture, exactly what we have defined as "the logic of a business model." Beyond the value loop, we can keep adding relevant choices and consequences to develop the Business model with increasing detail.
7. See Casadesus-Masanell and Ricart (2010), where the distinction between strategy and business model, and between strategy and tactics, is explained and illustrated in detail.
8. Amit and Zott (2010). See also Amit and Zott (2001); Amit and Zott (2007).

References

"Special Issue on Business Models," *Long Range Planning*, 43, (2–3) (April/June 2010)

"Special Issue on Business Models," *Strategic Entrepreneurship Journal* (Forthcoming 2015)

"Special Issue on Business Models," *Universia Business Review*, 23 (Third Quarter 2009)

Amit, R. and Zott, C. (2001) "Value Creation in E-Business," *Strategic Management Journal*, 22: 493–520

Amit, R. and Zott, C. (2007) "Business Model Design and the Performance of Entrepreneurial Firms," *Organization Science*, 18: 181–199

Amit, R. and Zott, C. (April/June 2010) "Business Model Design: An Activity System Perspective," *Long Range Planning*, 43 (2–3): 216–226

Andreu, R. (2014) *Huellas: Construyendo Valor desde la Empresa* (Barcelona: Editorial Dau)

Andreu, R. and Ricart, J. E. (2014) "The Genuine Responsibilities of the CEO: A Framework for Managing Today," *IESE Insight*, Fourth Quarter

Bartlett, C. A. and Ghoshal, S. (2000) *The Individualized Corporation: A Fundamentally New Approach to Management* (Chantam, Kent: Random House)

Casadesus-Masanell, R. and Ricart, J. E. (2010) "From Strategy to Business Models and Onto Tactics," *Long Range Planning* 43(2–3): 195–215

Casadesus-Masanell, R. and Ricart, J. E. (2011) "How to Design a Winning Business Model," *Harvard Business Review* 89(1–2):100–107

Casadesus-Masanell, R. and Ricart, J. E. (2012) "Competing on Business Models," Chapter of *Handbook of Research in Competitive Strategy* edited by G. B. Dagnino (Edward Elgar)

Casadesus-Masanell, R., Ricart, J. E. and Tarziján, J. (2015) "A Corporate View of Business Model Innovation," chapter 5 of *Business Model Innovation: The Organizational Dimension* edited by N. Foss and T. Saebi

Drucker, P. (2004) *The Practice of Management* (Oxford: Elsevier Butterworth-Heinemann)

Finkelstein, S. and Hambricks, D. (1996) *Strategic Leadership: Top Executives and their Effects on Organizations* (Minneapolis/St. Paul: West Pub. Co.)

Gassmann, O., Frankenberger, K. and Csik, M. (2014) *The Business Model Navigator: 55 Models that Will Revolutionize your Business* (United Kingdom: FT Publishing)

IBM Global Business Services, Global CEO Study 2006, 2008, 2010, 2012. The 2012 Study, (Available at http://www-05.ibm.com/services/es/ceo/ceostudy2012/) Accessed: 12 February 2015

Kim, W. C. and Mauborgne, R. (2005) *Blue Ocean Strategy. How to Create Uncontested Market Space and Make Competition Irrelevant* (Boston: Harvard Business School Press)

Kotter, J. (1982) *The General Managers* (New York: Free Press)

Llopis, J. and Ricart, J. E. (2013) *Qué hacen los buenos Directivos: El Reto del Siglo XXI* (Madrid: Pearson Education)

Martin, R. (2009) *The Design of Business: Why Design Thinking is the Next Competitive Advantage* (Boston: Harvard Business School Press)

Mintzberg, H. (1973) *The Nature of Managerial Work* (New York: Harper Collins)

Osterwalder, A. and Pigneur, Y. (2010) *Business Model Generation. A Handbook for Visionaries, Game Changers and Challengers* (New York: Wiley)

Porter, M. (1985) *Competitive Advantage. Creating and Sustaining Superior Performance* (New York: The Free Press)

Porter, M. (1996) "What is Strategy?" *Harvard Business Review* (November–December)

Ricart, J. E. (2012) "Strategy in the 21st Century: Business Model in Action" *IESE Technical Note SMN-685-E*

Ricart, J.E., Llopis, J. and Pastoriza, D. (2007) *Yo Dirijo: La Dirección del Siglo XXI según sus protagonistas* (Barcelona: Ed. Deusto)

Teece, D. (2009) *Dynamic Capabilities and Strategic Management. Organizing for Innovation and Growth* (USA: Oxford University Press)

Part III
Innovative Methodologies and Learning Processes to Foster Innovation

7
Design Thinking and Innovative Problem Solving

Srikant Datar and Caitlin N. Bowler

Genesis of the curriculum, curriculum overview and key assumptions

Can individuals learn to think more innovatively?

In 2010, professors Srikant M. Datar and David A. Garvin and research associate Patrick G. Cullen published *Rethinking the MBA: Business Education at a Crossroads*. *Rethinking the MBA* took stock of business education in the US in a way that had not been done since the Carnegie Corporation and Ford Foundation each published reports on the subject in 1959. The research revealed an educational establishment disconnected in significant ways from the businesses and organizations in which its graduates traditionally go to work. Through interviews with numerous high-level executives and corporate recruiters and deans from highly ranked business schools in the US and Europe, a picture developed of MBAs whose skills were unequal to the most pressing needs of 21st century employers. Tasked with executing on known strategy or operations, MBAs performed very well. But when faced with "unstructured problems, ambiguous data, rapidly changing environments, and information overload" (Datar, Garvin and Cullen, 2010)—the new normal in an increasingly complicated and global world—MBAs faltered. Hence the question, *Can anyone, including MBAs and executives with superb analytical skills, learn to think more innovatively and, if so, how might we go about developing these skills?* Executives and managers could then train their associates in these skills.

Many MBA programs have historically focused on cultivating analytical skills and specific knowledge (the "knowing" component in the "knowing-doing-being" taxonomy), producing excellent analysts and functionaries, but failing to produce enough of the effective leaders businesses need. Today's students and executives must "master a new set of skills: the ability to deeply understand what their customers need, find and frame problems, collect, synthesize, and distill large volumes of data; exercise creativity and imagination; and develop, test, and revise ideas" (Datar, Garvin and Cullen, 2010). These "doing" and "being" skills allow MBAs to thrive in a business world increasingly characterized by unstructured problems but require a very different pedagogy than the ones that have been traditionally used.

In this chapter we describe a new Harvard Business School course, Design Thinking & Innovation (DTI), built on the assumption that innovative thinking can be learned by anyone open and willing to practice and develop this skill. Design thinking is an approach to problem solving that is human-centered and uses qualitative research methods to get deep insight into those needs and user motivations. Through close observation of people in their environments, direct engagement with them through interviews and shadowing, and even attempts to experience the world as they do, researchers can gain deep understanding of users' motivations and needs and, using this knowledge, produce solutions crafted to address those needs directly. In the skill taxonomy of "knowing-doing-being," much of business education has focused on knowing skills, which can be developed effectively through lectures, case discussion and small seminar discussion. In contrast, innovative thinking is a "doing" skill that can only be developed through hands on engagement and repeated practice over time. Therefore, the curriculum is structured to provide students many opportunities to "learn by doing," featuring only two cases in favor of a variety of hands on exercises.

Through research into the literature and close collaboration with a number of highly skilled practitioners in the field of design thinking and design education, the authors identified tools or "props" that practitioners use at each stage of the innovation process to do work associated with that phase. To increase their chances for adoption by students and executives, these tools are self-contained and punctuate the curriculum. They provide tangible opportunities for students to practice and develop innovative thinking skills that, most importantly, are "portable" and intended to be practiced by students and executives in their careers across a range of industries.

The DTI innovation framework that anchors the curriculum is comprised of four main phases as follows and described in Table 7.1. (1) *Clarify* (clarifying and developing a deep understanding of the problem), (2) *Ideation* (using insights from discovery research and other tools

Table 7.1 Innovation framework phases

Process phase	Guides and activities
(1) Clarify	Clarifying and developing a deep understanding of the problem
(2) Ideate	Using insights from discovery research and other tools to generate ideas
(3) Develop	Building prototypes to test, iterate and develop solutions
(4) Implement	Incorporating stakeholders' interests and leveraging those strategically to bring concepts to life

to generate ideas), (3) *Concept Development* (building prototypes to test, iterate and develop solutions) and (4) *Implementation* (incorporating stakeholders' interests and leveraging those strategically to bring concepts to life). This framework builds directly from the *FourSight* model of creative process preferences developed by Dr. Gerard Puccio and colleagues at the Buffalo State International Center for Studies in Creativity (Puccio, Mance and Murdock, 2010), with modifications introduced through work done over three years with individuals from the major design-thinking practices and innovation firms, including IDEO, Continuum, Frog Design, LUMA Institute, SIT and Synecticsworld.

This framework and the tools and techniques introduced here will be relevant to any professional tasked with, in the words of Nobel laureate Herb Simon, transforming "existing conditions into preferred ones" (Simon, 1996). This includes individuals designing products, services or experiences for a customer or end user, whether external or internal to the organization, or overseeing those who do—essentially any executive working today. The remainder of this chapter examines each phase of the innovation framework and highlights tools or techniques associated with each phase that could be taught and practiced easily in corporate settings.

Innovation framework & human-centered design

In the context of the DTI curriculum, *innovation* is defined as anything (for example: product, service, business model, experience or process) that is both novel and useful (Amabile, 1998). The "useful" requirement serves to place the user, her needs and her desires squarely at the center of the innovation framework around which the curriculum is structured. As the curriculum ventures far afield to explore the various phases of the innovation process, from problem framing and breaking fixedness to idea generation and prototyping, this idea of "human-centeredness" serves as a beacon. No matter where one is in the process, focus always returns to the user, her needs and how the innovation process can produce products, services, experiences and business models to meet them. Many of the tools in *Concept Development* (Phase 3) and *Implementation* (Phase 4) focus specifically on how new ideas with promise, as well as problems, can be modified and developed to be successfully adapted. This dynamic underscores two key premises on which the course is built: (1) designs that build out from the needs of users—explicit and implicit, articulated and observed—are more effective and more widely embraced than those developed in other ways, and (2) it *will* take multiple iterative cycles to adequately develop an idea before it is adopted by users and succeeds in the marketplace.

The question of *desirability* of a given program or service, as perceived by users, is a primary consideration in this innovation framework (Goligorsky, 2012). How *desirable* is a proposed product, service, etc., from the point of view of the intended user? Does the design meet users' needs? Does it leverage motivations? *Desirability* is one of three dimensions in IDEO's framework for evaluating an idea's potential for success as measured through adoption, alongside *feasibility* (do the technologies or other conditions exist to bring the concept to life?) and *viability* (how sustainable is the innovation from a resource and economic perspective?). Given the importance of "usefulness" for an innovation to succeed, it is important for executives to develop the skill to evaluate the extent to which a concept might be desired by particular users. Typically, business students and executives are most comfortable analyzing issues around *feasibility* and *viability*. They are often less comfortable assessing issues of *desirability*, even though *desirability* is a vitally important condition to understand at the beginning of an innovation process because it is the most difficult to manufacture artificially if it does not already exist. Understanding *desirability* is a skill that can be developed in executives by paying explicit attention to user needs and actively considering issues and decisions from the end users' perspective.

Phase 1: Clarify

The discovery phase is dedicated to identifying user needs—explicit "pain points" articulated by the user as well as latent needs he does not recognize—and understanding the context that has produced them. The objective of this phase is to define and frame the underlying problem(s) as effectively and appropriately as possible (i.e. Are you solving the right problem?), based on the insights produced through research with users as well as relevant data from other available sources. The three discrete activities in the phase are (1) deep observation, (2) synthesis and insight generation, and (3) problem definition and framing.

The high-level prerequisite for success in this phase of the process is cognitive empathy—the ability to understand the experience of another person by putting oneself in that person's shoes. The ability to empathize with a user, especially when that user's world view, values, social, cultural and economic situations are different from one's own, is absolutely critical to developing the insights that lead to great and impactful innovations. Empathy is the foundation layer for this initial inquiry and key to the ability to make the deep observations on which insights and innovations build.

For practitioners at design firms such as IDEO and Frog Design, the first step in the observation stage is to identify *pain points*, defined as moments when a consumer/user experiences frustration, difficulty or uncertainty when using a product, service, etc. The presence of *pain points* indicates an unmet user need. Pain points can be *explicit*, such as when a call to customer service results in a circuitous slog through the phone trees of multiple departments (a customer can explicitly report that experience to be annoying and patently bad), or *latent*, such that the user does not recognize herself that an unmet need exists. A classic example of a latent need is the iPad. Prior to its launch, many laptop and netbook users were skeptical of a tablet computer without a keypad; its success, at least as predicted in the popular press, was hardly foregone. Now, nearly 260 million iPads have been sold since September 2010 (Statista, 2015) as users around the world breeze through media with the swipe of a finger. Clearly a latent need existed for this type of device.

Procter & Gamble is famous for its ability to use design research/ qualitative research to identify pain points among its customers and use insights from the research to develop new consumer products. One of the more recent and high-profile examples is the Swiffer, invented and developed in collaboration with design firm Continuum, which completely reconceived of the floor-cleaning process and eliminated the need for tools that had literally been in use for centuries. That the Swiffer, the need for which no customer had actively articulated prior to its initial launch by Procter & Gamble, generates annual sales of $500 million (Continuum, 2015) and again indicates just how prevalent these latent needs can be. This was a customer base one would imagine consumer products manufacturers would have already understood very well.

Just what were the pain points that Continuum identified? And more importantly, what was the process for identifying those pain points and identifying insights that led to Swiffer? The following description captures the essence of the process used by design research firms such a Continuum. This structured process can be replicated by any corporate team interested in collecting empirical observations about customer experiences through use of several simple tools.

First, a team must structure its looking, which can be accomplished by creating a *journey map*. A *journey map* is a graphic tool used to organize detailed information about an individual's steps through a process (Goligorsky, 2012) that allows the researcher to identify the various stages along a journey where unmet needs may exist. In the example of cleaning the kitchen floor, the user journey would start at the hall closet (or another typical storage location) where the mop, bucket and cleaning fluid are stored when not in use. As the user collected his tools and carried them to the kitchen, the map would note this change in physical locations (i.e. environments, contexts). In the kitchen, the *journey map* would capture a series of steps for cleaning the floor, such as preparing the cleaning solution and water in the bucket at the sink, mopping the kitchen floor (getting under furniture and under cabinet soffits), then cleaning the mop and bucket in the sink, letting them dry in the sink (or maybe in the hall), before changing locations back to the hall where the user returns the tools to their storage space. Each location on the map and step in the process represents an opportunity for detailed looking, both for pain points and for opportunities for improvement or innovation. The *journey map* structures the looking the research team will do across time and place.

Second, using the locations and stages charted out in the *journey map* as a guide, the team must identify exactly *what* it should observe. *AEIOU* is a tool to help researchers observe an unfamiliar (or, in this case, overly familiar!) environment much more carefully to develop a nuanced understanding of the context in which the activity, in this case, cleaning the kitchen floor, takes place. *AEIOU* is simply an acronym checklist of dimensions to think through that stands for Activities, Environments, Interactions, Objects and Users (Goligorsky, 2012). Researchers at IDEO use *AEIOU* as a guide as they make observations.

In the mop example, researchers might have used *AEIOU* to make the following list of elements to observe:

Activities	Retrieving the tools from the closet, filling the bucket with water, adding cleaning solution, mopping the floor, squeegeeing the mop, cleaning the mop once floor is clean, letting mop dry, putting mop and other tools away.
Environments	Hall closet, kitchen, sink area
Interactions	Asking for help to hold a stool so a person might reach high up places without falling down
Objects	Mop, bucket, cleaning solution, sink, rubber gloves (maybe)
Users	Person cleaning the floor

Third, using the structure around time and location created by the *journey map* and the elements to observe articulated through *AEIOU*, the team must then actually collect observations. There are three basic techniques for making observations. The first is *direct observation* ("looking") of a user performing a task, engaging with a service, or using a product. Observing individuals as they engage with a product or service can be useful in uncovering behaviors or needs, such as the challenge of an elderly person lifting a bucket of water from a sink. Second is individual or small group *interview* ("asking"), often in the environment where the person uses the product or engages the services; this is called *contextual inquiry*. *Contextual inquiry* also allows an interviewer to ask for clarification or further exposition *in the moment*, which is rarely possible in surveys where respondents are anonymous and, if follow-up is possible, may not recollect exactly what they were thinking when they answered specific questions. Third is engagement of the service, product, etc., by the researcher himself ("trying") (Goligorsky, 2012). By trying a product or service herself, the researcher collects information and generates insights through direct experience. For example, actually going through the process of mopping a kitchen floor and then cleaning the mop gives valuable insight into how a user might feel about cleaning a dirty mop. Trying a product or service also allows emotions to surface that might otherwise be hard to understand. Experiencing the frustrations of an inadequate product or flawed service focuses the mind on finding ways to improve it or eliminate its need altogether. Each method can produce different kinds of observations and insights.

Design research firms generally use all three methods or some combination therein, *triangulating* among sources. By analyzing a research question from multiple perspectives along multiple dimensions from multiple sources (e.g. different dimensions to explore would include methods of inquiry, data sources or theoretical approaches), researchers are able to check and establish the validity of conclusions. Adding multiple investigators is another way to triangulate (Berg, 2007).

Using a process that included hours of structured *looking* and *asking* at the entire floor cleaning process in 18 homes in Boston and Cincinnatti (Butterman, 2012), Continuum identified a number of related, but unique pain points. One, when filled with water, the bucket can be heavy and difficult to move, especially for smaller or older users. Two, water can spill as the person hoists the full bucket from the sink to the floor. Three, the mop gets so dirty in the process of cleaning the floor that it is questionable how clean the floor actually gets using this method. Four, the mop head itself must then be cleaned in the sink after it has been used to clean the floor. Five, the tools—bucket, mop (including damp mop head)—are bulky to store. These observations provided the raw data the team synthesized to generate actionable insights.

During synthesis and insight generation, a research team considers all of the data gathered from observations, interviews and its own experiences interacting with a product or service to identify themes, reconcile conflicting data and generate insights. At this step teams begin to think critically about what has been observed and may make plans to do further research to answer specific questions or fill gaps in knowledge. Based on its observations the Continuum team developed the following insight: Managing the tools required for a mopping process is laborious. *Users spend as much time preparing to mop and cleaning the mop as they do actually mopping the floor!* The team could now frame the problem in an actionable way: *How to create a method for cleaning floors that minimizes time spent cleaning the tools themselves and maximizes effectiveness of the cleaning implement?*

From this deep understanding the team could craft the *design principles* that would guide the design and development process. *Design principles* are a succinct articulation of those requirements or attributes that a solution needs to have to respond effectively to the identified pain points. Given the roster of pain points associated with traditional mopping, design principles to guide the team included:

- *Ease of use and convenience*—The new tool must be easier to use than the traditional mop and bucket.
- *Cleanliness*—The floor must be cleaner after being cleaned by the new tool than it would have been if cleaned by the traditional mop and bucket.
- *Reduce time to clean*—The process using the new tool must be faster than the old process.

A solution would be deemed provisionally acceptable if it adhered to these design principles. *Design principles* also allow for more comprehensive evaluation of designs and help identify and determine tradeoffs. In the computer security industry the two prevailing design principles that guide any product, system or policy developed are in direct and dramatic tension: robust security and ease of use. Those competing principles guide each development process and most decisions developers make are around negotiating that conflict to effectively balance the interests of their clients (Norman, 2009).

Design principles are also important because they link people working on a project who were not involved with the research directly to the user experiences and pain points originally observed and analyzed by the research team. During the ideation phase, teams generate ideas about how to satisfy design principles crafted from research in the *clarify* phase.

Phase 2: Ideation

Ideation, the generation of ideas, is the phase most associated with innovation. Practitioners take two broad approaches to this phase. The first group (generally design research firms) advocates going far, breaking boundaries and reaching toward "wild ideas" (Goligorsky, 2012). A second group (specifically Systematic Inventive Thinking, Inc.) advocates staying close to the problem and looking for opportunities within the problem space and among the materials and resources already at one's disposal (Stern, 2012). Both approaches have produced successful results in a corporate setting.

Although initially counterintuitive, the "stay close" approach resonates deeply with many students and executives because of its foundational assumption about innovation and barriers rooted in individual cognition that can be overcome systematically. *Systematic Inventive Thinking* (SIT) is a set of tools designed specifically to break the *cognitive fixedness* (Zynga, 2013) that limits individuals' ability to see alternatives to structures, relationships and uses than those that already exist. For instance, in the US prior to 2000 it was possible to rent a car for a day, though many (especially vacationers) rented for multiple days or weeks. Why was 24 hours the smallest increment for renting a car? In additional to whatever operational concerns justified this minimum, *cognitive fixedness* no doubt played a big role. ZipCar, founded by two women in Somerville, Massachusetts, in 1999, created a car-sharing service that allowed members to rent a car for a time period as short as 20 minutes, a duration perfect for running a quick errand in the city.

Traditional rental car companies had broken fixedness around owner-ship, but ZipCar broke fixedness around minimum size and flexibility around rental periods, blowing open a market aimed at residents and workers in densely populated areas who valued the flexibility these small time increments and network of shared cars provided (Tice, 2012). The SIT tool of *division* tells users to break a product, process or business model into its component parts and reconfigure them in different ways to create new opportunities (Stern, 2012). The premise is simple: Why stop at a 24-hour rental period when it could be divided even further?

Consider the process of mopping and all the tools and materials required, described in the last section. First, there is the mop, composed of a mop head of tightly wound fibers, along with a long shaft made of wood, plastic or light metal. Second is the bucket. Third is the cleaning solution. Fourth is the water. Each of these elements is subject to fix-edness by the observer. What if the shaft of the mop could be divided into smaller pieces that could fold up or collapse through a telescoping mechanism? This is *division* at work on a physical component. Once *division* has been applied to the shaft of the mop, such that it is col-lapsible, the researcher then needs to evaluate whether this new design addresses an existing need. In this case one could imagine a collapsible shaft making storage easier. Also, if a folding mechanism was intro-duced where the fold could be secured at a particular angle, it might make it easier to reach far under a table or corner with less bending required by the user, a feature that was eventually adapted into a Swiffer spinoff for dusting.

In the Swiffer example the Continuum team essentially applied SIT's *subtraction* tool, which requires elimination of a component deemed essential (Stern, 2012), when it eliminated the task of washing the mop after use—or even the mop head itself. Given the insight that people spend as much time cleaning the tools as they do cleaning the floors (and with questionable results), the team was confident this would be an attractive proposition. The challenge then became bringing this vision to life in accordance with the established design principles.

The SIT tools are prompts to take a moment and engage in thought experiments around different ways of breaking fixedness. In the context of rental cars, the question was: if this business process is *divided* and the segments rearranged, does an opportunity emerge? In the context of laptops, the question was: if the laptop keyboard is *subtracted* what remains? Does a laptop screen alone have value for some set of users? The appeal of SIT tools for many analytically minded executives is that these thought experiments are highly structured and can be performed quickly and on one's own. Practicing these tools at the office or on one's commute has no tangible cost except time and mental energy. When a tool produces an idea judged to have possible value for a user type—in other words, the idea might be *desirable*—the team must then begin to think carefully and quickly about overcoming questions around *feasibility* and *viability*. That is no small task. But in this case the tools are powerful in their ability to break fixedness and produce opportunities with potential to be deemed *desirable*, which is a critical first step.

Alternatively, there are several techniques to help individuals or teams to "go far" in their thinking. One method is alternate worlds, a tool to identify and use perspectives from different industries, organizations or disciplines to generate fresh ideas about a problem (Luma Institute, 2012). In 2005 Syngenta, the global agro-products company, looked to the affordable, single serve "sachet" packaging and distribution model for personal care products (e.g. shampoo) as it thought about ways to move into the market for smallholding farms in Kenya where excess cash is very tight. The company adapted the concept to develop and distribute single serve packets of crop-protection material that would be affordable enough to be accessed by thousands of very low-income farmers in the region. Farmers could purchase these sachets when small sums were available, empty one into a typical backpack with water tank and spraying attachment, and spray their fields. The company developed a sophisticated education and distribution program to support the product, but the initial idea came from looking to an alternate world (Anthony, 2012).

The most well-known form of "go far" ideation is brainstorming, a tool that encourages individuals or teams to think about potential solutions to problems in imaginative ways. The goal of the exercise is to encourage wildly different thinking along any number of dimensions related tightly or loosely to the problem area. The design consultancy IDEO cultivates cultural norms and actively promotes a set of behaviors among participants that "free" them up to think in unconstrained ways. IDEO's list of seven principles for effective brainstorming are: (1) defer judgment, (2) encourage wild ideas, (3) be visual, (4) go for quantity, (5) have one conversation at a time, (6) stay focused on the topic and (7) build on the ideas of others (Goligorsky, 2012).

Underlying these guidelines is recognition that the quality of the social environment is critical to the ideation process. Most importantly, people need to feel safe to be willing to publically voice "go far" ideas (guideline 1, Defer judgment). Having one conversation at a time (guideline 5) and staying focused on the topic (guideline 6) help groups maintain focus on the ideas and task at hand. Build on the ideas of others (guideline 7) encourages collaboration and a developmental approach to ideation. The group understands that the original idea voiced is just a starting point for discussion, and that group authorship is expected. Encouraging wild ideas (guideline 7) and going for quantity (guideline 4) push participants to move beyond their safe and favorite ideas in favor of wild and far. While the far ideas may not be useful as first articulated, each may contain a kernel of an idea with promise or it may spur another participant's thinking. The call to "be visual" (guideline 3) reflects the firm's roots in engineering and recognizes that quick sketches can often allow for fast exploration and communicate more with less.

Both the "stay close" and "go far" approaches to ideation can be effective for individuals and organizations. One important note is that the "stay close" approach practiced by SIT can easily be practiced by individuals with little support beyond personal initiative (although it is also practiced through professional facilitations), while the "go far" approach generally benefits from a structured process that requires more time and coordination among multiple participants.

Structuring an ideation process

Though there are a number of ways to design an ideation process, ideation is frequently organized around the creative matrix (Luma Institute, 2012), a structured format for triggering new ideas informed by design principles. Figure 7.1 presents the creative matrix. In the matrix (usually 3–4 by 4–5) the column headings are the design principles the team will use to develop the product ("What" the design should achieve), as articulated during the clarify phase. In the Swiffer example these principles were *ease of use and convenience, cleanliness* and *reduce time to clean*, so each of those would populate a column heading. The rows represent different ways to achieve the design principles (the "How"). The row headings suggest broad categories that the team might want to consider when developing solutions to achieve the design principles, in both structured and unstructured ways. For example, in the Swiffer example, row headings might be "Use of SIT techniques," "Technology" or "Reaching places that are difficult to clean," all of which are structured approaches to idea generation in that they indicate a particular tool, category or outcome to think about. In contrast, an unstructured approach would be "open brainstorming." The row headings are not solutions for addressing the design principles but rather "aide de memoires" to

DESIGN PRINCIPLES ("WHAT")			
	EASE OF USE & CONVENIENCE	CLEANLINESS	REDUCE TIME TO CLEAN
Reaching places that are difficult to clean			
SIT techniques			
Programs			
Technology			
Open brainstorming			

(AIDE DE MEMOIRES ("HOW"))

Figure 7.1 Creative matrix—Swiffer example
Source: Adapted from LUMA Institute (2012).

ensure that the team does not miss different ways of addressing the design principles. Without the "technology" row heading, for example, ideas such as using "robots to clean" may not come up, and without the "Reaching places that are difficult to clean" row heading, the team may not think about the need for the solution to clean corners, areas behind cabinets or objects attached to the ceiling.

Once the matrix is set up, for each design principle, team members suggest ideas that will help address that design principle using the row headings to spark their thinking. The team writes each idea it generates on a post-it note and then affixes that post-it to the cell at the intersection of the columns and row headings that sparked it. At the end of the exercise the creative matrix will be populated with many ideas on post-its with the range of ideas generated during the ideation session organized by the matrix. The next task is for the team to choose and combine the different ideas articulated on the creative matrix to create a concept that will address the design principles. During this combination and evaluation process, the team will inevitably make tradeoffs about the degree to which each design principle will be reflected in a particular concept. Helping to facilitate these tradeoffs is a key role of design principles.

With a rough concept in hand from the creative matrix process, a team can then use the concept poster to begin to think through and flesh out the basic details of the concept. Figure 7.2 presents the concept poster. Several sections comprise the concept poster. The first, background and insights, presents the main pain points and design principles that represent that logical underpinning of the concept. A second section describes that basic concept itself, including the value proposition and the functional and emotional benefits of the product. The third section identifies the key assumptions that would need to be tested regarding desirability, feasibility and viability, and may indicate possible ways to test these assumptions. Using the concept poster, the team can very quickly flesh out its idea to elicit feedback from potential users.

Phase 3: Concept development

The concept development phase is about improving and revising a concept through iterative production and testing. User feedback is critical to this process and the concept poster is a good first stage vehicle for doing this. Feedback is most effective when constructive (not only critical), and the Rose-Thorn-Bud technique provides a structured way

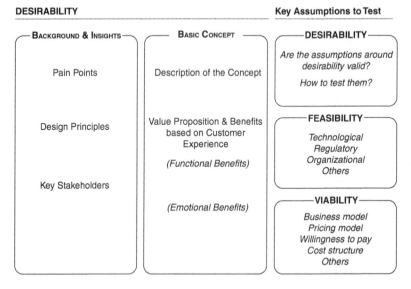

Figure 7.2   Concept poster
Source: Adapted from LUMA Institute 2012.

for a group of individuals to provide a good range of feedback (Luma Institute, 2012). To carry out Rose-Thorn-Bud users are presented with the concept poster and asked to comment on the aspects of the concept they view positively (rose), negatively (thorn) or see as promising (bud). Users write each comment on a color-coded post-it note that reflects the rose-thorn-bud, and affix the note to the area of the concept poster to which it refers. These comments give the designer-specific insights into how the concept might be enhanced or improved very quickly and cheaply and early in the process (Luma Institute, 2012).

In the next stage of concept development, teams begin to test ideas generated during ideation. A team may choose to explore several potential ideas first (using rough approximations) and, through the prototyping, testing, feedback and iteration process, ultimately decide to pursue one or two with increasing levels of fidelity to explore what a final offering might look like. Figure 7.3 presents the prototyping process.

Prototypes and rapid cycles of testing and feedback are at the heart of the concept development phase. With creative thinking, anything can be prototyped. Each prototype allows a practitioner to answer a different kind of question, from the very broad (e.g. Are people interested at all in this kind of offering?) to the very specific (e.g. Does the user understand how to navigate through this digital interface?). By prototyping early and often and soliciting feedback from actual users, the team can learn vast amounts, recalibrating key assumptions, answering critical questions and gaining important technical/practical knowledge as it goes.

After the Continuum team generated the idea for Swiffer, the team immediately set out to create a rough prototype. Initially, the Swiffer was imagined as a shaft with a disposable pad with cleaning fluid

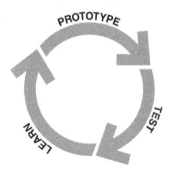

Figure 7.3   Prototype—Test—Learn
Source: Adapted from LUMA Institute 2012.

attached to the end as well as a nozzle to spray cleaning fluid onto the floor just ahead of the cleaning pad that would eliminate the need for the bucket, water and cleaning fluid. This nozzle and spray function would be controlled by the user. In a 2012 interview, Continuum CEO Harry West described this initial prototyping effort as follows:

> This whole thing is what you'd call a Frankenstein Model. We had an old broom, got paper towels, we found plastic tubes to spray water on the floor. We got a nozzle from a spritzer bottle, a little electric pump. Within a day, we hacked it. We're going to a model shop and cutting it up and getting it to fit. We created an ergonomically effective handle.
>
> (Butterman, 2012)

Though very rough and nothing to look at, the prototype solved the critical question of whether this kind of model could clean the floor more effectively than a traditional mop with a bucket of water and cleaning solution. Using a standardized evaluation process, the team determined that the prototype *was* more effective at cleaning, and decided to move the design and development process forward.

Such small experiments allow for big learning with minimal risk, preventing the worst-case scenario of fully developing a concept, rolling it out, only to find that many of the key assumptions underpinning it were simply incorrect. Learning to "fail small" is challenging for MBA students and executives who have advanced in academics and the workplace by performing well and explicitly *avoiding* failure. Leaders in an organization can take many concrete actions to build and maintain a culture where thoughtful prototyping, including the failures that will inevitably accompany it, is encouraged and practiced by individuals tasked with creating anything new. It will be uncomfortable at first, but over time, this approach produces more clarity about the final concept and minimizes the chances the team will fail big (and expensively) in the long run.

Phase 4: Implementation

Thinking about issues around implementation is critical to bringing well-developed concepts into the world where they will meet previously unmet user needs and improve experiences with products and services. Much of implementation hinges on understanding the various stakeholders in an organization or throughout the system that will be delivering the service or product. How will the team get the people it needs on board to support this new service? How will it get actors out-side its control, be they distributors or department managers, to execute as required so that the service is successful? Many of the principles and techniques of the *discovery* phase apply here. Although instead of "users" the subject of the practitioners' inquiry will be "distributors" or "managers," and the shape that inquiry takes might look somewhat different.

The *stakeholder analysis* tool is useful for addressing these important questions systematically. The first step is to simply identify all relevant stakeholders. Then, for each stakeholder, gauge their current levels of support (or opposition) and estimate where the support of each needs to be for the project/strategy to move forward or be adopted. (In Figure 7.4 below, the current level of support is indicated by an X, and the required level of support is indicated by an O.) The *stakeholder analysis* chart created through this process can then help to structure discussions of how to win the support of critical stakeholders (Puccio, Mance and Murdock, 2010).

Figure 7.4 illustrates a hypothetical analysis drafted by sales team at a company selling sophisticated and very expensive robotic inventory management systems. The analysis charts the positions of key stake-holders inside a potential sales company, the CEO, CTO and COO, and approximates where the sales team believes each would have to be to seriously consider purchasing its system. With this analysis in hand, the team can think creatively about ways to design the product, the terms of the contract, the service terms or any other flexible component to gain key individuals' support.

Even with effective stakeholder analysis, the innovator must over-come two major challenges associated with implementation. First, can the future user absorb the idea? In other words, can the designer com-municate the idea effectively, so that potential users or stakeholders,

STAKEHOLDERS	Strongly Oppose	Moderately Oppose	Neutral	Moderately Support	Strongly Support	Possible Actions
CEO		X —————	▶O			
CTO			X—————		▶O	
COO	X —————				▶O	

Figure 7.4   Stakeholder analysis
Source: Adapted from Puccio, G.J., Mance, M. and Murdock, M.C. (2010).

with no prior knowledge or familiarity with the concept, can understand it? It is surprisingly difficult for someone very close to an idea, having spent considerable time and energy developing it, to effectively adopt the consumers' uninformed point of view (Heath and Heath, 2006). To address the first issue, innovators try to arouse the curiosity of customers in the product, demonstrate how the product works and its value, and make it psychologically comfortable and easy to adopt.

The second challenge is rooted in the tension between customers' general tendency to prefer the status quo and the behavior change a user *must* embrace to adopt any new idea. The more behavior change is required the more difficult it will be for the innovator to convince users that the costs of behavior change outweigh the benefits of the innovation (Gourville, 2005). Products and services designed with this challenge in mind directly address felt pain points and provide clear functional and emotional benefits based on deep empathy and understanding. In doing so, they minimize the behavior change required and increase the likelihood they will be adopted. In a previous section of this chapter, we discussed how executives need to be more empathetic to user needs. As there, deep understanding and the human-centeredness of design is the best antidote to problems of implementation.

Conclusion

Established organizations succeed through execution, successfully managing their operations cycle, but to succeed in the long run they must manage the innovation cycle equally well. While the operations cycle encompasses everything related to performance and execution, the innovation cycle refers to those activities carried out to develop new products, processes, business models, etc. In recent years, the increasing pace of change in organizations has increased the organizational emphasis on the innovation cycle, which is where the human-centered, design-thinking approach is most relevant.

The difference in focus and mindset required of managers is very different for the operaitons cycles compared to the innovation cycles. The operation cycle is managed using rules, routines and procedures with laser focus on meeting performance measures. The innovation cycle is different, requiring greater attention to curiosity, speculation, connection-making, developmental thinking and experimentation. The danger is when someone highly skilled and successfully managing the operations cycle comes to manage people and activities in the innovation cycle using the mindset of the operations world.

For an organization to be successful, it must manage both cycles well. There is a long history and a series of best practices for managing operations, but the same is not true for managing innovations. The challenges are many: how to identify innovative individuals, how to organize the work and the teams, what managerial processes to develop, and what culture and climate to create? The social environment that these actions unleash can have profound impact on whether innovations are nurtured or eroded (Amabile, 1998). For innovation to succeed, organizations need innovatively minded leaders who have a vision for the future innovation landscape and ways to manage conflicts and differing agendas, while reducing the fear of failure among individual team members and recognizing and rewarding innovative work. Individuals trained in design thinking understand the innovation process deeply and so can be more effective in leading innovation. Fortunately, design thinking is a skill that can be learned with repeated practice, in business schools as well as within the corporate setting.

References

Amabile, T. (1998) "How to Kill Creativity," *Harvard Business Review* 76, no. 5, pp. 79–86.

Anthony, S. (2012) "The New Corporate Garage," *Harvard Business Review* 90, no. 9, pp. 44–53.

Berg, B. (2007) "Qualitative Research Methods for the Social Sciences," California State University, Long Beach.

Butterman, E. (2012) "Mopping the Floor with the Status Quo," *ASME.org*, Available: https://www.asme.org/engineering-topics/articles/product-planning/mopping-floor-the-status-quo (Accessed December 2012).

Continuum, "Swiffer: A Game-Changing Home Product," Available: http://continuuminnovation.com/work/swiffer (Accessed 15 January 2015).

Datar, S.M., Garvin, D.G. and Cullen, P.G. (2010) "Rethinking the MBA: Business Education at a Crossroads," Harvard Business School Press, Boston, MA.

Goligorsky, D. (8 December 2012) "Empathy and Innovation: The IDEO Approach," *Lecture*, Harvard Business School, Boston, MA.

Gourville, J. (2005) "The Marketing of Innovations: Module II: The Psychology of Innovations," HBS Case No. 506-016, Harvard Business School Publishing, Boston, MA.

Heath, C. and Heath, D. (2006) "The Curse of Knowledge," *Harvard Business Review* 84, no. 12, pp. 20–23.

LUMA Institute (2012) "Innovating for People: Handbook of Human-Centered Design," LUMA Institute, LLC., Pittsburgh.

Norman, D. (2009) "The Way I See It: When Security Gets in the Way," *Interactions* 16, no. 6, pp. 60–63.

Puccio, G.J., Mance, M. and Murdock, M.C. (2010) "Creative Leadership: Skills that Drive Change," 2nd ed., SAGE Publications, Inc., Woburn.

Simon, H.A. (1996) "The Sciences of the Artificial," 3rd ed., The MIT Press, Cambridge.

Statista, "Global Apple iPad Sales from 3rd Quarter 2010 to 1st Quarter 2015," Available: http://www.statista.com/statistics/269915/global-apple-ipad-sales-since-q3-2010 (Accessed 2 February 2015).

Stern, Y. (7 December 2012) "Systematic Innovative Thinking," Lecture, Harvard Business School, Boston, MA.

Tice, C. (2012) "Zipcar: Two Moms, a Business Idea and $68 in the Bank," *Entrepreneur*, Available: http://www.entrepreneur.com/article/223692 (Accessed 1 June 2012).

Zynga, A. (2013) "The Cognitive Bias Keeping Us from Innovating," *Harvard Business Review Online*, Available: https://hbr.org/2013/06/the-cognitive-bias-keeping-us-from (Accessed 13 June 2013).

8
Global Leadership Development and Innovation Inside

Pankaj Ghemawat

Introduction

As somebody who started teaching more than 30 years ago in what was then the General Management area at the Harvard Business School, I have long been interested in leadership development, broadly defined. In the last 15 years, my work has mostly focused on globalization and its implications for business, with a particular focus on business strategy and, more recently, leadership development. I discuss at some length my perspectives on the globalization of leadership development in a chapter included in Canals (2012). That chapter, "The ABCDs of Leadership 3.0," proposed a different way of addressing the distinctive complexities that leaders grapple with in a global (or international) context: by thinking through as well as experiencing the differences and distances between countries and acting on the implications (Ghemawat, 2012). The model was grounded in logic, empirical research, an AACSB-sponsored survey of academic thought leaders worldwide, participation in the AACSB's Globalization of Management Education Taskforce, and my experience teaching these ideas—and experimenting with them— over more than a decade.

When asked to contribute a chapter about integrating innovation into global leadership development, I first thought of companies that I know well attempting major innovations with a significant cross-border component or impact. But as I played around with these examples, I was also offering a massive open online course (MOOC) for the first time. And so it occurred to me that while innovation by exemplars out there is an important topic that deserves to be considered in detail in global leadership development, so is innovation *inside* such programs.

The first section anchors this discussion of "innovation inside" in my experience designing and first offering a MOOC, "The Globalization of Business Enterprise," under IESE Business School's auspices on the Coursera platform.[1] The second section explains why, based on this experience, I consider that to design MOOC or not to design MOOC is <u>not</u> the key question: I think the real threat/opportunity resides in rapidly improving online technology substituting, over time, for traditional face-to-face interactions. The third section suggests some confusions and cautions about business schools' responses to MOOCs/online technology. The fourth section shifts to normative mode: it discusses how a business school might try to orchestrate an effective response to an ongoing, evolving stream of innovation opportunities. The final section discusses the same broad issues from a company perspective, that is, from the vantage point of corporate leadership development programs. Section six concludes.

The "GLOBE" MOOC

Offering a MOOC was a recent step in a longer-run personal program of trying to use technology more effectively in my teaching—a concern that had already led to in-class use of voting devices, the development of cartograms, interactive displays and tools for my personal website, ghemawat.com,[2] the release of a globalization-related course-on-a-disk CD cobranded with AACSB International (the largest international accreditor of business schools) and the build-up of a modest presence on social media. So when the opportunity to offer a MOOC through IESE on Coursera came up—it was sparked by a meeting with Daphne Koller, one of the cofounders of Coursera, at TED Global in 2012, when we both spoke there—I was eager. *The New York Times* had branded 2012 "The Year of the MOOC" (Pappano, 2012), and so checking out this new and perhaps blockbuster technology seemed an interesting next step in my digital journey.

The MOOC that I developed, "The Globalization of Business Enterprise (GLOBE)," was based on an eponymous course that I had developed as a required course for the first-year of the MBA program at IESE Business School and offered for the first time in winter 2010. The face-to-face version of GLOBE, which continues to be offered at IESE, itself represents a case of "innovation inside" in terms of both content and structure. It was based on my participation over two-and-a-half years in a taskforce that AACSB International assembled on the Globalization of Management Education and, in particular, my authorship of the chapter in the taskforce's report that focused on what business schools should teach MBA students about globalization and how.[3]

In terms of content, the face-to-face version of GLOBE was intended to acquaint MBA students with basic facts about globalization, expose them to a broad view of the differences between countries that under-lie limited levels of cross-border integration and get them to begin to think about the broader implications of such differences for public and business policy—and for their own personal development. In terms of structure, the 12 sessions in IESE's required curriculum allotted to GLOBE were meant to serve as a cross-functional platform for follow-on discussions of globalization in other core courses—an objective bolstered by the requirement that follow-on functional courses have a 10–20 per cent cross-border component that would interlock with the GLOBE platform. This interlock approach recognizes and accepts that schools and curricula are generally partitioned by function, rather than requiring them to completely transform themselves.

The GLOBE MOOC retained the content and the cross-functional perspective of its face-to-face precursor although, obviously, the inter-lock structure itself could not be migrated to the Coursera platform. The MOOC was first delivered in February–March 2014 under IESE's auspices on Coursera. A total of 22,361 students from 163 countries signed up.[4] The sign-up patterns for those students whose locations we could identify are summarized in Figure 8.1. I will elaborate on the sign-up patterns by country because they help illustrate one of the core frameworks underlying the course itself: my CAGE distance framework.

The CAGE framework, widely taught at leading business schools, is based on research clearly indicating that international interactions are dampened by cultural, administrative (or political), geographical and economic distance (hence the CAGE acronym)—or, equivalently, that they are disproportionately concentrated among country-pairs that are close in such terms.[5]

The CAGE framework also seemed to apply to sign-up intensities—that is, the number of people signed up divided by total enrolment in tertiary education in the country in question. A multivariate regression that explained nearly one half of the variation in sign-up intensities indicated that they were likely to be twice as high in English-speaking countries as in others. They also dropped off by 25 per cent for each doubling of geographic distance from the US. A dummy variable indi-cating emerging-economy status faded from significance once the other variables were taken into account; however, it did carry a consistently negative sign, reflecting the fact that while 47 per cent of the enrolled

142

1. U.S.A.   17%
2. India   12%
3. Spain   9%
4. China   5%
5. U.K.   4%
6. Germany   2%
7. France   2%
8. Canada   2%
9. Mexico   2%
10. Brazil   2%

Figure 8.1 Sign-up patterns for the GLOBE MOOC on Coursera

students were from emerging economies, such economies account for 75 per cent of the total university students. Note that this particular finding raises some doubts about what *The New York Times*, in its "Year of the MOOC" article, characterized as "[t]he shimmery hope ... that free courses can bring the best education in the world to the most remote corners of the planet" (Pappano, 2012). And the week before my course went live also provided a stark reminder of the importance of administrative/political factors: US export controls forced Coursera to pull the plug on students in Iran, Syria, Cuba and Sudan, affecting two dozen prospective students who had already signed up. I should also mention that in addition to the variables cited above, sign-up intensities were strongly and positively related to the country-level globalization index that I prepare annually with Steven Altman.[6]

In addition to these country-level influences, individual/institutional factors also mattered. Thus, the three countries from which the most students signed up were the three I have spent the most time living in: the US, India and Spain. And Spain is, of course, also where IESE Business School is headquartered, although it has multiple locations around the world.

So much for course content and sign-ups. What were the kinds of issues that came up when the twain met?

The first issue, and the one that is probably most talked about in a MOOC context, has to do with the level of commitment of the students. Commitment levels clearly were lower than in a face-to-face, fee-paying context. Of all the students who signed up, 14,049 looked at *some* course materials, implying that a one third had literally zero engagement with the course. However, more than two thousand were still active in the last week of an eight-week course—a bit better, overall, than the averages reported in a Wharton meta-analysis of MOOCs (Terwiesch and Ulrich, 2014).

This somewhat higher level of stickiness reflected strenuous efforts to mitigate the effects of low student commitment. Probably the most effective of these devices was beginning most of the (in-studio) lectures with footage of me foreshadowing session themes from iconic locations where I found myself (for other purposes): Trondheim, the Viking capital of Norway; Times Square and the UN building in New York; Copacabana in Rio; the Capetown waterfront; the Jetee de l'Eau in Geneva; la Boqueria market in Barcelona; the British Parliament as the backdrop in London. ... Of course, this would have made less sense if I weren't teaching a course about globalization. And I must also admit that given the work involved in trying to build stickiness, I was a bit unhappy that it didn't rise above the levels that it did reach. MOOCs are inherently a low commitment medium.

A second, somewhat related issue had to do with limitations to the depth of the discussion online. Consider a case I wrote specifically for my MOOC—a two-pager on a designer backpack company from Colombia expanding into more than 20 foreign countries, mostly through franchising. Most of my business cases (descriptions of business situations meant to serve as the basis for class discussion) run ten to 15 pages. But this norm was upended not only by Coursera students' limited willingness to engage but also by my realization that I had very limited control—relative to the conventional classroom setting—of online case discussions. As a friend with prior experience put it, "Running a case discussion online is like going to class with a case, being there for the first five minutes of the discussion, but then having to leave." Thus, simpler material that allowed less room for things to go entirely off-track seemed advisable, even if it did take a toll in terms of the depth of the discussion. But despite such attempts at simplification, I was still surprised at how quickly discussions could veer off course.

A third issue involved collaboration—or rather, restrictions on it—on the Coursera platform. Given the subject matter of the GLOBE course and the focus of main multi-week course assignment on country-level analysis, it was frustrating to be unable to direct submissions by students on particular countries to peers from those countries for purposes of eliciting feedback. But fortunately, given the topic of the course, there *were* other things that could be done to leverage this large, globally diverse group of students. They yielded the largest sample to date for surveys that I have run with many groups about perceived levels of globalization—one that permits analysis of cross-country variation. And my IESE colleague, Sebastian Reiche, and I also tested our new survey instrument on global intelligence on this group.

The real threat/opportunity

Looking across the issues mentioned in the last section, I came away with the sense that learning outcomes were significantly worse for the students enrolled in my MOOC—even those who dropped in regularly instead of dropping out—than for students whom I teach face-to-face. Much of the literature that purports to analyze the degree of threat that MOOCs and other online educational technologies pose to traditional classroom instruction starts—and stops—with consideration of learning outcomes. But while they are one interesting measure of benefits delivered by MOOCs and other online models, they are not all that matters.

For one thing, from a student-centric perspective, one must supplement measures of learning content/quality with considerations of time spent, flexibility on the time dimension, and so on. And from an instructional perspective, the ability to "convene" a large, geographically dispersed group of students can be very valuable in and of itself—for example, in a course focused on globalization and perceptions of it, such as my MOOC.

Broadening the basis of comparison beyond the usual focus on learning content to look at some of these additional benefits expands the possibility of online technology looking better than, or at least more comparable to, traditional educational models. This is especially true when one takes account of segmentation by country, institutional or individual characteristics (cited in the analysis of sign-up intensities). And maybe by field. Thus, according to one source, "studying business has always led the way in this respect, with one-third of the nearly three million on-line students pursuing business degrees."[7]

A second caveat around focusing on learning content is that any competitive analysis should look at relative costs as well as relative benefits—and to split the former into recurring and nonrecurring costs. MOOCs tend to have very low recurring costs unlike traditional classroom instruction. And while the nonrecurring costs associated with developing a MOOC are large compared to conventional course development, (a) they are ideally to be shared across multiple offerings, and (b) a focus on incremental course development costs misses out on the capital-intensity of a traditional university structure which, especially when one capitalizes and includes the present costs of multiyear—in the case of tenure, indefinite—contractual commitments to faculty, is quite high. Overall, looking at relative costs as well as relative benefits likely makes MOOCs/online technology look comparatively more attractive.

A third caveat, and probably the most important one, is that to focus on relative positions right now is to forget about technological change that can shift them over time—which, again, will likely make online models look more competitive. To fully appreciate this point, think of MOOCs not as standalone offerings but as a particular point on a decades-long trajectory of increasing effectiveness for online education. Conventional classroom education, in contrast, is a mature technology. While the benefits of online education may currently be lower, they are likely to increase faster: think of changes such as more sophisticated

collaboration platforms, increased Internet access in emerging economies in particular and improvements in videoconferencing technology,
to name just a few. And the different rates of progress are likely to continue: will, for instance, the difference between face-to-face and online
remain as large once hologram technology is mastered?

Turning to the cost side, MOOCs *will* experience some cost pressures.
Coursera, for instance, apparently still needs to develop a revenue
model: thus far, it has depended on venture capital plus the willingness
of its partner institutions to pay for the required investments in content development. But that is nothing compared to the cost escalation
experienced by and projected for conventional higher education: in the
US, the cost of college has risen by almost five times the rate of infla-
tion since 1983, while the salaries of college graduates have been flat for
most of the last decade ("Is College Worth It?," 2014).

Or consider higher education in business—the part of the educational
sector that I know best, and one long considered relatively immune to
pricing pressures. The 2013 Application Trends Survey conducted by
the Graduate Management Admissions Council (GMAC) reports that
in 2013, 53 per cent of part-time MBA programs in the US experienced
a decline in applications, while another 18 per cent reported stagnant
volumes (GMAC, 2013b). Note that part-time MBA students, who are
typically working—and more than three-quarters of whom, according to
GMAC data, stay in their existing jobs after graduating—are apt to value
convenience more and socialization and certification less than full-time
MBA students, that is, are comparatively more likely to find online
models attractive (GMAC, 2013a). But even full-time two-year MBA
programs (again, in the US) aren't immune. While 52 per cent of them
reported an increase in applications in 2013, which can be seen as just a
rebound from several years of declining applications, 2013 was the first
year since 2009 that the majority of such programs reported an increase
in applications (GMAC, 2013b)! Superimposing the advent of improved
online models on such dismal application statistics has led some to
predict a major shakeout in higher education in business: thus, according to Richard Lyons, dean of UC-Berkeley's Haas School of Business,
"Half of the business schools in this country could be out of business
in ten years—or five" (quoted in Clark, 2014). And while those at the
top 20 business schools sometimes feel that such dire warnings apply to
everybody except themselves, it is worth noting that Northwestern and
Michigan have recently announced reductions in the size of their full-
time MBA programs, and Stanford has decided to expand its one-year
Sloan masters program significantly, apparently because of concerns

about the pressures on two-year MBA programs. So once again, the sense of safety at the top may be overdone in at least some quarters.

Responses and nonresponses at business schools

The previous section argued that online technology more than MOOCs does present a significant threat/opportunity for business schools. What kind of responses in terms of innovation inside has it elicited from them? There are no systematic sources of information on this topic, but one can make some broad generalizations as well as talking through a few cases that have attracted particular attention.

First, there do seem to be many cases of nonresponse. While such outcomes may reflect effort-aversion or myopia, they can also arise from the purest of motives. Many faculty and staff continue to see online learning as an inferior version of face-to-face education. In the face of such beliefs, getting people to expend the extra effort required to engage with new technology—as opposed to doing what they have always done—is difficult. And the difficulty is reinforced by the fact that many institutions have yet to develop the capabilities and skills required to support online learning (Ladkin et al., 2009).

Second, there are clearly also many institutions that are dabbling with new technology by, for instance, experimenting with MOOCs. And while the conclusions they are drawing may differ somewhat, most still seem to be struggling to orchestrate a coherent strategic response to new technology.

Third, there are institutions that have sought to insource MOOCs as a way of reducing costs. One (unsuccessful) example is provided by San Jose State University, which, suffering from resource constraints and citing its location in Silicon Valley, tried to get departments to switch some courses from classroom to online. A controversy around attempts to mandate, in particular, an online course on social justice by Michael Sandel of Harvard forced the university administration to backtrack, leaving San Jose State's professors to decide when to swap-in online content for their in-class appearances (and employment levels). But despite this example, a degree of swapping-in may be something that *must* occur if productivity challenges in the educational sector are to be addressed.

And fourth, there are a few institutions with the resources to start significant development initiatives of their own. Two that have attracted particular attention are Harvard Business School (HBS) and Wharton. HBS has decided *not* to embrace one of the existing MOOC platforms, but rather, to invest heavily in a proprietary platform, HBX. Its first offering will be an online, for-pay CORE or Credential of Readiness, which will comprise three courses—business analytics, economics for managers and financial accounting—to be aimed at a pre-MBA population. Wharton, in contrast, has embraced MOOCs with a vengeance, making ones out of all its core courses with star professors, reasonable production values, and so on. And there has been much debate about which is the better approach for those wealthy institutions. Michael Porter of Harvard Business School favors the HBS approach, but Clay Christensen, also of HBS, the Wharton approach.

My own perspective is that the obvious differences between the HBS and Wharton approaches mask an important similarity—and limitation. HBS is using its online platform to target a set of students—pre-MBAs—whom it doesn't currently serve. And Wharton-style models, according to the school's research, "seem to attract students for whom traditional business school offerings are out of reach" (Christensen et al., 2014). In other words, both schools treat their online efforts as relatively self-contained rather than with connections to what goes on in their traditional classrooms.

As a result, the risk of making serious efforts to rethink the "core" of such programs in light of online technology is not happening. This is compounded by the prevalent emphasis on cocooning new initiatives from existing ones. But for online development efforts to have the potential to contribute to blending the new and the old outside their own narrow areas, there must be a path for them to influence the core. This requires efforts to create strong linkages through mechanisms such as cross-staffing, multiple points of contact and unification of reporting/decision structures at some meaningful level. And since resistance typically rears its head before key commitments are made—that is, in the experimental phase—experimentation both in the core and in new areas requires these mechanisms to be used relatively early in the process, before the way forward is entirely clear.

A simple way of framing the change required—although it is quite complex in all its implications—would be as a shift from thinking about face-to-face time as a bucket to be filled to thinking about it as a scarce resource to be rationed. Schools should ideally focus the roles of online and in-class interactions around their comparative advantages. In particular, in-class interactions should be favored when:

- judgment and socialization are important;
- discussion of the reasons behind competing interpretations is critical to transformative learning, and is best facilitated by face-to-face contact;

- it is important to have a nexus to tie together not just homework, but fieldwork (or other activities pursued in the course of activity learning); and
- promoting presentation/discussion skills is important.

Conversely, don't do in the classroom what can be done as effectively online. Technology already offers some obvious ways to improve on traditional classroom interactions. For example, don't drone through a presentation in class: posting video lectures based on such materials for viewing before or after can free up class time for general discussion as well as questions and answers. And the even higher hope for technology is that it can help in enhancing some of the approaches emphasized in constructive theories of learning—discovery, hands-on, experiential, collaborative, project-based, task-based, and so on—so as to help with concept engagement, regardless of whether they take place within the classroom or outside it.

In the specific context of global leadership development, the experiential component has achieved some salience, so the potentially powerful role that technology can play in assisting with it is particularly worth highlighting. Global leadership development programs that mix experiential and conceptual components typically have participants visit one or more locations that are foreign to most of them. Having all key faculty follow such groups around the world creates several types of difficulties. Being able to use technology to relax these constraints would be enormously valuable. And in fact, my next set of experiments with technology, after MOOCs, have involved remote delivery of a module (culminating in project presentations) remotely, from Barcelona to participants in IESE's Global Executive MBA program who are visiting China.

Innovation inside business schools

Given the variety of possible responses highlighted in the previous section, it is worth emphasizing the role of **experimenting**—not just with recombining, but across a broad range of strategies, only some of which were discussed above. Given the amount of ambiguity in the environment and how quickly it is evolving, there are large opportunities to learn about online learning. This is particularly true if one thinks of all the developments in digital space on which companies currently seem to be focused (even though educational institutions generally lag behind): changes that include mobility, social media and the proliferation of devices in what used to be a computer-centric space.

Of course, I am not the first person to suggest experimentation as perhaps the best way to think about how universities should engage with new technology: former MIT President Susan Hockfield, for instance, made that the central theme of a recent discussion on designing the university of the future (Hockfield, 2014). But simply running a lot of experiments is no substitute for having a set of principles to guide such efforts. While the responses to online technology in higher education are, as noted above, subject to many contingencies, it is possible to specify at least a few imperatives—or, if you will, procedural tips—based on my experiences at IESE that merit attention from most institutions of higher education:

1. Start with an inventory of existing efforts. Any large educational institution is likely to have dozens if not hundreds of projects—admittedly of very different scale and scope—undertaken or under way that are relevant to its online journey.
2. Work on a number of small projects rather than a megaproject. My MOOC is just one of more than a dozen initiatives at IESE aimed at improving teaching within IESE's programs through the use of technology, particularly before and after a residential session.[8]
3. Think strategically about where to get started. In a multiprogram context, in particular, picking the right program to start out with greatly increases the likelihood of success. At IESE, the focus of the early technology-development efforts is not on the flagship, fully residential two-year MBA program, but on the Global Executive MBA (GEMBA) program, with residential sessions in Europe, North and South America, and Asia. At other institutions, focus on the part-time rather than the full-time MBA may be appropriate because the former may have greater receptivity of improvements online.
4. Maximize the learn-to-burn ratio, which implies not only picking promising areas to work in, but also doing so on the cheap (see Ghemawat, 1991). Thus, while it is routinely asserted that "the cost of MOOC production ... can reach hundreds of thousands of dollars" (Straumsheim, 2013), I can say that IESE Business School's total investment in developing the GLOBE MOOC did *not* reach six figures (although the figure excludes the opportunity costs of my own time). That said, there will be competition for resources between existing and new activities; thus, setting an overall percentage target for total investments dedicated to new initiatives will help prevent them from getting crowded out by existing ones.
5. Emphasize the development of usage-flexible resources—in this case, not only digital content (most business schools are still very much

stuck in the stage of online distribution of static documents) but also the capabilities and skills to support new initiatives in environments that are still geared toward delivering classroom-based learning (for a detailed discussion of usage-flexible resources, see Ghemawat and Sol, 1998). With regard to the development of such usage-flexible resources, issues related to intellectual property rights loom large and still need to be resolved at most institutions (including IESE) to enlist the full cooperation of even those faculty who are inclined to move in this direction—typically a small fraction of the total.

6. Put organizational mechanisms in place to ensure focus on new initiatives and to facilitate coordination not only *across* these initiatives but also *between* them and the "mainstream"—important given the considerable sources of inertia that might otherwise block progress (also see below). At IESE, a Learning Innovation Unit that reports directly to the School's Executive Committee was set up in spring 2013 for this purpose.

7. Sequence activities and reviews adjust rapidly, including abandoning them if exit triggers are hit. At IESE, since we are still in the early stages of this process, it remains to be seen how well this particular stage will be managed.

8. Enhance learning through personnel choices, information-sharing, post-audits, and so on, as well as through deliberate attempts to also learn from other companies—outside as well as within one's specific industry segment.

Innovation inside corporate education

There seems to be a relative dearth of literature on online learning in the executive context. Overall, however, the adoption of online learning seems to have been much more limited in executive education programs than in degree programs. Examination of the offerings of the world's top-ten executive education providers (see "Executive Education Rankings 2013," 2013) indicates that almost all courses being offered, both short and long, are offered face-to-face. More broadly, it seems that executive education providers have limited themselves to creating stand-alone e-learning modules that are meant to be auxiliary to classroom-based core experiences. And leadership development programs, in particular, are supposed to be unique in that they typically require minimal mastery of factual knowledge and are based more on constructive and collaborative methods, so one would expect particularly low levels of online penetration there.

Of course, some of the same points about the limitations of online technology could be made about degree programs in business schools, so current patterns in corporate education may simply reflect similar lags. And there *are* some signs that some of the pressures that are driving change in degree programs are also leading to changes in the corporate space. A *Forbes* contributor reports that, "in a recent Future Workplace survey, completed by 195 corporate learning and HR professionals, 70 per cent of respondents said they saw opportunities to integrate MOOCs into their own company's learning programs" (Meister, 2013). And market research conducted by McKinsey & Company shows that learning leaders have clearly felt the effects of the financial crisis.

Finer grained analysis of the possibilities (see the text box) suggests that although significant experimentation is underway with MOOCs, they also seem to have marked limitations. As a result, the broader point about thinking strategically about how to integrate technology into leadership development is as much an imperative for corporate education as for business schools—although the optimal answers to the questions about what to do about/with it may differ.

MOOCs: Perspectives from Corporate Learning Leaders

Giuseppe Auricchio[9]

My research on the current use of blended learning in executive leadership programs, involving in-depth interviews with 43 senior HR executives from leading firms in North America and Europe, has revealed mixed opinions amongst learning leaders about the relevance of MOOCs to corporate learning and development needs. When I asked interviewees about their impressions of the MOOC phenomenon and how it was impacting their organization's learning and development agenda, two key findings emerged.

First, while popular press indicates that the use of MOOCs in a business context is gaining rapid acceptance, the research suggests that many HR leaders are still familiarizing themselves with the concept of what a MOOC is, and reflecting on how they might be able to use it. As put by one interviewee, "It's fairly new to a lot of us ... and so as I learn more about that, I'll get more comfortable with making decisions on whether or not we should really dive into the use of MOOCs or not." Real experiments with the use of MOOCs in a corporate context are few and far between. Indeed, most HR executives seem to be in a state of exploration, rather than experimentation, as described by another interviewee. "I think it's something that is certainly worth exploring more, but I don't have the answer to it and I haven't jumped on the bandwagon ... I don't know if it's successful or not; I'd rather kind of watch it."

Second, those HR leaders that are familiar with MOOCs are dubious as to whether MOOCs achieve the learning impact demanded by corporate programs. Most recognize a MOOC as "a convenient delivery method" that provides "easy access to a library of content." But fewer are convinced that real learning is taking place. "I think this is definitely overestimated. You're just watching a speech on TV—that's basically what MOOC is." For these HR executives, MOOCs are missing some elements that make corporate learning experiences effective. First, MOOCs "don't require deep presence, with real peers who are deeply embedded into a learning experience." As a result, participation in any form is good enough, to the detriment of real engagement. Moreover, MOOCs promote learning in isolation. "A development program is one of the most communal, bonding, socially generative contexts we have. What MOOCs do is isolate learners. They create separate spaces both physically and mentally, which isolate people." Such isolation is not helpful for HR directors, who recognize that for corporate learning to be effective it needs to be anchored in a work context, in which employees can learn from each other, solve problems together and collectively make sense of the behavior their organization asks of them.

As a result, with respect to their use of MOOCs for employee development, most HR executives believe that "while it's potentially an important phenomenon and you should be aware of it, you should also be aware of its limits." Consistent with these beliefs, the research confirms that some companies are exploring how to leverage the different aspects of learning design that characterize MOOCs to create experiences for their customers. "Where I see the opportunity is we have a lot of customers who would like to be healthier and we have a lot of health expertise. And so you can see a lot of value in maybe putting together a MOOC that would offer health-related education to the masses." This intuition fits with the general sense that MOOCs, while perhaps effective at distributing knowledge, do not—taken in isolation—fully meet corporate learning needs.[10]

Some of these differences revolve around the role of corporate learning leaders, who must take an organizational perspective on the costs and benefits of online education, in contrast to the primarily individual-level perspective, at least on the demand side, emphasized in the rest of this chapter. On the one hand, these corporate learning leaders tend to share the same preferences as business schools for face-to-face executive leadership development. But they also have to worry about the organizational costs of sending participants to residential programs—which typically exceed the costs in an individualized, self-pay model because of the opportunity costs to the organization of having key individuals away from work for extended periods of time. These costs are compounded by increasingly dispersed and diverse target audiences within companies that have expanded across industries and geographies, forcing many of them to conclude that they may need different learning architectures. Thus, a survey conducted in the spring of 2012 shows that half of the respondents reported that their organizations are currently offering global learning or planning to do so within three years (ASTD Research, 2012). And finally, casual evidence suggests that companies are increasingly demanding experiences that boost both the individual's and the organization's performance—implying, among other things, learning experiences that increasingly occur within the context of work, often over an extended period of time so as to facilitate real applications (Hernez-Broome and Hughes, 2004).

These considerations constrain not only the dispatch of participants to residential programs but also other traditional expedients such as flying in star professors or, in the case of very large companies, in-house provision of leadership development programs (think of GE Crotonville, for instance). Such constraints point toward the idea of grounding programs in diverse work contexts. Interest in this regard is boosted by the conclusion from one of the more rigorous studies about blended learning and leadership development, that, "paradoxically, distance learning can offer a significant advantage to those aiming to develop highly situated practices, such as leadership capability" (Ladkin et al., 2009). The idea, very simply, is that online learning allows direct application of ideas to workplace contexts since participants spend much (or all) of their time in the workplace during the term of the course. And this supplies another reason why technology may be (even) more valuable for global leadership development than it is for leadership development programs in general.

Conclusions

My MOOC experience was incidental to the basic messages of this chapter. It started, in effect, with the basic strategic principles of thinking broadly about competitive position and sustainability: taking a broad rather than a narrow view of benefits to students, looking at the relative costs as well as relative benefits and reckoning with how relative costs and benefits are likely to shift over time. If you do all that, the threat/ opportunity associated with online technology will become much clearer, or so I have argued.

In terms of responding to online technology, I have argued that there is no one-size-fits-all strategy for business schools, and that given evolving technologies and other sources of ambiguity, a portfolio of initiatives may make more sense than one big commitment. There should, however, ideally be a focus on treating face-to-face time as a scarce resource, to be rationed, rather than a bucket to be filled—and there should be a path for it to lead to changes in the core and not just at the periphery. And in the specific context of global leadership development programs, technology can also play a very important role in mediating their experiential components.

Some of the same principles apply, of course, to leadership development programs within companies. But there are some differences as well. In particular, global companies may be particularly interested in the potential of online technology to tie together multiple company locations while minimizing travel and job disruptions and allowing for projects grounded in actual work contexts.

Notes

I am grateful to Giuseppe Auricchio, Head of the Learning Innovation Unit at IESE Business School, for numerous helpful discussions and for his contributions to Section five in particular, to Dean Jordi Canals for his comments and to the 22,000+ students who signed up for the first offering of my Globalization of Business Enterprise (GLOBE) course on the Coursera platform.

1. Coursera course "The Globalization of Business Enterprise" https://www.coursera.org/course/globe.
2. Pankaj Ghemawat's official homepage: http://www.ghemawat.com.
3. For a more detailed description of the AACSB-related work, see Ghemawat, P. (2011) "Responses to Forces of Change: A Focus on Curricular Content," *Globalization of Management Education: Changing International Structures, Adaptive Strategies, and the Impact on Institutions: Report of the AACSB International Globalization of Management Education Task Force.* Bingley:

Emerald, pp. 105–56. My action research in the classroom is described in more detail in Ghemawat, P. (2011) "Bridging the 'Globalization Gap' at Business Schools: Curricular Challenges and a Response," in Canals, J. (ed.) *The Future of Leadership Development: Corporate Needs and the Role of Business Schools*. Basingstoke: Palgrave Macmillan, Chapter 2.3.

4. 11,580 students of the total who signed up—2 per cent of the total—could be classified to one country; the analysis that follows is based on this subsample.
5. For the original discussion of the CAGE framework, see Ghemawat, P. (2001) "Distance Still Matters: The Hard Reality of Global Expansion," *Harvard Business Review* (8), 137–47.
6. See Ghemawat, P. and Altman, S. A. (2013) "Depth Index of Globalization 2013," Available: http://www.ghemawat.com/dig/ and Ghemawat, P. and Altman, S. A. (2014) "DHL Global Connectedness Index 2014," Available: http://www.dhl.com/en/about_us/logistics_insights/studies_research/global_connectedness_index/global_connectedness_index.html. There is, in particular, a strong relationship with depth on the informational pillar of the overall globalization index (Accessed 1 February 2015).
7. Kip Becker at Boston University Metropolitan College (BU MET), one of the world's largest providers of on-line business education, cited in Simmons, E. (2014) "To MOOC or Not to MOOC?," *Connect*, 22 April 2014. Available: http://www.thecasecentre.org/educators/casemethod/resources/features/moocs. (Accessed 1 February 2015).
8. While McKinsey & Company has developed a 'portfolio of initiatives' approach that may seem similar to what is advocated here, I do not rely on it since it essentially misses out on the key considerations related to commitment versus flexibility that motivate points 4 and 5 below. To see this, consult Bryan, L., Elder, R., O'Brien, B. and Rutherford, S. (2010) "A Dynamic Strategy for Uncertain Times," *McKinsey Quarterly* (Spring), 56–63, and particularly their summary Exhibit 3, p. 62.
9. Executive Director, Learning Innovation Unit at IESE Business School.
10. This box is based, in large part, on 'Introduction and Conceptual Framework', Chapter 1 in Auricchio, G. (2014) *A Study of the Views of Senior Learning and Development Professionals in Flagship Global Companies Regarding Their Use of Blended Learning in Executive Leadership Development Programs*. Ed.D. Thesis, University of Pennsylvania. Available at: www.Proquest.com.

References

ASTD Research (2012) "The Global Workplace: Learning Beyond Borders," (Vol. 4, No. 2). Available at: https://www.td.org/Publications/Research-Reports/2012/2012-Global-Workplace. (Accessed 1 February 2015).

Canals, J. (2012) *Leadership Development in a Global World* (Basingstoke: Palgrave Macmillan).

Christensen, G., Alcorn, B. and Emanuel, E. (2014) "MOOCs Won't Replace Business Schools—They'll Diversify Them," *HBR.org*. Available at: https://hbr.org/2014/06/moocs-wont-replace-business-schools-theyll-diversify-them. (Accessed 1 February 2015).

Clark, P. (2014) "Online B-Schools Threaten the Traditional Classroom," *Bloomberg Businessweek*, 5 May 2014, pp. 51–2.

"Executive Education Rankings 2013," (2013) *The Financial Times: Business Education.* Available at: http://rankings.ft.com/businessschoolrankings/executive-education-open-2013. (Accessed 1 February 2015).

Ghemawat, P. (1991) "Flexibility: The Value of Recourse," *Commitment: The Dynamic of Strategy.* (New York: Free Press), pp. 109–34.

Ghemawat, P. (2012) "The ABCDs of Leadership 3.0," in Canals, J. (ed.) *Leadership Development in a Global World: The Role of Companies and Business Schools.* (Basingstoke: Palgrave Macmillan), pp. 62–89.

Ghemawat, P. and Sol, P. D. (1998) "Commitment Vs. Flexibility?," *California Management Review*, 40(4), 26–42.

Graduate Management Admission Council (GMAC) (2013a) "2013 Alumni Perspectives Survey." Available at: http://www.gmac.com/~/media/Files/gmac/Research/Measuring%20Program%20ROI/alumni-2013-web.pdf. (Accessed 1 February 2015).

Graduate Management Admission Council (GMAC) (2013b) "2013 Application Trends Survey." Available at: http://www.gmac.com/~/media/Files/gmac/Research/admissions-and-application-trends/2013-app-trends-survey-report.pdf. (Accessed 1 February 2015).

Hernez-Broome, G. and Hughes, R. J. (2004) "Leadership Development: Past, Present, and Future," *Human Resource Planning*, 27(1), 24–32. Available at: http://www.ccl.org/leadership/pdf/research/cclLeadershipDevelopment.pdf. (Accessed 1 February 2015).

Hockfield, S. (2014) "Former MIT President: Experimentation Heart of Universities' Future," *Georgetown Speaker Series on Designing the Future(s) of the University.* Available at: http://www.georgetown.edu/designing-the-futures-of-the-university/speakers-series/hockfield/. (Accessed 1 February 2015).

"Is College Worth It?," (2014) *The Economist*, 5 April 2014. Available at: http://www.economist.com/news/united-states/21600131-too-many-degrees-are-waste-money-return-higher-education-would-be-much-better. (Accessed 1 February 2015).

Ladkin, D., Case, P., Gayá Wicks, P. and Kinsella, K. (2009) "Developing Leaders in Cyber-Space: The Paradoxical Possibilities of on-Line Learning," *Leadership*, 5(2), 193–212.

Meister, J. (2013) "How MOOCs Will Revolutionize Corporate Learning and Development," *Leadership*, 13 August 2013. Available at: http://www.forbes.com/sites/jeannemeister/2013/08/13/how-moocs-will-revolutionize-corporate-learning-development/ (Accessed 2 February 2015).

Pappano, L. (2012) "Year of the MOOC," *The New York Times*, 2 November 2012. Available at: http://www.nytimes.com/2012/11/04/education/edlife/massive-open-online-courses-are-multiplying-at-a-rapid-pace.html?pagewanted=all. (Accessed 1 February 2015).

Straumsheim, C. (2013) "Confirming the MOOC Myth," *Inside Higher Education*, 6 December 2013. Available at: https://www.insidehighered.com/news/2013/12/06/mooc-research-conference-confirms-commonly-held-beliefs-about-medium. (Accessed 1 February 2015).

Terwiesch, C. and Ulrich, K. T. (2014) "Will Video Kill the Classroom Star? The Threat and Opportunity of Massively Open on-Line Courses for Full-Time Mba Programs," *Mack Institute for Innovation Management at the Wharton School*, 16 July 2014. Available at: http://ssrn.com/abstract=2467557. (Accessed 1 February 2015).

9
Innovation, Blended Programs and Leadership Development: Key Success Factors

Eric Weber

The blended program learning space

The digital revolution has impacted almost every aspect of modern day life. Education is no exception. What we learn, how we learn and where we learn have been profoundly affected. And while distance learning has existed for decades to provide individuals in remote locations with their basic right to education—be it by correspondence, radio, TV or satellite—it was not until the advent of the information age, and in particular the widespread adoption of the Internet as a means of communication and information transmission, that learning outside of a traditional classroom setting skyrocketed.

Today education takes place somewhere along the continuum that ranges between pure online programs and pure face-to-face instruction. And while there are no standards or universally agreed-on definitions of how this space is distributed, some praxis has been established over time.[1] One such type of program is commonly referred to as a blended or hybrid program.

Blended programs are those that combine traditional face-to-face instruction and delivery with some portion of the course delivered online or outside the realm of the residential portion of a program. I will, for the most, refer to this component of a blended program as "distributed learning" instead of the more widely used elearning term. I use the term "distributed" in part because material and content delivery and provision of learning can occur in a variety of ways during this period, not just through the Internet, and in part to avoid the possible negative connotations of placing an "E" in front of anything that uses the Internet (Mendelson, 2002).

Much has been written about the blended management education model, with a trove of supporters and of course detractors in similar numbers. Halverson et al. (2014) look at what the conversations on blended learning have been about over the first decade of blended learning research.

Beyond the educational merits of blended learning, however, we find that key arguments in support of a blended model are, directly or indirectly, associated to the economics that a blended model offers over a traditional face-to-face model of instruction. Economies of scale in content distribution and dissemination, standardization of key processes of the learning experience and scalability of the e-learning portion of a blended program can in fact lead to significant cost savings. On the flip side, if blended learning is adopted solely for the intended economics of this particular educational model, the student or participant experience, in many cases, is also watered down because of the anonymity that may result in the non-residential portion of the program.

One of the main misconceptions regarding blended programs is that they are closer to fully online programs than traditional face-to-face programs. Research into the matter has found that "blended learning is generally not part of an institutional transition strategy from face-to-face to fully online courses (or programs), but rather a discrete option that institutions choose on its own merits" (Allen et al., 2007).

In this chapter I posit that blended programs can be designed to deliver an impactful experience to participants and that technology-based instruction can aid in developing new management capabilities. I will also provide some insight on how to enhance the learning experience through the blended model by achieving learning and development outcomes that are not necessarily possible in a traditional face-to-face learning model. Finally, I will discuss some criteria for the successful delivery of a blended program. I will at times refer to the experience of the Global Executive MBA program at IESE Business School, a program I helped develop 15 years ago at the height of the dot-com bubble. For a summary of the genesis of the Global Executive MBA program, refer to the Appendix.

The design imperative of a blended program for impact

Programs can be designed and offered for many different reasons, and as pointed out above, blended programs are often thought of as a means to achieve economies of scale or significant cost reductions when compared to an all face-to-face version of the same program. While such an objective can be a noble one, I will focus on the design of blended programs that seek impact and learning outcomes rather than economies of scale or cost savings. This implicitly entails that the non-residential or distributed portion of the program will be used for more than just content delivery and will constitute the focus of what follows. I highlight below some design imperatives for successful blended programs.

Mission. It is obvious that any blended program should fit, and be a reflection of, the institution's mission. The more explicit the mission is, the easier it will be to assess the success of the program. It has also been found that faculty are more engaged and willing to support blended program initiatives when the efforts they are asked to make are mission driven and supported by the institution (Moloney et al., 2010). IESE Business School is a mission-driven school where all programs, activities, staff and faculty try to develop the school's mission, so it was rather straightforward to come up with a list of mission-specific criteria that would allow the institution to benchmark the new program. The need to design a program of the highest professional standards that would have a deep, positive and lasting impact on its participants was paramount.

Learning model. A key design imperative for any program is the learning model it seeks to implement. An understanding of how that learning model works in the leadership development process is usually assumed as the institution has developed it over the course of time. The translation of that very learning model from face-to-face instruction into the distributed learning portion of a blended program should not be taken for granted, however.

IESE adheres to an interconnected learning model that focuses on knowledge, capabilities, interpersonal skills and attitudes (Canals, 2012), also referred to and written about as "Knowing"—"Doing"—and—"Being" Datar, Garvin and Cullen, 2010) (Figure 9.1).

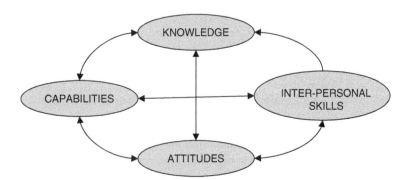

Figure 9.1   An interconnected learning model
Source: Canals (2012).

While programs are usually designed around courses, as any traditional MBA program for example, with academic disciplines shaping the core courses to be taught, a program that seeks impact on participants would not be focused solely on transmission of knowledge, but also on the formalization of learning processes and building of habits in an attempt to develop behaviors and skills that cut across courses and disciplines. This constitutes one of the biggest challenges in the design of a blended program—as the merits of technology applied to the learning process are, for the most, focused on the knowledge dimension—the transmission of content.

Technology has effectively turned content into a commodity, available for free from a host of quality providers. How to use technology to go beyond the mere transmission of content—into the capability development space—and beyond, into the attitudes and values domain, acting also in the development of inter-personal skills, should be a key program design challenge that should not be taken lightly. I will refer back to the implementation of the learning model in a blended program in the next section.

Continuous assessment of learning outcomes. Measuring program effectiveness is key to the success of a blended program. Assessing learning outcomes of the distributed learning portion of a blended program will require careful development of new metrics, and typically, a constant monitoring system to check for participant engagement and commitment. Dropout rates in internet-based instruction are alarmingly high (more on this later), and leaving participants to themselves during the distributed learning portion of a blended program almost certainly leads to disengagement from a significant portion of the cohort. This is particularly true in non-credit bearing Executive Education courses where participants are usually not formally assessed, but surprisingly also in credit bearing courses, such as a blended Executive MBA program, where students are assessed and typically will be assigned a grade for their work in the online portion of the program.

The role of technology. By definition, blended programs depend critically on technology to deliver the distributed learning portion of the program. The easy part is designing and implementing a technology-based content distribution system, but as already discussed, this is not the primary purpose of the blended programs we are contemplating. Technology is to be an enabler of the learning process, including the development of capabilities and inter-personal skills, and the platform for reflection needed to address attitudes and the potential consequences of doing so.

The academic goals and the administrative needs of a blended program justify the use of technology and not the other way around. It is easy to fall into the temptation of using the latest technologies because they are the latest technologies, or adopt alleged industry standards because they exist at this point in time. Whatever technology is adopted—usually a combination of industry standards and latest technologies—it should be chosen because together these tools enable the institution to fulfill the needs of the program.

Entrepreneurial spirit. The combination of strategic positioning, program design, content production, program delivery, platform support and geographic scope that the new technologies allow a development team to contemplate when designing a blended program are both exciting and daunting at the same time. The possibilities to experiment are endless, but at times, the track record of many of the new product offerings and the companies that provide them are non-existent. Thus, except for in the most basic cases, an organization that embarks on creating a blended program with an aspiration to have an impact on participants should approach such a project with an entrepreneurial spirit.

Development of leadership competencies in a blended program

Aware of the potential limitations of a blended program format where participants are "away"—potentially for significant periods of time—from the learning environment and support system that any campus constitutes, attempts should be made to minimize the impact of these limitations on the learning process and on the learning outcomes. One approach to doing so is the "four Cs" model as applied to blended learning, conceptualized by IESE Business School for the design of the Global Executive MBA program. This approach consists on focusing explicitly on four key aspects of any good learning experience: Collaboration—Continuity—Community—Competencies.

The first area of focus is to create a *collaborative learning environment*, both in the residential face-to-face periods of the program and in the technology-based distributed learning periods. Learning and development occur best in collaborative settings, where individuals can learn not only from the instructor or professor but also from the experiences of peers. In addition, when sufficient credibility and trust has been built up, the process of recognizing and accrediting learning and achievement is enhanced. Thus, the necessary feedback needed to support effective participant learning occurs naturally and comes not only from the instructor or professor but also from peers that are undergoing the same learning experience.

A collaborative learning environment occurs naturally in the residential face-to-face periods of a blended program, particularly in programs where the case method is the predominant means of instruction. While it may seem counterintuitive at first, one innovation that has proven successful at IESE is to extend the case method of instruction into the distributed learning periods of our blended program.

IESE engaged educational consultants at the beginning of the design phase of the Global Executive MBA, consultants with experience in blended program design, program delivery and platform development. The recommendation for the distributed periods was clear: to standardize the entire process, from design to delivery, and all the way through assessment and feedback. Each professor or instructor was to follow a cookie-cutter process that would guarantee a consistent learning experience for the program participants, while allowing for a cost-efficient solution. Most of the steps of the process would be provided and supported by the technology platform. It was acknowledged that not all residential face-to-face faculty "translated" well into the distributed learning space, but that the standardized process would help achieve certain homogeneity in the delivery of distributed learning. Furthermore, we were told that experience had shown that some faculty that underperformed on the residential periods would actually excel in the distributed learning periods.

While the above design logic has merits and is well suited to cases where content delivery and a focus on knowledge are the primary purpose of the distributed learning portion of a blended program, it is less adequate for a program that seeks to achieve more during those periods.

Thus, an alternative course of action is to give faculty complete freedom to innovate and create meaningful distributed learning activities within the possibilities the technology and the chosen platform allow. Research has shown that one of the characteristics of success in blended programs is allowing faculty to control the design mix of online and face-to-face experiences for themselves and students (Moloney et al., 2010). Having a learning expert—with technology-enabled learning platform experience—to assist faculty in their course design and to create a repository of distributed learning experiences is key to the success of this approach. This repository of experiences should not only contain the different types of distributed learning activities that faculty employ but also the feedback of what works particularly well, and under what circumstances, and what does not work that well or requires an inordinate amount of faculty time and/or effort. Part of the learning expert's time should be devoted to sharing these experiences amongst the program faculty, both individually and collectively in faculty seminars, and encouraging them to innovate and build on the experiences of their peers. Thus, not only is a collaborative learning environment created for the program participants, but also for program faculty.

Implemented this, the distributed learning space can be transformed into a virtual learning environment where teaching—discussing—creating and distributing content, and assessing learning—development and progress—is obtained.

Over the years we have been able to corroborate that the communication and learning that take place in many of the online discussions often reach greater depth than traditional classroom discussions. Participants can spend more time reading and reflecting before carefully preparing and submitting their responses, whereas in a classroom setting participants often feel pressured to quickly say whatever comes to their mind, which may not always be what they would have really wanted to say.

Faculty, on the other hand, have found that while successfully overseeing these online discussions can be a significant time commitment, they are able to cover many more aspects of a case than in a face-to-face classroom session that is limited by a finite time for discussion. I do not venture to say that online discussions are better or worse than face-to-face discussions, but rather, that if adequately designed and delivered, these online discussions can complement face-to-face instruction in a way that allows for learning and development beyond what one can achieve in the classroom. This is consistent with Garrison and Kanuka (2004) who state,

> A concomitant property of learning with Internet communication technology is that it has a significant educational implication resulting from the emphasis on written communication. Under certain circumstances, writing can be a highly effective form of communication that encourages reflection and precision of expression. When thoughtfully integrated with the rich dynamic of fast-paced, spontaneous verbal communication in a face-to-face learning environment, the educational possibilities are multiplied.

Furthermore, positive experiences in one blended program can later serve as an incubator for technology-enabled learning that can be transferred to other programs and activities at the host institution. Interestingly, much of the development work can be scaled and translated between different types of programs, credit bearing or not. In the case of IESE, the Global Executive MBA program continues to be the program where learning innovation occurs most frequently, aided now by a Learning Innovation Unit that was created in 2013 to serve all IESE programs and learning and development initiatives.

The second area of focus is to provide a *continuous program experience*, despite the inherent modular format of a blended program. Effort should be placed in creating a seamless learning experience that lasts throughout the entire duration of the program as opposed to a collection of intense, but unrelated, residential modules that potentially could lead to an "on-off" learning experience. A "pre-residential—residential—post-residential" program format, together with a careful design and timing of the non-residential activities, can create a natural program flow with few, if any, program interruptions.

The collaborative nature of the distributed learning activities helps to reinforce the sense that participants are always "in" the program, regardless of time, place or space. Participants from different countries in different time zones are involved in engaging collaborative assignments and activities, irrespective of where and when they connect to the learning platform. Online communication bridges the residential face-to-face periods so that the program is really a continuous long program, rather than a collection of isolated modules. Faculty and staff involvement during the distributed learning periods reinforce the sense of "presence," achieving an integration of contexts in which learning and development takes place.

One aspect worthy of mention is the *timing of activities* during the distributed learning periods that critically aids in achieving program continuity. Experience and research has shown that self-paced learning requires a high degree of commitment and focus, and that dropout rates are extraordinarily high. While transparency in elearning is increasing, the real dropout rates are still somewhat of a secret. It is not uncommon to hear that 50–60% of people that start an elearning course drop out, with percentages in the high seventies also being quoted. Regardless of what the dropout rates in elearning really are, most learning experts agree that it is significantly higher than in face-to-face learning environments (Lee and Choi, 2011).

What we have learned over the years from a participant engagement point of view is that initial response to online activities is very high, reaching a peak of interest in a relatively short period of time, but that if nothing "new" happens, participant interest drops precipitously (Figure 9.2).

Conscious of this reality, activities in the distributed learning space have to be adequately timed so that the peak of interest over a period

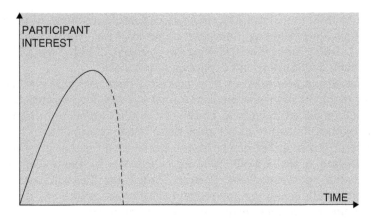

Figure 9.2   Participant interest in distributed learning activities over time

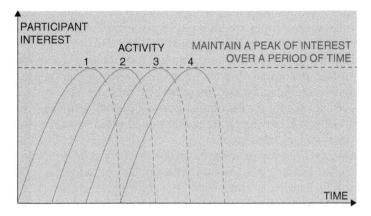

Figure 9.3   Timing of distributed learning activities to maintain participant interest

of time is maintained. This can be done within a given course or subject matter, or across all activities that take place in any given distributed learning period. Coordination of workloads, submission dates, synchronous activities (if applicable), etc. during these periods is key to the success and the achievement of learning outcomes, and requires a considerable amount of planning to get right (Figure 9.3).

The third area of focus, or the third C, is to build a *sense of community*. In the same way that a physical campus constitutes a learning community for the full-time students and participants that partake in the residential programs offered, the technology platform for a blended program has to enable the hosting institution to maintain an equivalent campus spirit and create a global community of learners that sustains the learning community achieved during the residential periods of the program throughout the periods of distributed learning. The effective integration of Internet technology with the most valued characteristics of face-to-face learning can lead to a sense of engagement in a community of inquiry and learning (Garrison and Kanuka, 2004).

Experience and research has shown that blended programs that are adequately designed produce a sense of community that is as strong and at times stronger than traditional face-to-face programs (Rovai and Jordan, 2004).

Furthermore, it is this very sense of community, together with the trust and knowledge of the other participants as individuals, with their strengths and their weaknesses, which allow program participants to develop their interpersonal skills. This is certainly true in the residential setting, where face-to-face learning is complemented by the power of face-to-face communication; where elements like empathy, tone of voice, emotions, body language, judgments, eye contact, feelings, etc., impregnate the immediate feedback with additional meaning. But it is also a good opportunity to develop interpersonal skills in the remote technology-enabled space provided by the distributed learning periods where the immediacy and intensity of the feedback given by the face-to-face communication is watered down, and other aspects—the training of a discussion, such as the strength of the written word, which remains over time, the tone of voice in verbal communications, etc.—become key in interacting with others and getting a persuasive message across. As organizations become more and more global, and in the process find the need to create virtual teams that are required to interact across the world with the aid of technology, these newly acquired interpersonal and leadership skills prove to be invaluable.

Some of the more recent innovations in the Global Executive MBA would be next to impossible to implement if they did not feel they were part of a close-knit community where participants trust one another. Such is the case of the In-company project, where participants group together, based on professional interests, around a real company problem or situation that needs to be solved. One of the participants brings this problem to the group from his or her company and must include a signoff from someone in the participant's firm. On other occasions, the In-company project focuses on a new business idea or an entrepreneurial project that an individual participant might be working on.

Regardless of the origin of the project, the confidentiality or non-disclosure agreements that are signed, such projects would not take place if an atmosphere of trust and collaboration were inexistent.

Note that the previous two Cs, collaboration and continuity, are key in creating a sense of community, and that all three Cs together create a virtuous circle of learning in the distributed learning space. This leads naturally into the last C of the framework.

The last area of focus and fourth C is to place special attention to the particular *competencies* that can be developed in the non-residential period of a blended program. This connects back to the learning model that the institution has adopted, described in the previous section, and the particular competencies that the institution desires to develop or foster in the participants of its programs. But regardless of the details of the learning model adopted, a deep analysis of the specific competencies that are unique to the technology-enabled learning space must take place.

Without trying to be comprehensive, the following are some of the competencies that we have discovered translate particularly well into the distributed learning component of a blended program: critical thinking, communication skills—particularly written communication—, self-management, intellectual inquiry and curiosity, integrity, tenacity, persistence and perseverance—particularly in self-paced activities—, negotiation in virtual settings and virtual teams, work across time zones both synchronously and asynchronously, provide feedback both individually and collectively in remote settings, develop distributed decision-making capabilities, manage across cultures and manage global business complexity.

Even though the purpose of a blended program is rarely to teach participants about technology per se, one additional role attributed to the use of cutting-edge technology is to help participants develop their skills and abilities to perform in new work environments that use these new technologies and to enable them to take some of the learning on the use of these technologies in the workplace back to their organizations or future employers.

In closing, let us not forget that teaching in the distributed portion of a blended learning program commands a set of specific competencies that faculty require or need to develop. Institutions that adopt blended learning programs need to assess what level of training and development their faculty and instructors will need to be successful in this teaching environment. Research into the matter has shown that between 20 and 30 new competencies need to be acquired to effectively manage instruction in the online space (Ragan et al., 2012).

Some closing thoughts

The temptation to reduce technology-enabled learning to content distribution is as alive and well today as it was at the beginning of the elearning craze, and unfortunately on some fronts we, as a learning society, as institutions and as individuals, have not evolved as much as we could have in this time.

The possibilities of incorporating technology into the learning process today far outpace what was possible just a few years ago. Yet, despite the advances and the technology options we face today, the fundamental underlying questions remain the same. How can one incorporate technology-based learning solutions into existing programs and create new ones to enable a more convenient and higher impact learning environment and learning process that truly develops leadership competencies? Designing meaningful blended programs is certainly a step in the right direction.

Appendix

The genesis of the Global Executive MBA program

In spring of 2001, IESE Business School decided to launch an executive MBA program for seasoned managers with a minimum of 10 years of management experience. It was to be targeted at an international audience as opposed to a regional one, as was the focus of the existing Executive MBA program.

The intent was to serve companies that required an increasingly global talent pool and employees that could manage and operate globally, and to further develop individuals with global responsibilities or about to take on such responsibilities in their organizations. Consistent with this focus, and after a few iterations, the program was ultimately called the Global Executive MBA.

Targeting global managers required coming up with an innovative program format that would allow working managers from around the globe to attend the program while continuing to work full-time for their companies. A blended education model was chosen, a format that would combine intense face-to-face residential modules with pre-module and post-module distributed learning periods.

It was clear from the beginning that this new program would rely heavily on technology to offer the non-residential portion of the program. The challenge was to use technology to recreate, and potentially improve in some key aspects, the learning experience of the full-time MBA.

A handful of equivalent programs offered by top-tier business schools already existed, but these programs were far from being an established program category in the degree granting management and leadership development space. The existing programs differed widely in program format, geographic scope, instruction methods, target audience and in their use of technology.

What we now refer to, with 20/20 hindsight, as the Internet dot-com bubble had just peaked in March of 2000, with the NASDAQ reaching an all-time high of over 5,000 points. Internet companies were the call of the day, and the education sector was no exception. The Internet, it was claimed, would disrupt and change the way institutions conceived, designed and delivered their programs, the way content would be generated and disseminated, and ultimately, the way students would learn.

The resultant design was a 15-month blended program divided into 7 modules, which were again divided into 3 periods. Each module started with a 2-week "Pre-Residential" period where the participants did the necessary reading and preparation for their coming face-to-face classes. Then there was a 2-week "Residential" period where the actual face-to-face sessions occurred. The residential periods were intended to be very intense and also the periods in which the relationships were established between professors and participants. These residential periods took place in Barcelona, Silicon Valley, Shanghai and Madrid. Each module ended with a 4–8 week "Distributed Learning" period in which the participants continued their studies from their place of residence with the aid of the Internet. While the Distributed Learning period was fully dependent on the use of technology, it is important to note that we used our technology platform during the other periods as well. From a credit point of view, the initial program design contemplated roughly the same amount of work in the residential periods of the program as in the pre- and post-distributed learning periods combined.

Technology has evolved at an incredible pace over the course of these last 15 years in almost all domains that affect learning. Some of the "innovative" solutions implemented at the beginning of the Global Executive MBA as "cutting-edge" have been proven obsolete, while other technologies—already of age 15 years ago—have withheld the passing of time and the pace of technological innovation rather well. As an example let me name the Newsgroup technology, used as a platform for discussion forums, that is as valid today as it was 20 years ago. Other advances—such as the overall speed of the Internet and the possibility to stream large amounts of information in a cost-effective way; high definition multi-media; the always and everywhere connected devices and the multi-platform learning possibilities (desktop, tablet and mobile)—are realities today that we could only dream about, or outright did not exist, just 15 years ago.

The program has been redesigned several times since it was launched, including the introduction of elective courses, an in-company project, new venues (New York and Sao Paulo) and the addition of the America's Track where participants commence the program in New York instead of Barcelona and where IESE's campus in New York becomes their "home" campus instead of IESE's campus in Barcelona.

Note

1. An example of a prototypical course and program classification is given below (Allen et al., 2007):

- *Traditional* course or program with no online technology used; content is delivered in writing or orally—0% of content delivered online.
- *Web facilitated* course or program which uses web-based technology to facilitate what is essentially a face-to-face course—1 to 29% of content delivered online.

- *Blended/Hybrid* course or program that blends online and face-to-face delivery. Substantial proportion of the content is delivered online, typically uses online discussions and typically has some face-to-face meetings—30 to 79% of content delivered online.
- *Online* course or program, where most or all of the content is delivered online. Typically have no face-to-face meetings—80+% of content delivered online.

References

Allen, I. E., Seaman, J. and Garrett, R. (2007) "Blending in: The Extent and Promise of Blended Education in the United States" (Needham, MA: Sloan Consortiium.)

Canals, J. (2012) "Rethinking Global Leadership Development: Designing New Paradigms," in Canals, J. (ed.) *Leadership Development in a Global World: The Role of Companies and Business Schools.* (Basingstoke: Palgrave Macmillan): 29–61.

Datar, S., Garvin, D. and Cullen, P. (2010) "Rethinking the MBA: Business Education at a Crossroads" (Boston, MA: Harvard Business School Press.)

Garrison, D. R. and Kanuka, H. (2004), "Blended learning: Uncovering its transformative potential in higher education," *The Internet and Higher Education, 7 (2)*: 95–105

Halverson, L. R., Graham, C. R., Spring, K. J., Drysdale, J. S. and Henrie, C. R. (2014) "A thematic analysis of the most highly cited scholarship in the first decade of blended learning research," *The Internet and Higher Education, 20*: 20–34.

Lee, Y. and Choi, J. (2011) "A review of online course dropout research: implications for practice and future research," *Educational Technology Research & Development, 59 (5)*: 593–618.

Mendelson, A. (2002) "E-Learning at IESE," *Internal Working Paper IESE Business School.* (Barcelona, Spain).

Moloney, J. F., Hickey, C. P., Bergin, A. L., Boccia, J., Polley, K. and Riley, J. E. (2010) "Characteristics of successful local blended programs in the context of the Sloan-C Pillars," *Journal of Asynchronous Learning Networks, 14 (1)*: 71–89.

Ragan, L. C., Bigatel, P. M., Kennan, S. S. and Dillon, J. M. (2012) "From research to practice: Towards the development of an integrated and comprehensive faculty development program," *Journal of Asynchronous Learning Networks, 16 (5)*: 71–86.

Rovai, A. P. and Jordan, H. M. (2004) "Blended learning and sense of community: A comparative analysis with traditional and full online graduate courses," *International Review of Research in Open and Distance Learning, 5 (2)*: 1–13.

Part IV

Innovation at Business Schools: Creating an Entrepreneurial Learning Context for Leadership

10
Entrepreneurship and Innovation: Business Schools as Drivers of Change

Bernard Ramanantsoa

Introduction

We have to acknowledge that the desire to start one's own business has gotten stronger and stronger among MBA students. A growing number of participants are convinced that creating a business is a sure way to create value and employment in this time of crisis in the world. Nearly 20 per cent of the HEC Paris MBA graduating class prefers taking a chance with a completely new business rather than trying to move up in a consulting firm or in a classic multinational corporation.

We also have to acknowledge, sadly enough, that actually doing so is not all that common. Only 10 per cent of our participants actually specialize in entrepreneurship during their MBA program, and only a few graduates actually launch a start-up once graduated from the school. Most are quite sincerely hungry to learn but in the end put off the project for a few years for down-to-earth considerations, like reimbursing their student loans and stabilizing their personal situation.

This is an important issue and a genuine challenge to be taken up, given that entrepreneurship is a key factor in the situation we face today. Entrepreneurship is therefore a major challenge we must all address. To do so, however, we need a sound, objective conception and analysis of it, stripped of all the ideological presuppositions and incantations that cloud the concept and our vision of it. According to Drucker (2007), a reference on such matters, the main misconception is that entrepreneurial spirit is a natural, almost innate phenomenon and that if it does not appear spontaneously in companies, it is because the latter are repressing it, whether consciously or not. We share his opposition to this particularly unhelpful view because, in our opinion, the spirit of enterprise is neither natural nor spontaneous. It is the fruit of constant efforts, of disciplined thought and action and of daily practice. In this respect, it is not the sole prerogative of a few gifted individuals, but requires a variety of knowledge, abilities and attitudes which can be taught, developed and put to use in schools like ours or businesses as they exist today.

This point is of particular importance for business schools because it raises a key question: How should entrepreneurship be fostered as a discipline and how should it be taught in business schools?

In the same way that the entrepreneurial spirit does not seem to us to be an innate feature specific to certain individuals, we would reject any sort of approach consisting in defining a standard profile for entrepreneurs. Even if entrepreneurship is indeed, as we believe, a discipline of mind and action, it can be characterized by a more or less complete combination of qualities and abilities in the person of the entrepreneur. That is what we will begin by conducting a critical but constructive analysis of the main myths (Ramanantsoa and Moingeon, 1997) on the subject of entrepreneurs, which lead business school faculty to have doubts as to the possibility of developing the entrepreneurial spirit others. On this basis, we will then conduct an analysis of the specific context of business schools and examine their strengths and weaknesses in terms of entrepreneurial spirit. This is a necessary step on the way to defining what and how we should teach to foster entrepreneurship among our students.

The six great myths about entrepreneurs[1]

1. Are entrepreneurs driven by power and money?

When we observe entrepreneurs building and running companies, whether small or large, we can easily imagine that they are driven by the power of managing and dictating their will to others as to what should or should not be done (Astebro, 2012). However, many studies on entrepreneurs have demonstrated that the great majority of them are driven mainly by a profound desire to achieve things, and that their motivations in terms of power and affiliation are significantly less than those of a given population of managers. Real entrepreneurs are motivated by the desire to achieve sometimes unique performances and to leave their mark. They do not reject power, however, but only those of its attributes that are of no interest to their will to achieve. Power is of interest to them as a source of influence in order to facilitate their projects, or as a source of freedom to conduct and complete them by obtaining the necessary resources, and the best of them know how to make use of it. Likewise, money is not a matter of indifference to them, be it as an enabler or as a reward (Hamilton, 2000). But money is not the reason for their action; it is merely the indicator of their success as an entrepreneur. If they are given an opportunity to accomplish something or to achieve their project, entrepreneurs will do the work no matter what the terms. Paradoxically, money is, meanwhile, a great incentive to work for those who are not entrepreneurs. Strong motivation, a powerful need to achieve and the determination to leave their mark, these are the cornerstones of entrepreneurship.

2. Are entrepreneurs dreamers and dilettantes, incapable of accepting the discipline of an organization?

While it is true that their usual behavior rarely complies with institutional standards—unusual working hours, lack of respect for organizational rituals and routines, ignoring line management rules, personal ways of working—questions remain about the reasons behind such attitudes (Gort and Lee, 2007). Are they due to the naturally abnormal character of these individuals, or might it not be that these rituals and routines serve only to preserve the existing situation within organizations and therefore constitute resistance to the novelty and originality that underlie entrepreneurial action? Is it the freedom of the innovator's behavior that is abnormal or the organization's resistance to anything new? (Blanchflower and Oswald, 1998) As for whether they are dreamers, in the light of the analysis above, it is fortunate that they are sufficiently so to imagine that their organization may eventually accept and reward their action, and to continue their fight within it. For this is the only area in which they may be tasked with a certain short-sightedness. For the rest, although they are motivated by great achievements, they generally prefer realism, knowing that the success of their project relies on it having a firm footing in the realities of the field, pushing them to proceed systematically by trial and error and multiply their contacts with the real world. They are also hard workers, "work addicts" who may take some liberties with working hours but who are also capable of working through the night in their laboratories or offices to take their project forward, when necessary, or keep at it until it succeeds. Original they may be in some ways, but only as concerns the modus operandi of their organization, because entrepreneurs are relentless workers with a strong sense of responsibility whenever they can throw themselves into motivating projects.

3.   Are entrepreneurs not averse to taking risks and outright optimists?

It is true that they do not have the natural risk aversion of many corporate executives, and are indeed more disposed than most to accept risks (Astebro, 2003). This is subject to two caveats, however: that those risks should be assessed and calculated, and that they must feel capable of controlling them because they fall within their scope of competence. Although the targets they set themselves are ambitious and stimulating, entrepreneurs do strive to keep risks down to the minimum by choosing areas in which there is more margin for error and applying strategies that offer them an "undue advantage," meaning that they may still succeed even if everything does not go to plan, and by anticipating any obstacles through lots of preparatory work and contacts in the field. It is this experience and familiarity with the field that impact the level of risks they perceive, which may be lower than in other individuals. In this respect, contrary to what many might imagine, they are not ingenuous and eternal optimists, even though they do have great confidence in themselves and their ability to succeed. It is precisely this ability to make a fair assessment of their skills that leads them to accept risks they consider they can control, and which attracts investors. Their philosophy of "nothing is impossible" combined with foresightedness and their ability to make a fair assessment of the dangers ahead leads them toward original solutions in which they believe that they can control and mitigate the risks that are inherent to any innovation.

4.   Do entrepreneurs tend toward an off-the-cuff approach, for lack of analytical abilities?

The fact that they have intuition and know-how to use it does not mean that they are devoid of analytical abilities (Hartog, Van Praag and Van der Sluis, 2010). Once they have made the intuitive leaps forward that are so mystifying to those around them, most of them take the time to reflect upon and analyze their ideas, and to try to conceptualize and test them, either empirically or scientifically. The great entrepreneurs are both intuitive and analytical, thereby explaining that they can "act as a man of thought and think as a man of action," as Bergson put it.

5.   Are entrepreneurs all-out individualists, egoists and control freaks?

Although strongly committed to their project and focused on its success, the entrepreneur will always give priority to the project's demands and the work to be done to carry it forward (Berlin, 1953;

Astebro and Thompson, 2011). They have a natural tendency to focus on tasks, rather than individuals, and their targets, capacity for work and demanding approach are often such that it is difficult to find any individuals, other than themselves, who are capable of meeting requirements. Given that their project is global and uncertain by nature, the entrepreneur will tend to gather together and control all the resources they need. In this respect, their ability and readiness to delegate to others will be naturally and circumstantially limited. However, the innovative nature of their idea and the spirit of adventure of the project constitute two particularly powerful forces of attraction for certain individuals. Thanks to their ability to convince others and their natural leadership, the latter being a frequent trait of entrepreneurs, the innovator will therefore have little difficulty putting a team together. It may be a team that is somewhat particular in nature, being almost entirely focused on a sole objective—the project—and particularly motivated by achieving it. It is precisely this feature of the team, however, that will enable the entrepreneur to manage it without any great difficulty, all the more so because as the originator and creator of the idea, they will benefit from a certain aura and natural power within the team. It will be up to the entrepreneur to put the team together according to key criteria—voluntary participation, multidisciplinarity, autonomy and total commitment—and to manage it in a way that fosters an atmosphere of freedom and continuity. Although naturally individualistic with a tendency to centralize power, the entrepreneur may thus succeed in composing and motivating a team that is dedicated to the project.

6. Do entrepreneurs have any moral sense and do they "manipulate" their organizations?

Profoundly dedicated as they are to their project and driven by a quest for performance, entrepreneurs do indeed take great liberties in their interpretation of the rules that govern any organization. They do not hesitate to bypass line management, to breach any guidelines that might be contrary to the interests of their project, to carry out tasks that do not go with their function, to develop a prototype, product or activity in secret, or to get specialists in different departments of the organization dedicating time to the project that should be reserved for their day-to-day work. In a word, they knowingly apply the rule that "it is easier to apologize after the fact than to ask permission beforehand" and seek to mobilize all the resources of their organization for the benefit of their project by all means that might be necessary. And yet all venture capitalists acknowledge that the characteristic feature of entrepreneurs is their honesty and integrity. Toward themselves, first of all, pinpointing problems and tackling them head on to resolve them. Toward their partners, too, in that they will not try to hide things from them. And, finally, toward their host organization, because even if they do overstep the rules, it is with the sole aim of fulfilling their project, for their own pleasure and profit admittedly, but also within and to the great advantage of their organization, if the latter does not reject them. An entrepreneur is a natural rebel in an organization that is not conducive to innovation and originality, but he or she is also profoundly honest and upright. For entrepreneur and organization alike, success requires a compromise that takes them outside the bounds of the traditional ways of functioning.

The specific context of business schools

MBA participants are often budding entrepreneurs but rarely inventors

The strong international leaning of the MBA population (more than 80 per cent non-French at HEC Paris) requires a special interactive teaching approach, open on the world, with the support of digital technology. In addition, participants who choose to study *entrepreneurship* have professional experience and a technical profile (average age of 30 years, 6 years of work experience and 70 per cent engineers). They know that a project is more likely to succeed if it is innovative, is difficult to imitate or reproduce and has a distinct technological advantage. On the other hand, even though some MBA participants want to start their own business and are aware of the importance of technological innovation, they are rarely inventors themselves.

Insufficiently integrated, innovative teaching

Once they have joined their business school, students find themselves in a teaching framework that, once again, may not always favor the skills and qualities of the entrepreneur.

The curricula in today's business schools are based on the progressive learning of management techniques and methods. The rule is that of division into subjects and teaching of each of those subjects in their own right. The more integrated teaching that is so necessary for managing a project is rare and is generally designed as a catch-up mechanism or a quick, partial overview. It is naturally perceived by students as being a sort of artificially developed patch. The subjects that are taught give priority to techniques and present solutions that are known and applied by companies deemed to be high performers in management terms. They systematically give their preference to managing existing systems, for lack of elements to grasp the new and the original. In this respect, the case study approach may be pernicious in two ways, firstly in that it generally aims to find future solutions for known, existing activities and secondly because although it does require the involvement of the student, it is only to find solutions and never to implement them. If the general portrait brushed here really is not conducive to the spirit of enterprise, there are, however, in each of the schools, exceptions to the mainstream route and a number of pedagogical alternatives that are being developed, often on the margins, to address the principles of entrepreneurship.

Professors of management with little in the way of natural entrepreneurial spirit

Faculty may not be exactly living, idealizable examples of the spirit of enterprise, whether by their personal characteristics or by the way they work and teach. If anything, they are quite the opposite in their great majority (Astebro, Bazzazian and Braguinsky, 2012). It must be acknowledged that if they have chosen to go into teaching, it is probably, in most cases, to avoid becoming a manager or executive. This may admittedly be seen as a rejection of normality, but that is often as original as they get. The taste for risk is not one of their qualities, and teaching, consisting in passing on reproducible methods and behaviors, does not predispose them to being or learning to be original. Trained as they are in hypothesizing and deduction, in particular by the research work that is the main criterion sought for in business school teaching staff, they are structurally analytical, rational and keen on logic and little inclined to intuition. The structure of the schools and academic recognition also lead them to be specialists rather than generalists, to opt for a discipline-based approach to the detriment of the more cross-cutting view that is a fundamental trait of entrepreneurs. As for the academic context, it is little focused on innovations and more concerned by the scientific aspect of the approach.

This analysis reveals all the difficulties surrounding the teaching of entrepreneurship in our institutions and explains their mediocre results. Does that mean that this situation is inherent to our system and insurmountable? We do not believe so, and certain pedagogical experiments have provided ample proof to the contrary. However, favorable conditions need to be created, and the teaching structure—in its content and form—needs to be adapted to the imperatives of the entrepreneurial spirit.

Teaching entrepreneurship

Necessary environmental conditions

Two key conditions are necessary in our institutions to avoid such teaching being little more than a gadget or a decoy for the outside world, hiding an inability to foster entrepreneurship:

First, the institution needs to promote entrepreneurship very clearly and officially as a key component of its vocation, and secondly, it must translate this into operational fact in its rules and procedures. While the first condition is fulfilled in almost all business schools, it is on the second that efforts are still required.

Regarding the students, first of all, we must accept atypical profiles that do not fit the mold. Perhaps we could modify our selection system: tests for originality, self-confidence and consistency could make an advantageous addition to our range of selection tests for the examination. We very certainly need to adjust things in the course of our tuition, too, as is already done to some extent by HEC Paris: by accepting courses that depart from the usual norm; taking account of entrepreneurial experiences, whatever their outcome, in the overall assessment of the student; allowing our students freedom to experiment in areas and sources of personal and professional motivation and investment; and including an "originality" component in their course assessments.

In terms of teaching, next, opportunities must be created and time allowed for more cross-cutting, multidisciplinary teaching, alongside subject-based courses. Ideally, a pedagogical system would be constructed in which general teaching would form the backbone of the approach. Courses on individual subjects would then be incorporated progressively, as a means of resolving the problems encountered by the students, which would only motivate them all the more to learn those disciplines. This would constitute a genuine revolution, in both senses of the term. It would not be simple to achieve, but like for any entrepreneur, the only risk lies in not giving it a try.

As regards teaching staff, finally, it is essential that the teaching component should once again be given a value at least equal to that of the research component, by avoiding the current near-monopoly of the research-PhD system in recruitments and accepting the alternative profile of the entrepreneur, by fostering opportunities to work in multidisciplinary teams and by developing, alongside the academic system based on cutting-edge expertise and scientific methodology, a mechanism rewarding teachers who experiment, innovate and uphold the entrepreneurial spirit.

The second is that the institution must also show flexibility, open-mindedness and great rigor.

Flexibility and openness are required if we are seeking to create a climate of freedom that is conducive to pedagogical experimentation and alternatives, for teachers and students alike. But without rigor and a demanding approach on the part of the institution, the objectives of learning the knowledge and know-how necessary for effective management may not be met. Is there not the risk, in seeking to learn to dare, that we might dare to forget learning and teaching? A genuine entrepreneur is not just a firebrand but also a good manager. Rigor is required in our vocation as teachers of management and should not be forgotten, at the risk of developing poorly structured "phony" courses without any real material that can be taught and which are likely to attract and develop the least motivated and conscientious of our students, rather than a population of entrepreneurs. This is a major risk in teaching entrepreneurship and the most frequent cause of its disappearance or depreciation. The risk is all the greater if the view is taken that the theoretical and experimental foundations of entrepreneurship are largely inexistent. That is not our view, and although those foundations are not necessarily obvious, we will now attempt to explain them.

Entrepreneurship-specific courses

Aside from learning the management methods and techniques that form the heart of our teaching and are the indispensable foundations for any manager, and therefore any entrepreneur, teaching entrepreneurship should, in our opinion, be structured around four essential dimensions, in the light of the analysis of entrepreneurs above:

Identifying (and selecting) opportunities

This is the major distinctive feature of entrepreneurs within a population of managers. They have the ability to distinguish that which most managers cannot see, or to see it more quickly than the others, and most importantly, this ability to pinpoint opportunities is not on a one-off basis but is permanent. This explains why students also need to learn to analyze each of the opportunities that are detected in order to select the best ones. It may not be obvious how to teach this, but there are three possible directions to work in:

1. Cultivating and fostering curiosity, by opening our students up to the outside world and teaching them, through "discovery work" (on certain sectors or activities), to multiply opportunities for encounters,

learning things and collecting information, and to nurture a taste for discovery.

2. Learning to reason by similarity and analogy in order to acquire an ability to clarify the confused situations which are naturally conducive to opportunities and to see analogies between the circumstances or models they observe and known situations, in order to foresee "creative" opportunities.

3. Using concepts and methods which can take a small amount of essentially qualitative, imprecise information and use it to provide a clear operative view of the situation. In this respect, strategic analysis tools are extremely relevant.

As for learning to select opportunities, steps must be taken to counter the omnipotence of financial models, in favor of identifying the necessary resources, in their broadest sense, and analyzing the degree of control the entrepreneur can exercise. (This opportunity dimension is now the subject of a course as part of the "Business Plan" track in our MBA.)

Developing entrepreneurial strategies

These in fact relate to two generic strategies (cost and differentiation) that we teach in our strategy courses. They are, however, specific adaptations of those strategies for innovations or small entities that we generally do not go into in our teaching which is focused mainly, particularly in our cases and examples, on the issues of large groups and mature sectors. The "judo business strategy"—exploiting opportunities arising from the weaknesses of the opponent—and "aiming for small, specialized and hidden," to take just two examples, are worthy of our attention, however, and of a proper place in our teaching. Should they be incorporated into our mainstream strategy teaching or should a special course be developed using specific teaching materials? That is a question of policy to be answered by each institution, but it does need an answer no matter what. Seeking differentiation, entrepreneurial strategic alternatives and identifying the resources necessary and risks related to each of these strategies constitute a new pedagogical challenge.

Managing a project

This kind of teaching is generally absent from our syllabuses, and yet entrepreneurship is naturally and intimately linked to the notion of the project. Constructing this kind of teaching should not pose a major problem, however, as long as we do not focus only on the technical aspects, which may indeed be necessary but remain insufficient. The human dimensions of project management must be given preference (we will emphasize this point more particularly later), as should the political dimension. Two aspects merit our attention and a transfer of know-how: negotiation skills and influence within an existing structure, in order to guarantee the chances of survival of a project, and the ethical dimension required of those managing change.

Managing a team

The aim here is to work on the behavior and attitudes required of the effective entrepreneur. Leadership, self-confidence and consistency seem to us to be three personal dimensions that are of capital importance for the entrepreneur to succeed. We are convinced that these are not necessarily innate qualities and that they can be fostered in our students by the right teaching and training. As for the methods and techniques of teamwork, they are not a new discipline: they just have to be taught with a focus on tasks and managing teams on a project.

Managing the link between innovation and entrepreneurship

This relationship (Dussauge, Hart and Ramanantsoa, 1992) is probably of the most significance and equally the most difficult to define. We will concentrate on describing the way in which we have been trying to cope with this challenge at HEC Paris. It clearly represents a new pedagogical approach, for which admittedly we do not yet have evaluated results; we therefore cannot ascertain to what extent they can be applied to other contexts.

HEC Paris has a unique, competitive vantage point due to its physical location as part of the Saclay plateau south of Paris, benefiting from a concentration of some of the top scientific and technical institutions, be they domestic, European or from around the world. The launching of our new *entrepreneurship* curriculum comes at a crucial time when the Université Paris Saclay is coming together to form the greatest technological cluster in Europe, and where SATT (Sociétés d'Accélération de Transfert de Technologie) are being created in what is turning out to be perfect synergy with our program.

The Paris Saclay project and the coinciding acute interest from our students have led us toward opting for contents which strongly emphasize *technological innovation* and for a pedagogy founded on *action-learning*.

Students who choose the *entrepreneurship* specialization are submerged in full-scale experimentation in a specific place, the **eLab**,[2] the "e" standing for both "entrepreneurship" and "electronic." It offers a context and the high tech functionalities favorable to creativity, team work and communication: the highest speed technological networks, airplay, video conference, whiteboard painting, mobile structures, furniture and equipment arranged according to teaching needs, user-friendly and cozy meeting space.

HEC Paris MBA students come to the eLab to learn how to start a business. Rather than request that they innovate on their own, we can count on our Saclay partners to feed the eLab with technology and patents having strong differentiation potential, to give the students a chance to transform them into value-added economic activity.

We remain in a strictly teaching framework: the eLab is not an incubator. After the program is finished the students are free to enter an incubator or not, to create a start-up or not.

Professors bring along the necessary teaching and coaching skills. International experts (entrepreneurs, lawyers and investors) come to share their know-how and their best practices to complete student instruction. Going well beyond classic course work as such, the manner of teaching in the eLab is a complete system of action learning where the courses, the team work, the meetings and structured sharing facilitate taking initiatives and using open source resources.

The students work in teams of four for virtual startups, each participant taking on a specific role: CEO, CTO, CFO & VP Sales/Marketing. They are coached for 4 to 8 months by experienced business leaders with international profiles.

The virtual start-up projects rely on innovative technology and, if possible and even better, on disruptive innovation, identified as such with the help of the professors specialized in teaching entrepreneurship at the core of the entrepreneurial ecosystem of HEC Paris (as much in France as abroad) and notably on the Saclay plateau where the opportunities for disruptive technology are particularly great.

In January 2014, we launched a complementary awareness campaign for first year MBA students, with the cooperation of the entrepreneurship clubs from both the MBA and the pre-experience masters programs so that, upstream of the entrepreneurship track, students play an active role in identifying the projects on the Saclay plateau and at the heart of the SATT that would be able to feed their work in the eLab their second year. In the end, the objective would be to insert our initiative between the SATT and the incubators in order to link technological innovation and the creation of enterprise. Creating a link like this allows a business school like HEC Paris to play a more decisive role. In fact, this link is anything but automatic: inventors are not necessarily entrepreneurs and entrepreneurs are not necessarily inventors. Our added value would be to create a fruitful dialog between them to enhance innovation by entrepreneurship.

Perspectives to foster the entrepreneurial spirit

Quite naturally, the method that lends itself best to developing the entrepreneurial spirit is project-based teaching, consistent with managing entrepreneurial initiatives. It makes students accountable and motivates them strongly, provided that the selected project themes are proposed by students or by tutors who are particularly involved and concerned. It is especially productive for learning when based on projects that have a firm footing in reality, requiring constant back and forth between analysis and the field, but also when supporting teaching—courses or follow-up by a generalist tutor—is provided as back-up. We need to teach our students to use the resources at their disposal and to generalize and capitalize, in their future action, on the lessons learned from experience. Finally, we need to create strict constraints in terms of form, dates, resources and budget that the students will learn to manage or juggle, in order to place them in a normal business situation. This method can be applied to the teaching itself and/ or it can be proposed and used to structure extra-curricular projects decided upon by the students.

In addition to using this project-based approach, we can conclude by asserting that the way that we teach also needs to be challenged and adapted—by focusing our course materials on managing new and innovative products and services, in order not to end up teaching students to manage "future dead branches"; by educating our participants to detect and analyze varying scenarios and alternatives, rather than finding "the" solution; by imagining original solutions that get off the beaten track and hopefully distance the future entrepreneur from applying classical methods in all situations (and passing on this bad habit) and by focusing our new teaching materials on young, innovative start-ups: in short, by putting a message across in which the focus is decidedly on innovation, seeking to inoculate the virus of originality to offset the natural tendency of teaching toward imitation and reproduction.

Notes

1. The typology of myths regarding entrepreneurs was first presented by Michel Santi (1994).
2. The **eLab** was created thanks to the generosity of HEC Paris Foundation donors (Pascal Cagni, Jean-Luc Allavena, and Pascal de Jenlis).

References

Astebro, T. (2003) "The return to independent invention: Evidence of risk seeking, extreme optimism or Skewness-loving?," *Economic Journal*, 113(484): 226–239.

Astebro, T., Bazzazian, N. and Braguinsky, S. (2012) "Startups by recent university graduates and their faculty–implications for university entrepreneurship policy," *Research Policy*, 41: 663–677.

Astebro, T. and Thompson, P. (2011) "Entrepreneurs, Jacks of all trades or Hobos?" *Research Policy*, 40: 637–649.

Berlin, I. (1953) "The Hedgehog and the Fox." (New York: Simon and Schuster)

Blanchflower, D.G. and Oswald, A.J. (1998) "What makes an entrepreneur?" *Journal of Labor Economics*, 16(1): 26–60.

Drucker, P. (2007) "Innovation and Entrepreneurship: Practice and Principles." (Oxford: Butterworth-Heinemann).

Dussauge, P., Hart, S. and Ramanantsoa, B. (1992) "Strategic Technology Management." (John Wiley & Sons).

Gort, M. and Lee, S.H. (2007) "The Rewards to Entrepreneurship." (Buffalo, NY: State University of New York).

Hamilton, B. (2000) "Does entrepreneurship pay? An empirical analysis of the returns to self-employment," *Journal of Political Economy*, 108: 604–631.

Hartog, J., Van Praag, C.M. and Van der Sluis, J. (2010) "If you are so smart why are you not an entrepreneur? Returns to cognitive and social ability, entrepreneurs versus employees," *Journal of Management Strategy*, 19(4): 947–989.

Ramanantsoa, B. and Moingeon, B. (1997) "Understanding corporate identity: The French school of thought," *European Journal of Marketing*, 31(5–6): 383–395.

Santi, M. (1994) "L'entrepreneuriat: un défi à relever in L'Ecole des Managers de demain." (Paris: Economica).

11
Road Signs for Business and Business Education: Navigating the Geography of Social Value Creation

Peter Tufano

Introduction

In many ways, MBA programs and management education more broadly are like advanced driving schools. Our required curricula teach students *how* to operate one of the most powerful engines in the world: business. We teach how this engine must be finely engineered (operations), how it needs special fuel (finance) and how the elements need to work together (organizations and leadership). We teach how to monitor the gauges carefully (accounting) to keep track of internal performance. We instruct how to monitor external elements (marketing) to steer our vehicles at high speeds and through rough weather (strategy). We teach our graduates to design, build and operate one of the most complex and amazing pieces of equipment ever created by mankind—the business organization. As a field, we should be proud of our progress, in that we can identify accomplished alumni who have "gone far" and who acknowledge that their achievements are attributable in part to the business education they received.

Despite this good work, we need to go far beyond teaching "how" to drive performance in order to meet the high expectations of students and society. These additional requirements flow directly out of our thinking about leadership and innovation. On the leadership front, we now insist that business not only be profitable but also be responsible (or sustainable or inclusive or other terms). In brief, we now dare to ask "Why do and should businesses exist?" This question tends to entail recognizing broader social responsibilities of business which then begs a seemingly simpler query: "Where should we do our work?" By thinking about where we *locate* our work in broad terms, we quickly realize the importance of innovation, as some of the most interesting "locations" of business activity that are responsive to social needs will demand that firms act in new ways and serve their customers' needs in new ways. "Location" can be geographic—for example, frontier economies with poor infrastructure—but it can also be defined by sectors and the nature of the need being met—for example, reducing the level of chronic illness related to obesity or addressing climate change. In both cases, re-orienting the activity of the firm will likely require involve innovation. Moving our thinking and teaching from *how* to *why* to *where* can improve the practice of business education.

Step 1: From "how" to "why?"

If driving is the metaphor, recently driving our school curricula have been supplemented with a module on "*Why* do we drive?" Comparing my own student MBA experience from more than three decades ago with the experiences of MBA students today, there is considerably greater attention on this existential question. In the early 1980s, "why business" occupied relatively little time in MBA classrooms because we were led to believe elegant (and simplistic) concepts like Friedman's dictum that "the business of business is business" (Friedman, 1962) or the mandate that the firms' only job was to maximize shareholder value. My own PhD thesis chair was famous for his concept that a firm was merely a nexus of contracts, and that financial incentives like high-powered debt and that executive stock options would suffice to improve business.

We have worked down the "Why" reading list, moving from Adam Smith's magnum opus, "The Wealth of Nations" (Smith, 1776), which introduces many key concepts of economics, to his more complex work, "Theory of Moral Sentiment" (Smith, 1759), which muses about "sympathy" and the responsibilities of individuals and business. We are entering into more nuanced debates that draw upon faith-based traditions such as Catholic social theory, legal principles like fiduciary duties, philosophy and social norms to understand the responsibilities of business. For example, groups like Blueprint for a Better Business are laying out principles under which firms would address their responsibilities.[1] While partly drawing on economics, the thinking of this group is grounded more broadly: "The provenance is derived from philosophy and faith teachings, supported by emerging work on economics and organizational theory and social and behavioral science." This particular group of like-minded companies adopt five principles to guide their organizations:

- Honest and fair with customers and suppliers
- A responsible and responsive employer

- A good citizen
- A guardian of future generations
- Has a purpose that delivers long-term sustainable performance

We now embrace messy notions that businesses may have responsibilities not only to shareholders but also to bondholders, customers, employees and future generations as well as the planet. By one count, there are over 130 different groups set up to discuss or advance new models of business that speak to new models of business, that is, new "Why" notions. The "Renewing Capitalism" project done by the Doughty Centre at Cranfield University has assembled a list of these "organizations, initiatives and time-limited projects" that address questions of the future of capitalism.[2] The "why" element of these initiatives is clear from the language they use, seeking to induce companies—and business in general—to be more responsible—or alternatively inclusive, moral, ethical, progressive, sustainable, creative or conscious. In different ways, these initiatives are pushing forward a discussion of how a new conception of business ("why") can and should affect the actions of businesses.

In some cases, governments are turning these responsibilities into requirements. For example, India has recently passed revisions to its Companies Act that mandate that large firms spend 2 per cent of their pre-tax profits on corporate social responsibility projects. Acceptable CSR projects are defined by these rules, which also dictate that a new Board Committee oversee the process.[3] While this is an extreme example, it is similar in spirit to requirements placed on US banks by Community Reinvestment Act, which under its service requirements encourage banks to contribute to the development of the communities in which they operate.[4] In the UK, the Department of Health has created a voluntary "Public Health Responsibility Deal" whereby firms pledge specific action to improve the public health of their customers and employees through changes in food and eating, drinking, physical activity and health at work.[5]

Appropriately, business education now spends far more attention on "why" or the rationale and responsibilities of business. We have replaced the simplicity of the 1980s with a far less comfortable set of discussions. Our leadership courses do not stop at understanding how to be merely effective but now ask whether a leader is responsible. The questioning about "why we drive"—and the relationship of how we conduct business to why we conduct business—is a healthy and overdue aspect of business education.

For example, at Oxford, this commitment to discuss "why" runs from our mission statement to our admissions practices and core curriculum, to our elective curriculum and through to our co-curricular and extra-curricular activities. If we are to meet our ambition, as a community to "tackle world scale problems," then we must admit students who share this goal. Our two most generous scholarship programs are reserved for applicants who have demonstrated a commitment to social entrepreneurship or to careers that seek to address social needs. Our required curriculum includes a course on "Responsible Business" where students are challenged to think about different theories of business, and then about the practical implications of these notions on business behavior. Another required course, "Global Rules of the Game," sensitizes students to the written rules and unwritten norms that determine acceptable behavior. Our elective curriculum has an innovative offering where business school professors team teach with counterparts from the humanities about leadership with an emphasis on responsibility. Our extensive co-curricular activities around social entrepreneurship, run out of our Skoll Centre, and our hosting of the Skoll World Forum give students role models of businesses and business people who do far more than maximize profits. I would hope that students find it difficult to graduate from our MBA program without spending considerable time thinking about "why business exists" and pondering practical implications for business.

Step 2: Moving from "how" to "where"

"Why" is an elegant question and thus fitting for thoughtful professors and students. But perhaps our driving metaphor might illustrate an important intermediate step that we missed. Are we racing on an oval track, or are we hauling a full load on the open road? On the track, only speed matters: the "destination" is clear and we don't need directions. But, if the proper image is of a fully loaded truck, hauling precious cargo, we need to ask: *Where* are we headed?

Apart from schools that orient themselves and their students to particular occupational destinations (financial service or consulting jobs) or geographic destinations, management education has been agnostic about the question of *where*. I would argue that this failure to directly address "where" has two unintended and perverse outcomes. First, by failing to be explicit about *where* we have been complicit with accounting standards and ranking schemes which preference some destinations or activities over others. Second, by failing to be explicit about *where*, we have missed major opportunities to restructure our programs to be consistent with the rich conversations about "why" and the responsibilities of business. I will briefly discuss the former and spend most of my time on the latter point.

Implicit "where biases"

As a finance professor, I taught my students many different types of models that turn various inputs into the value of securities: net present value models, real options models, binomial option pricing models and many more. In each case, we would go over how models are imperfect, but useful, representations of reality. They omit certain elements and overweight others. We should always be careful in how we use models, for a blind reliance on them can lead us to make massive mistakes, and my field of financial engineering is replete with examples.

For businesses, short-term earnings are a metric that can drive the evaluation of businesses. Much has been written about short-term thinking driven by pre-occupation with quarterly earnings. However, to link to the prior discussion, market forces tend to ask "How much?" rather than "How did the firm earn that money?" or "Was the behavior that produced those earnings consistent with the purpose of business?"

There are a substantial set of initiatives that seek to create metrics that capture these more nuanced questions. For example, the International Integrated Reporting Council seeks to advance the reporting of an extended set of metrics:

An integrated report is a concise communication about how an organization's strategy, governance, performance and prospects, in the context of its external environment, lead to the creation of value in the short, medium and long term.[6]

Returning to the driving metaphor, traditional accounting metrics capture "how fast" the vehicle is moving. However, if we embrace the "why" questions about business, we need a richer set of metrics. Integrated reporting helps outsiders to determine *on which road* the vehicle is driving, where location is measured not by reference to GPS coordinates but rather to a set of environmental, social and governance metrics.

While business schools may critique short-termism, they are subject to equally short-term measures. For business schools, rankings are the models that turn various inputs into a measure of the value of a program or a school. Related research demonstrates the elasticity of applications to rankings in college application decisions (Luca and Smith,

2013). Some ranking schemes of MBA programs are highly dependent on three-year salary and salary growth, accounting for 4 per cent or more of the ranking. Unduly focusing on this metric leads schools to preference applicants and graduates who are likely to go into the highest paid careers. I recently had dinner with one of my recent graduates who had been successful at a major investment bank before coming to Oxford but who planned to embark on a post-MBA stint working for a social enterprise. While I applaud her passion and fully support her, I would be naïve not to acknowledge that she will damage the ranking of our program by heading to the "wrong" destination in salary and rankings terms. No matter how fulfilling her career is—or how useful it is for the world—we are penalized for her choice.

While we rail against short-termism by corporations, we are complicit in accepting a system that uses short-term salary to judge our value. By ignoring "where" both businesses and business education suffers.

Curricular "where" indifference

The failure to address "where" damages our curricula. I believe that the core values of a program are reflected in its core curriculum. Essential items are not optional, but rather mandatory, elements of the student experience. In virtually every MBA program, Strategy is a core course, along with Marketing, Accounting, Operations and a short list of topics.[7] Strategy courses teach students which industries and firms will be the most profitable over a long term. Presumably, we do this because firms seek to maximize their profits and values, and hence we need to be able to help students learn where opportunities lie. Michael Porter's famous "five forces" analysis, introduced in 1980, is a textbook case study of a curricular element designed to help students identify opportunities (Porter, 1980). Since we were primarily focusing on maximizing shareholder value, we needed content that helped to identify where that value could be found.

Advancing the clock a few decades, we say that we now seek to drive businesses to not only to create private value but to do more. "More" might involve less damage to the planet, or it might involve addressing unmet consumer needs that will increase social welfare. Integrated reporting seeks to measure how much more firms are doing. In business education, our core curricula should help students understand where these broader opportunities lie.

In simple terms, we must do more than motivate students and businesses about contributing to the solutions of global problems—we must direct them to the areas where business can have the most impact on humanity. We must challenge them to understand "What are the fundamental forces that are changing society?" and "How might businesses play a role to address these mega-trends?" These are locational questions that turn the social "why" question into more practical "where" questions.

In my meetings with business executives, especially CEOs, I ask them to list the forces that will fundamentally alter society—and hence business—over the next quarter century. Reports like the World Economic Forum's Global Agenda Report (WEF) or the Oxford University report "Now for the Long Term" (Oxford) lay out these issues, although often for shorter time horizons.

Their responses are remarkably consistent. For example, it is patently obvious that falling birth rates and increasing longevity are altering the age composition of countries and the world. The impact on virtually every sector of business will be vast. The aging in the US, Western Europe, China and Japan will confront health care systems, financial markets, housing markets and consumer goods industries. Natural resource scarcity and climate change are acknowledged by most business executives as real long-term challenges to business and society. Even topics like inequality creep into the lists of CEOs, when they reflect on the long-run phenomena that will alter society and business.

Should MBAs and business executives think about these trends, which might help them answer the "where" questions? I asked a new class of Oxford MBAs at the start of their program whether they felt that this type of material was appropriate for their educations. Their unrehearsed answer was a resounding "Yes!" If experienced CEOs and new MBAs both see this sort of grounding as useful or essential, why has this type of orienting material—examining the intractable and pressing big issues been absent from our programs—and from board rooms?

Explaining "non-phenomena"—dogs that don't bark—is exceptionally difficult. I would offer a few explanations, however, for the current circumstance, at least in management education. Perhaps we don't teach this material because it doesn't get rewarded by employers or rankings or students—perhaps no one really wants the students to learn this. This explanation is inconsistent with my students' enthusiasm, however, not their satisfaction with having learned it. I would contend that we don't teach this material because we are captives of our organizations and their mindsets.

Our excellent professors teach "how": finance, operations, accounting, marketing and the like. Like driving instructors, teaching "where" is neither their jobs nor their specialties. There is nothing in the curricula of PhD programs, nor in the development of business school professors, that equips us to teach this sort of material. Teaching this type of "where" material would require schools to have experts in a variety of different areas. Schools simply lack experts in phenomena like demographics, natural resource scarcity, new technologies, geopolitical change, justice and other topics. Just as we manage what we measure, we teach what we know. We don't require our students to know this material—locating the where of social opportunity—because we don't have the capabilities to teach it. This problem is most pronounced at stand-alone, resource-constrained and small business schools, where these faculty constraints are more severe. They can also paradoxically be pronounced in some rich and very proud schools, which see themselves as distinct from their parent universities. There is a relatively simple solution to this absence of "where" in our curricula. We must introduce material into the core of business school curricula that is the social equivalent of Porter's five forces, for example, that locates the opportunities for social value creation. This material should help to identify areas of unmet consumer and societal needs over the business horizon of the students. While the immediate business horizon of an MBA may only be a year or two (for example, the term of their first post-MBA job), the horizon for our social landscape exercise should be over the business lifetime of the student, which is at a minimum 25 years. By definition, the areas of unmet consumer and social need are likely to be large and complex, and thus a reasonable goal would be to create an introduction to these subjects in order to encourage further deeper investigation. Given the forward-looking nature of this material, it is important not to present any of these topics with certainty, but rather in the spirit of scenarios.

At Oxford, we seek to be fully "embedded" in the University, so we naturally seek the help of our colleagues in other fields, such as demographers and environmental experts to address these issues. These experts have both the knowledge and the passion to communicate the essence of their fields to our students, and then we, as business schools, need to do the translation from technical expertise to business opportunity.

There are a variety of ways to introduce this material systematically into the education of students, whether in MBA or Executive classrooms. One could do this through lectures, case studies or newer methods of education. At Oxford, our colleagues worked with us to curate materials (new videos, Khan Academy style whiteboards, readings, infographics) on a digital platform to educate the entire community of faculty and students and alumni. Together, we designed a course that looks intensively at megatrends, starting with demographic change, big data and water scarcity.

For example, in our demographic unit, students learn the basic elements of demography. Populations grow as birthrates rise and life expectancy increases. The former factor is a function of medical progress and family choices. The latter is primarily a function of lifestyle choices and medical progress. Countries such as the US, the UK, Japan and China will experience substantial demographic deficits—large numbers of older citizens supported by a smaller fraction of working-age individuals. Countries in Africa and parts of South Asia will experience demographic dividends, with large numbers of young, potentially employable people.[8]

The needs—and hence business opportunities—in demographic deficit countries will increasingly focus on health care, elder care, retirement dissaving, changing patterns of real estate and transportation demand, and possible intergenerational strife. For example, over the next quarter century it would not be unrealistic to see the emergence of a large and successful elder-care sector in China, nor to see rapid advances in health care monitoring that allow older people to live in longer in their homes. The particular form of business opportunity might not be obvious, but the general category can be understood. Conversely, in the countries with demographic dividends, there are substantial business opportunities in education and skills training, and comparative advantages to firms that can profitably employ young labor forces.

To deliver this material to students, alumni and others, we have adopted a blended learning approach. The material that we *do know*, for example, frameworks, facts and underlying trends—that comes from experts in the field—is captured on a digital platform. For an example, the opening video on our demography module is a 10-minute film with high production values that lays out the core facts and issues about demography in an easily accessible manner.[9] The narrator of the video and most of those talking on camera are non-business school professors who are experts in demographic change.

In a flipped classroom, face-to-face time is devoted to intense interaction with students. Oxford has historically used tutorials to encourage critical thinking, by having the students produce work regularly and meet with their tutor in very small groups to sharpen their thinking. Using this approach, our students work in small groups with tutors to explore these types of issues. They produce essays, video interviews, presentations and fully developed projects that speak to the potential business implications of the phenomena we are investigating. These implications can be both broad and narrow. At the broad level, we ask them to consider what sectors of the economy will be most affected by demographic change or how the conceptions of privacy affect "big data" businesses. At the narrow level, we challenge them to think about specific products and services that can meet consumer and social needs over the next quarter century. It was the first time that many of them had taken the time to consider such issues: most 28-year-old business students don't think much about fertility rates, old people, immigrants or water scarcity. The results were insights into new forms of housing for the elderly, health care monitoring for senior citizens or ways to simplify immigration processes—valuable contributions for both businesses and policy-makers. Our recent graduates have already seen the power of this approach—a student who went to work for a global logistics firm in Asia wrote to say that the themes in the course gave him deep insights into the workings of his firm.

If strategy courses help students to locate the geographies of private value creation, then we need new types of courses to help students navigate the landscapes of long-term social value creation. Collectively, we are in our infancy in understanding this material. We run the risk of being mindless "futurists" who will inevitably get some, or all, of our predictions wrong. Rather, we need the expertise to understand the plausible futures that might create opportunities, and the humility to know that our understanding is imperfect.

Our Oxford course is called "Global Opportunities and Threats: Oxford"—GOTO. The name is more than an acronym—it symbolizes two things. First, MBAs should be the "goto" women and men in their organizations, the ones that others turn to for results. Second, we subtly were giving students sign posts about the places where opportunities lie, where businesses might not only make a great deal of money but also have the greatest impact.

Going beyond the classroom

I contend that this sort of broader grounding in the potential for social value creation is just as helpful for senior business leaders as well as business students.

To the extent that boards are called upon, as they are in India, to oversee that their firms address social needs, they need to understand the landscape of these needs. What are the most pressing social issues, what have been the existing solutions to these problems, how successful have these initiatives been and where is the best point for leveraging real improvement? In India, it is estimated that firms will collectively funnel $2 billion (US) into existing and new CSR activities each year. It seems obvious that the overseers of this stream of funding need some training to locate "where" it is best deployed.

Even in countries where responsibility is not mandated by law, business executives would benefit from systematically thinking about the location of social value opportunities. Of the 130 organizations and initiatives identified in the Cranfield research study cited earlier, some linked their activities to specific targets (for example, the UK's Public Health Responsibility Deal and public health), while others, such as Blueprint for a Better Business, are far less directive. Assuming that a firm decides to take on these responsibilities, it's not clear where it should direct its energies.

The payoff?

Moving from a broader concept of business (Why) to thinking about the location of social opportunity (Where) should strengthen the world through addressing world-scale problems. For example, slowing down the rate of the warming of the planet is now widely recognized as an urgent imperative, and with businesses focused on this goal, hopefully we will be more successful at staving off the potential disastrous consequences.

Some studies show that companies that adopt a more expansive definition of performance—a broader notion of why—and which target specific objectives, for example, the where of environmental sustainability, end up performing better on traditional metrics. For example, a recent Oxford University working paper reviewing over 190 sources finds a remarkable correlation between diligent sustainability business practices and economic performance. The first part of the report explores this thesis from a strategic management perspective, with remarkable results: 88 per cent of reviewed sources find that companies with robust sustainability practices demonstrate better operational performance, which ultimately translates into cashflows. The second part of the report builds on this, where 80 per cent of the reviewed studies demonstrate that prudent sustainability practices have a positive influence on investment performance (Clark et al., 2014).

Beyond the potential direct benefits of helping students and businesses locate sources of social value, there may be an ancillary unintended benefit. My predecessor, John Kay, who was the Dean of

Oxford's fledgling business school from 1996–1998, has written a book on a concept he calls "obliquity" (Kay, 2011). In brief, he argues that the most effective route to an outcome may be the indirect route. It's not those who seek to become the richest that actually do—rather the most successful in this dimension are often seeking to do something else, such as address a large unmet consumer need.

In business school terms, the history of my former school, Harvard Business School may demonstrate this phenomenon. Twice in its history, HBS deviated from its "track" and in both cases it emerged far stronger. In 1920, 12 years after its founding, it reached out to the Law School to adopt a new teaching method: case studies. Perversely, being a bit more like a law school made the school a better business school. A few decades later, during World War II, the school was closed while the campus was turned over to the military for officer training. Some of the elements of the modern MBA were created when the school stopped training business men. By increasing the stakes—from making profits to winning a war and savings lives—it became a stronger business school (Cruikshank, 1987).

In a similar way, perhaps obliquity will produce a better outcome for business schools and businesses that orient their communities to thinking about these bigger issues—while not losing sight of delivering job-ready graduates and profits. If business students and business leader can think about, and perhaps even master, the solutions to preposterously large problems, then the business challenges they face may seem less daunting.

The link to innovation

Taking "where" seriously will take us to complex, difficult and dangerous terrains. Avoiding environmental calamity or dealing with the imminent train wreck of demographic change is a challenging work. If these were simple problems, we would have already solved them. Almost by definition, by orienting part of our efforts towards these opportunities for social value creation, we will be forced to think in new and creative ways. Students and business leaders will almost inevitably try out new ideas and approaches in thinking about how to address these issues. I suspect that this new thinking must lead to innovation. In the financial innovation space, there is evidence of a financial innovation spiral, for example, failed innovations often provide the basis for subsequent innovations, some of which will succeed (Merton, 1992). Similarly, here there will be many false starts, which will in turn spur on others. Challenging students and business leaders will almost surely unleash new creativity.

There is a truism that you can't get to your destination unless you know where you are going. Increasingly, businesses are concluding that they exist to address a wide range of issues beyond simply earning profits and maximizing shareholder value for owners. Increasingly, business schools are adopting the same approach. If our "destination" is entrepreneurship, low-income countries and finding business solutions to the future's vexing problems, then focusing on "where" is the next topic on our agenda of improving business and business education.

Notes

1. See http://www.blueprintforbusiness.org/ (date accessed 12 January 2015).
2. See http://www.som.cranfield.ac.uk/som/p20852/Research/Research-Centres/ Doughty-Centre-Home/Research/Renewing-Capitalism (date accessed 17 January 2015).
3. For a description of the revisions to the Companies Act, see http://www.pwc. in/assets/pdfs/publications/2013/handbook-on-corporate-social-responsibility-in-india.pdf (date accessed 14 December 2014).
4. See https://www.fdic.gov/regulations/laws/rules/6500-2515.html#6500hcda 1977 (date accessed 10 December 2014) for the CRA rules.
5. For details, see https://responsibilitydeal.dh.gov.uk/ (date accessed 17 January 2015).
6. See http://www.theiirc.org/ (date accessed 17 January 2015).
7. See Datar et al. (2010) for a relatively recent review of the core courses in major business schools.
8. For brief summaries of these issues, and examples of the types of sourced materials we ask students to read, see Bloom (2011) and Harper (2013).
9. The video is available at http://www.sbs.ox.ac.uk/community/global-community/global-opportunities-and-threats-oxford-goto/goto-demo-graphic-change (date accessed 17 January 2015).

References

Bloom, D.E. (2011) "7 Billion and Counting," *Science*, 333(6042): 562–569.

Clark, G., Feiner, A. and Viehs, M. (2014) "From the Stockholder to the Stakeholder: How Sustainability Can Drive Financial Outperformance," Unpublished working paper, *Smith School of Enterprise and the Environment*, Available at SSRN http://papers.ssrn.com/sol3/papers.cfm?abstract_id=2508281 (Accessed 16 February 2015).

Cruikshank, J.L. (1987) "A Delicate Experiment the Harvard Business School 1908–1945" (Boston: HBS Press).

Datar, S.M., Garvin, D.A. and Cullen, P. (2010) "Rethinking the MBA: Business Education at a Crossroads" (Boston: Harvard Business Press).

Friedman, M. (1962) "Capitalism and Freedom" (Chicago: University of Chicago Press).

Harper, S. (2013) "The End of Youth," *The World Today*, 69(3).

Kay, J. (2011) "Obliquity: Why Our Goals Are Best Achieved Indirectly" (London: Penguin Press).

Luca, M. and Smith, J. (2013) "Salience in Quality Disclosure: Evidence from the U.S. News College Rankings," *Journal of Economics & Management Strategy*, 22(1): 58–77.

Merton, R.C. (1992) "Financial Innovation and Economic Performance," *Journal of Applied Corporate Finance*, 4(4): 12–22.

Porter, M.E. (1980) "Competitive Strategy" (New York: Free Press).

Smith, A. (1759) "Theory of Moral Sentiment" (London: Penguin Classics).

Smith, A. (1776) "The Wealth of Nations" (London: Penguin Classics).

12
Developing Entrepreneurship Capabilities in the MBA Program

Franz Heukamp

Introduction

Entrepreneurship has been widely recognized as an important source of economic growth (Caree and Thurik, 2002) and job creation (Wiens and Jackson, 2014). It has been considered "at the heart of national advantage" (Porter, 1990, p. 125). Successful entrepreneurs command a lot of public attention and are considered examples of great life achievements. Many of the economically most successful individuals are entrepreneurs and important contributions to society in terms of new products and services that can be enjoyed, as well as purely social contributions are due to the "entrepreneurial leadership" of entrepreneurs (Kuratko, 2007). Entrepreneurs are also more satisfied with their lives than the average individual (Schneck, 2014). All things together, fostering entrepreneurship is clearly an important and worthwhile objective.

An MBA program is a leadership development program, typically in a university setting, which aims at enhancing the knowledge and capabilities of individuals in management and at contributing to the positive and sustainable development of society. In this chapter we study how an MBA program can contribute to grow entrepreneurship capabilities.

What is an entrepreneur? Can entrepreneurship be taught?

According to Drucker, an entrepreneur "always searches for change, responds to it, and exploits it as an opportunity," and "entrepreneurship, then, is behavior rather than personality trait. And its foundation lies in concept and theory rather than in intuition" (Drucker, 1985). Also, according to Kuratko, at the heart of entrepreneurial success is "entrepreneurial leadership" (Kuratko, 2007). This suggests that education, of some sort, in order to change behavior and improve outcomes and to strengthen leadership capacities, is likely to affect positively the capacity of an entrepreneur. Hence, an MBA program can make a contribution as developing leadership capabilities is at the heart of its objectives.

However, Zhao et al. (2010) showed in a meta analysis of several personality studies that conscientiousness, openness to experience, emotional stability, extraversion and risk propensity are all positively related to the intentions of individuals to become entrepreneurs. This suggests that despite Drucker's claim above, there are at least some personality traits that make an entrepreneurial career more likely. In fact, further research by Leutner et al. (2014) showed that an "entrepreneurial personality" can be established as a set of relatively narrow personality traits that *in part* predict entrepreneurial success. Thus, not everything about successful entrepreneurship can be trained; some people will be more inclined and prepared by personality for a career in entrepreneurship. Still, in line with the cited studies, an important part of entrepreneurial outcome is the result of actions and behaviors that can potentially be improved through specific leadership programs.

The popular image of an entrepreneur

Mainstream media often transmit an image of an entrepreneur as a tech "geek" who dropped out of college to start a company that turned out to be very successful. Examples of this are Bill Gates and Mark Zuckerberg, among others. The implicit message is that in successful entrepreneurship there is no room for people who start a company after obtaining a college degree or a master's degree or at a later stage in life, for that matter.

In reality, most entrepreneurs have earned at least a college degree and many times they start as entrepreneurs based on an insight that they had while working for a company as an employee. "Founders are young but seldom fresh out of school," as Goodwin (2015) puts it. Frick (2014) gives a similar insight and shows that the average age of entrepreneurs at founding in a sample of Silicon Valley firms (of the surviving firms) was 31. There is also a growing phenomenon of "Senior Entrepreneurship," that is, senior professionals who start their own venture (Kreamer and Guillies, 2015).

Many times, having deep knowledge about an industry or a technology and business processes is critical to start a new and successful venture. Acquiring this knowledge requires time, relevant experiences and is likely to be enhanced by an adequate training process. For example, an important part of participants in Executive MBA programs—people who have 10 or more years of professional experience—report that they are looking for a general business expertise in the MBA program in order to be ready to launch their own company.

Is an MBA a good preparation for starting entrepreneurial ventures?

Often we have been asked whether doing an MBA is a good preparation for starting one's own business. Sometimes the same question is asked in an even more dichotomized way: "Do I need to have an MBA to start my own company?" Obviously, the answer to the latter question is no. There are many examples of successful entrepreneurs who do not have an MBA education. Also, one would not expect to have one-size-fits-all recipes for entrepreneurship preparation.

Greer (2010) explains in a reflection on his own entrepreneurship experience that he started his venture without an MBA but that many of the problems that he ran into could have been avoided if he had had a more thorough business education, like the one you get in an MBA program. Many common issues in leading an organization such as leading people, managing projects, negotiating with partners and clients, etc., are critical to the success of a business, but they are not necessarily part of the skill set of the entrepreneur as she sets out to put her idea into practice.

Jeroen Kemperman, an IESE MBA alumnus and founder of Treeveo, also mentions the lack of business knowledge and skills as a reason to study for an MBA as a preparation to launch his own business (Head to Head, 2015). Moreover, most MBA programs teach in dedicated courses how to set up a business plan, how to look for financial resources, or what legal considerations to keep in mind on.

In summary, without claiming to be the only way to successful entrepreneurship, an MBA program can be helpful for the following reasons:

- It teaches business knowledge and business functions and skills that are useful to lead a business organization.
- It develops personal leadership abilities.
- It equips the entrepreneur with specific knowledge and capabilities about the entrepreneurship process, for example, with respect to funding techniques, business plans, negotiations, and so on.

- An MBA provides a rich environment for the first prototype development.
- Many MBA programs provide an ecosystem of advice, access to financing options, feedback on the venture, etc.
- It provides a network of classmates with experiences in many different sectors and business functions.

How successful are MBA programs at developing entrepreneurs?

Before discussing the distinct elements of education and support that MBA programs can provide for future and current entrepreneurs, we may want to look at the available data on how many MBA graduates start their own businesses and how they fare with it.

The Financial Times surveyed in 2014 the 2011 graduates of full-time and Executive MBA programs and reported that "just under a third of professionals who graduated in 2011 ... started businesses themselves or are in partnership with others." For full-time MBA graduates of 2011, this number stands at 22 per cent (Moules, 2014). These percentages show that entrepreneurship careers are popular among MBAs. The lower percentage for full-time program graduates may be due to the significantly lower age upon graduation, compared to Executive MBA programs. If we extend the picture to 10 years after graduation, we see, for example, that 50 per cent of the alumni of Dartmouth's Tuck school become entrepreneurs,[1] and for IESE Business School's MBA this number stands at 35 per cent.[2] Other top MBA schools have similar percentages and confirm the importance of entrepreneurship in the careers of MBA graduates.

The number of MBA graduates who start their own business immediately upon graduation used to be relatively small but has been growing over the past years. Rampell (2014) reports that 7.4 per cent of Wharton's class of 2013 launched their own venture, up from 1.6 per cent in 2007, and that 20 per cent of Stanford's class of 2013 was starting their own business, a historical record. Other schools, such as the Haas School of Business at Berkeley, also had around 10 per cent of the class of 2013 embark on an entrepreneurial project, and those rates "appear to be by choice" (Rampell, 2014) and not because of lack of other opportunities.

In the same direction, Moules (2015) states that "while becoming an entrepreneur is still a minority pursuit among business school students, the FT's analysis could also be read as evidence that an MBA education will help a wannabe entrepreneur's chances of start-up success." In fact, the survival rate of businesses started out of the MBA is above the general start-up survival rate. Eighty-four per cent of the companies launched by MBA graduates of the class of 2011 that were surveyed by the FT were still in business three years later (Moules, 2015).

Anecdotal evidence (Rampell, 2014) suggests that launching ones' own venture and maybe having to give up after some time has become much less of a stigma in one's career. Quite on the contrary, many corporations seem to like candidates who have shown entrepreneurial drive and who by failing to succeed in their start-up have made very valuable experiences that will serve them in other career paths.

How can MBA programs develop entrepreneurial capabilities?

We suggest dividing the entrepreneurial process of starting a new venture into five phases[3]:

1. Identification, exploration and evaluation of the opportunity
2. Development of a business plan
3. Determination and acquisition of required resources
4. Managing the new venture
5. Making the firm sustainable: growth strategies

For each of the five phases, we will discuss how an MBA program can contribute in the development of the specific capabilities associated with them.

Identification, exploration and evaluation of the opportunity

New opportunities are identified in many different ways by entrepreneurs and require attention from the entrepreneur to an unmet need or some other kind of opportunity. This can be part of a systematic search process or the result of a more spontaneous discovery or simply the result of many years of experience working in a business and noting recurring problems that could provide a business opportunity.

The identification and evaluation of new business opportunities can be taught by providing a framework of evaluation and reflection and discussion time based on case studies of entrepreneurs and how they went about it. This process also implies questions about the acting person and whether she sees herself as an entrepreneur. This part of the training process is about "Adopting an Entrepreneurial Mindset" and about developing an entrepreneurial spirit, a skill that is of value to managers and entrepreneurs alike.

An MBA program also helps developing the capacity to understand new opportunities by equipping the potential entrepreneur with learning about markets, customers, strategy and operations. Discussion about real business problems fosters appreciation about impact of changes in any of the basic variables of a business model, as, for example, through changes in technology or regulation, etc.

Development of a business plan

In the second phase, the new business needs to be "designed," and thus the original idea translated into a functioning business model and expressed in a clear and coherent business plan. In this phase, quality work is very important as a good idea can be poorly applied and fail if the business model is not well thought through. "A good business model remains essential to every successful organization, whether it's a new venture or an established player" (Magretta, 2002). The two key elements for a good business model are the "narrative test" which asks the question whether the story the model tells makes sense and the "numbers test" which asks the question whether the economics of the story are viable (Magretta, 2002).

The capacity to find good business models and express them well in a business plan can be developed by asking students to prepare business models in different contexts and giving feedback on how they do it. This process is complemented with learning that is stimulated by readings and reflections on the importance of business models and its specific contents and on how to develop business plans for which checklists have been elaborated (Sahlman, 1997). In addition, the general business savvy that MBA students acquire by studying successful and not successful businesses in the context of many courses and real cases provide a good background against which they can elaborate and evaluate new business models. This is a point where the contribution of an MBA program to entrepreneurship capabilities is very strong: MBA students acquire a broad set of business concepts in the areas of marketing, operations, strategy, finance, and so on, which provide a background for the evaluation of new business models.

As mentioned above, this "accelerated experience" that MBA participants acquire by studying many cases of business decisions is particularly relevant in Executive MBA programs where learning about existing businesses and their business models helps the participants to see more clearly the strengths of their own incipient business ideas.

Another way of stimulating learning about business plan development is business plan competitions. Many MBA students participate in business plan competitions that involve industry experts and sometime considerable financial prizes.[4]

Determination and acquisition of the required resources

The new venture will need people and resources—technological resources, finance, and so on—that need to be attracted. In this phase the entrepreneur will need to be both personally convincing and savvy in the specific financing possibilities that exist and how they can be acquired and put to work.

The combination of the capacity to convince and negotiate with the knowledge about specific financing processes and procedures is suitable for training in an MBA program.

Self-management and the corresponding interpersonal skills and emotional intelligence are trained in good MBA programs—along with negotiation skills. In addition, the specifics of venture capital are taught in MBA programs.

A very effective way of training future entrepreneurs in MBA programs for dealings with the resource question of new businesses is the *Venture Capital Investment Competition* (VCIC).[5] VCIC is a student competition that was started in 1998 at the University of Northern Carolina and today involves more than 70 business schools. Students work in small teams as venture capitalists, evaluating real business plans and elaborating term sheets. The students are then evaluated in their performance by actual venture capitalists. The process is organized as a competition, first at the school level, then at a regional level and with a final worldwide competition.

Some of the learning about required resources for the venture takes place in business angels and venture capital forums that are linked to MBA programs. This is where the network of industry specialists, many times alumni of a program and faculty members who can give advice, is helpful. Some specific example will be discussed below.

Managing the new venture

Starting to manage a new venture requires practical management skills, with an emphasis on managing a small company, many times with high growth rates. Managing a small company often involves dealing with peculiar difficulties such as almost endemic shortages of resources, the danger of short termism and potential conflicts between personal goals and the needs of the new business.

An MBA program is again well positioned to provide the tools to manage the incipient and growing business and to monitor the effect of the growth on the different critical parts of the new venture.

In addition, an MBA program provides the general management and leadership education that is needed to successfully lead any business. MBA programs emphasize personal leadership skills related to leading people, the capacity to work in teams and to lead teams. Moreover, questions of governance, organizational structures and policies are addressed and their importance for the mid and long term identified.

Making the firm sustainable: Growth strategies

After a successful launch and starting to manage the new venture, sustainability and growth become critical. The fact that many companies "switch" from the founder to a different manager in the growth phase of a new company suggests that there are specific capabilities required. Managing growth and making the firm sustainable involves strategic thinking, adaptability to circumstances and making short- and long term-needs compatible. Many MBA programs have courses in their entrepreneurship offering that are centered on growing new ventures. We present some examples in the following sections.

Core entrepreneurship education

Before discussing some specific examples of entrepreneurship offerings in MBA programs and how they can help build the corresponding capabilities, we should discuss very briefly how much of an entrepreneurship education any MBA graduate should receive. So far in this paper, we have focused on the ways in which an MBA education can contribute to prepare for entrepreneurial activities. However, we argue that every MBA graduate should learn some aspects about entrepreneurship, no matter what his or her career plans are.

Looking at the elements of typical entrepreneurship processes, as we have just done above, we can distinguish specific tasks and procedures in the creation and growth of a venture. In order to master these tasks and procedures, an entrepreneur will require some specific knowledge and skills that can be transmitted in a training process.

In addition, many people have argued that there is general leadership capacity associated with entrepreneurship but not only with the creation of a new venture or specific step in the process of starting of developing a new project. This general leadership capacity is rather associated with taking forward new initiatives, innovative projects and critical processes, sometimes in very well-established and, maybe even

big, organizations. This general capability of managerial action is sometimes called "entrepreneurial spirit" (Smith, 2013) or "entrepreneurial
mindset"[6] or "entrepreneurial leadership" (Kuratko, 2007).
Several MBA programs have acknowledged the need for basic entrepreneurship education and the need to foster entrepreneurial leadership
for all MBAs by requiring some coursework in the area, usually in the
first year of the MBA program. Examples of this are Babson College,
Harvard Business School and IESE Business School, among others. (see
Exhibit 12.1)

Exhibit 12.1 Examples of required entrepreneurship courses in MBA programs

Babson College	Entrepreneurship & Opportunity

This course provides an overview of the entrepreneurship method that will
enable you to create, identify, assess, shape and act on opportunities in a variety
of contexts and organizations. The method, called Entrepreneurial Thought
and Action® (ET&A), is teachable and learnable, but is not predictable. This is
a results-oriented course that emphasizes early action in order to test and refine
new venture concepts.

Harvard Business School	The Entrepreneurial Manager (TEM)

This course addresses the issues faced by managers who wish to turn opportunity
into viable organizations that create value, and empowers students to develop
their own approaches, guidelines and skills for being entrepreneurial managers.
The course teaches students how to:

- Identify potentially valuable opportunities.
- Obtain the resources necessary to pursue an opportunity and to create an
  entrepreneurial organization.
- Manage the entrepreneurial organization once it has been established.
- Grow the business into a sustainable enterprise.

Create and harvest value for the organization's stakeholders.

IESE Business School	Fundamentals of Entrepreneurial Management

"Fundamentals of Entrepreneurial Management" is an integrative capstone
course in entrepreneurship. It is based on the insight that in today's business
environment entrepreneurial management skills are key for general managers
and entrepreneurs alike. The course introduces cutting-edge materials—tools,
frameworks and perspectives—that allow you to acquire the basics of entrepreneurial management. At the same time, the course encourages you to adopt a
holistic perspective on building new businesses, and it asks you to synthesize and
apply what you have learned in previous first year MBA courses.

(*continued*)

Exhibit 12.1   Continued

IESE Business School	Fundamentals of Entrepreneurial Management

Specifically, the course helps you to:

- Turn an idea into a revenue-generating business, in various contexts: for example, in a corporate setting, family business, or start up.
- Acquire guidance and management tools for your future careers as business leaders.

Address your potential concerns and doubts about whether you "have what it takes" to be an entrepreneur.

Source: Babson, Harvard Business School and IESE Business School.

Research on the effectiveness of entrepreneurship training shows very encouraging results: Glaub et al. (2014) report, as part of their study, an increase in entrepreneurial success after a short training program.

Some cases of MBA programs' entrepreneurship offerings

MBA programs have introduced entrepreneurship offerings in the past decades, and in this section we briefly describe some of the different offerings that leading schools currently make (see Exhibit 12.2).

At the MIT Sloan School of Management,[7] MBA students do not have a required course on entrepreneurship. Students can choose an Entrepreneurship and Innovation (E&I) Track which offers a special certificate if certain course requirements are met, plus the participation in a business plan competition. Courses that are offered include[8]

- The Business of Software and Digital Platforms
- Design and Marketing New Products
- Dilemmas in Founding New Ventures
- Disruptive Technologies: Predator or Prey
- Early Stage Capital
- Energy Ventures
- Entrepreneurial Strategy
- New Enterprises
- Product Design and Development
- Social Innovation and Entrepreneurship

- Strategic Decision Making in the Life Sciences
- Technology Sales and Sales Management

At the Stanford Graduate School of Business, students can choose from a large offering of courses in entrepreneurship-related topics that are offered by different schools of Stanford University. The courses are divided in the following areas[9]:

- Experiential Courses
- Startup Foundations
- Marketing and Sales
- Building and Leading a Team
- Finance and Funding
- Product Design and Manufacturing
- Computing
- Legal Frameworks
- Search Funds

At IESE Business School, besides the required course in entrepreneurship in the MBA Program mentioned above, many optional courses are offered, including the following[10]:

- Entrepreneurship Summer Program: Students who are considering starting their own venture can take advantage of the summer term between the first and second year of the program and spend time validating their business idea, search and refine a business model and start building a prototype. The summer program takes place under the guidance of entrepreneurs and faculty and offers a fertile ground for exploration and a head start for students' projects. Throughout the second year, students can continue to work on their venture and refine their project, taking advantage of the following courses in this list.
- Entrepreneurship: Creating and Implementing Ventures 1&2
  This course focuses on the start of the entrepreneurial process: Finding a business idea, developing a business model and starting the fund-raising process. A student can take the two courses in a row and has ample time to develop her business model and prototype throughout the MBA program.
- Leading Growth: Strategies and Challenges
  The course deals with "growth" as an objective for both established firms and new ventures. The different settings in a new firm with its typical challenges of funding, finding the right people and resources

and in an established firm that needs to strengthen its innovation capacity are discussed.

- Working for a Start-Up
  Students are matched with a startup and gain first-hand experience about working in a new business.
- Business Model Innovation and Entrepreneurial Design
  Introduces a framework to analyze business models and discusses how to choose the business model appropriately for a new enterprise.
- Creativity for Managers
  Theoretical and practical approach at being more creative through cases studies, discussions with leading business people and creativity exercises.
- Financing Entrepreneurial Opportunities 1-2-3
  A sequence of courses around the financing of new ventures. Students are taught how to assess an investment opportunity, how to value an unquoted company, how deals are structured and what the exit strategies of investors are. The themes are discussed from the perspectives of the entrepreneur and the investor.
- Search Funds—Managing Creativity
  A course around "entrepreneurial acquisitions," that is, the search for an opportunity to invest in and lead a small to midsize company and thus become an entrepreneur. The specific elements of this search process are discussed, such as finding the right industry and company, evaluating investment opportunities, structuring the investment, negotiations, transitioning into the leadership roles, etc.

How else can MBA programs foster entrepreneurship? Offerings surrounding MBA programs

As an immediate consequence of the interest MBA programs and business schools at large have shown in entrepreneurship, many people with that same interest are brought together. The resulting network and environment, which is sometimes referred to as an "ecosystem," is one of the additional strengths of MBA programs with respect to fostering entrepreneurship.

The ecosystem typically includes,[11] besides academic coursework, access to mentors, the organization of business plan competitions, student clubs with networking events and exposure and interaction with business angels and venture capitalist.

For example, at the Stanford Graduate School of Business, many different entrepreneurship activities are regrouped in the Center for Entrepreneurial Studies.

At IESE Business School, the "Entrepreneurship and Innovation Center" (EIC) fosters research in the area of entrepreneurship and helps establish best practices. In addition there is a venture capital fund (FINAVES[12]) and a Business Angel Network, working with MBA students and alumni on their business plans offering mentorship, investors relationship and potential funding.

FINAVES was founded in the year 2000 and offers an important link between the different phases of startup growth and the corresponding financing needs and a link between the business school community and alumni. FINAVES takes a temporary stake in companies in a startup phase and which IESE alumni lead. These stakes are minority stakes between 10 per cent and 30 per cent and with a time horizon of the fund of 10 years. Since 2000, 40 companies were created.

Conclusions

Entrepreneurship and entrepreneurial activities are important for the economic development of society and offer a tremendous potential for personal growth and life satisfaction as an entrepreneur.

Business schools and specifically MBA programs can contribute to this important task for society by offering education in the capabilities associated with entrepreneurship. This includes specific knowledge about elements of the entrepreneurship process but also general leadership abilities that are crucial for the successful entrepreneur.

An MBA is not the only way to prepare for an entrepreneurial venture, but it has a good track record in "producing" entrepreneurs and providing many possibilities.

A crucial element in the contribution of MBA programs to entrepreneurship also lies in the hub formation for people who are interested in different elements of the entrepreneurship process.

Exhibit 12.2 Examples of elective entrepreneurship courses in MBA programs

---

INSEAD

- Building Businesses in China (Field Trip)
- Building Businesses in India (Field Trip)
- Building Businesses in Silicon Valley (Field Trip)

(continued)

216

Exhibit 12.2   Continued

INSEAD

- Emerging multinationals from Brazil (elective followed by field trip)
- Entrepreneurship in Action
- Corporate Entrepreneurship
- Effective Fundraising for entrepreneurs
- Entrepreneurial field studies
- Entrepreneurial strategies in emerging markets
- Leveraged buy-outs
- Managing Corporate Turnarounds
- New Business Ventures
- Technology Venturing Practicum
- Realizing Entrepreneurial Potential
- Your First Hundred Days
- Social Entrepreneurship & Innovation
- Business Planning Workshop
- Private Equity

MIT SLOAN

- The Business of Software and Digital Platforms
- Design and Marketing New Products
- Dilemmas in Founding New Ventures
- Disruptive Technologies: Predator or Prey
- Early Stage Capital
- Energy Ventures
- Entrepreneurial Strategy
- New Enterprises
- Product Design and Development
- Social Innovation and Entrepreneurship
- Strategic Decision Making in the Life Sciences
- Technology Sales and Sales Management

STANFORD GSB

(This list is a selection limited to the area of "Startup Foundations" and the GSB)

- Creating High Potential Ventures in Developing Economies
- The New Business Ideas Workshop
- Entrepreneurship from the Perspective of Women
- Disruptive Innovation
- Problem-Solving and Creativity
- From Launch to Liquidity
- Starting and Growing a Social Venture
- Formation of New Ventures
- Aligning Startups with their Market
- Strategic Management of Nonprofit Organizations and Social Ventures

(continued)

Exhibit 12.2   Continued

STANFORD GSB

- Entrepreneurial Acquisition
- Ensuring Social Innovation Scales: Across Borders, Across Sectors, and Across "the Valley of Death"
- Small Business Strategy
- Entrepreneurial Opportunities in Developing Economies
- New Business Models in Emerging Markets

Source: INSEAD, MIT Sloan and Stanford GBS.

Notes

1. See http://www.topmba.com/blog/entrepreneurship-mba-stats-mba-facts (date accessed 18 February 2015).
2. IESE Alumni Magazine (2015), 136:41.
3. Similar proposals have been made, for example, by Hisrich et al. (2005).
4. A well-known example is the MIT $100k business plan competition. See http://mit100k.org (date accessed February 2015).
5. See http://www.vcic.org (date accessed February 2015).
6. Defined in the FT Lexicon as: "Entrepreneurial mindset refers to a specific state of mind which orientates human conduct towards entrepreneurial activities and outcomes. Individuals with entrepreneurial mindsets are often drawn to opportunities, innovation and new value creation. Characteristics include the ability to take calculated risks and accept the realities of change and uncertainty." See http://lexicon.ft.com/Term?term=entrepreneurial_mindset (date accessed February 2015).
7. See http://mitsloan.mit.edu. (date accessed February 2015).
8. From http://entrepreneurship.mit.edu/course (date accessed February 2015).
9. See http://www.gsb.stanford.edu/ces/entrepreneurial-courses (date accessed February 2015).
10. See http://www.iese.edu/en/mba/program-structure/ (date accessed February 2015).
11. See http://mitsloan.mit.edu/mba/mit-sloan-community/entrepreneurial-ecosystem/ (date accessed February 2015).
12. See http://www.iese.edu/en/companies-institutions/supporting-startups/finaves/ (date accessed February 2015).

References

Babson (2015) "Babson MBA One Year Curriculum" Available at: http://www.babson.edu/program/graduate/Documents/gradadmissions/babson-mba-one-year-program-curriculum.pdf (date accessed 20 December 2014).

Caree, M.A. and Thurik, A.R. (2002) "The Impact of Entrepreneurship on Economic Growth," *International Handbook of Entrepreneurship Research*, edited by Acs, Z. and Audretsch, D., (Norwell: Kluwer Academic Publishers), pp. 437–471.

Drucker, P. (1985) "Innovation and Entrepreneurship" (New York: Harper and Row).

Frick, W. (2014) "How Old Are Silicon Valley's Top Founders? Here's the Data" *Harvard Business Review* Available at: https://hbr.org/2014/04/how-old-are-silicon-valleys-top-founders-heres-the-data. (date accessed 20 December 2014).

Glaub, M.E., Frese, M., Fischer, S. and Hoppe, M. (2014) "Increasing Personal Initiative in Small Business Managers or Owners Leads to Entrepreneurial Success: A Theory-Based Controlled Randomized Field Intervention for Evidence-Based Management." *Academy of Management Learning & Education*, 13(3): 354–379.

Goodwin, M. (2015) "The Myth of the Tech Whiz Who Quits College to Start a Company" *Harvard Business Review* Available at: https://hbr.org/2015/01/the-myth-of-the-tech-whiz-who-quits-college-to-start-a-company. (date accessed 20 December 2014).

Greer, S. (2010). "Does an Entrepreneur Need an MBA?" *Harvard Business Review* Available at: https://hbr.org/2010/11/does-an-enterpreneur-need-an-m. (date accessed 20 December 2014).

Harvard Business School (2014) "Required Curriculum" Available at: http://www.hbs.edu/mba/academic-experience/curriculum/Pages/required-curriculum.aspx (date accessed 20 December 2014).

Head to Head (2015) "Head to Head: Do Entrepreneurs need an MBA?" *Financial Times* Available at: http://www.ft.com/intl/cms/s/2/01b04504-b2ee-11e4-b0d2-00144feab7de.html#axzz3Wj8ejAfe (date accessed 16 February 2015).

Hisrich, R.D., Peters, M.P. and Shepherd, D.A. (2005) "Entrepreneurship" (New York: McGraw-Hill Irwin).

IESE Business School (2014) "MBA Program Structure" Available at: http://www.iese.edu/en/mba/program-structure/ (date accessed 16 February 2015).

INSEAD (2014) "MBA Elective Courses" Available at: http://mba.insead.edu/the-insead-mba/documents/INSEAD_MBA_ElectiveCourses.pdf (date accessed 16 February 2015).

Kreamer, J. and Guillies, W. (2015) "Mapping Our Future: The Exciting Road Ahead" *Kauffman Thoughtbook*.

Kuratko, D. (2007) "Entrepreneurial Leadership in the 21st Century." *Journal of Leadership and Organizational Studies*, 13(4): 1–13.

Leutner, F., Ahmetoglu, G., Akhtar, R. and Chamorro-Premuzic, T. (2014) "The Relationship Between the Entrepreneurial Personality and the Big Five Personality Traits" *Personality and Individual Differences*, 63: 58–63.

Magretta, J. (2002) "Why Business Models Matter." *Harvard Business Review*, 80(5): 86–92.

MIT Sloan (2014) "MIT Entrepreneurship" Available at: http://entrepreneurship.mit.edu/course (date accessed 15 November 2014).

Moules, J. (2014) "Starting a Business" *Financial Times* Available at: http://www.ft.com/intl/cms/s/2/4c21ada2-634e-11e4-8a63-00144feabdc0.html#axzz3Wj8ejAfe (date accessed 15 November 2014).

Moules, J. (2015) "Start-up Costs for MBA Graduates Pay Off" *Financial Times* Available at: http://www.ft.com/intl/cms/s/2/3d3f48f8-95cb-11e4-be7d-00144feabdc0.html#axzz3Wj8ejAfe (date accessed 15 February 2015).

Porter, M.E. (1990) "The Competitive Advantage of Nations" (New York: Free Press).

Rampell, C. (2014) "Ready, Willing and Able to Take a Risk" *Washington Post* Available at: http://www.washingtonpost.com/opinions/catherine-rampell-ready-willing-and-able-to-take-a-risk/2014/06/09/521a2334-f011-11e3-bf76-447a5df6411f_print.html (date accessed 15 February 2015).

Sahlman, W.A. (1997) "How To Write A Great Business Plan." *Harvard Business Review, July-August:* 98–108.

Schneck, S. (2014) "Why the Self-employed are Happier: Evidence from 25 European Countries." *Journal of Business Research,* 67: 1043–1048.

Smith, C. (2013) "Don't Hire Entrepreneurs; Hire Entrepreneurial Spirit" *Harvard Business Review* Available at: https://hbr.org/2013/02/dont-hire-entrepreneurs-hire-e (date accessed 15 February 2015).

Stanford GSB (2014) "Entrepreneurial Courses" Available at: http://www.gsb.stanford.edu/ces/entrepreneurial-courses (date accessed 15 February 2015).

Wiens, J. and Jackson, C. (2014) "The Importance of Young Firms for Economic Growth" *Entrepreneurship Policy Digest,* Kansas City, Missouri: Kauffman Foundation.

Zhao, H., Seibert, S.E. and Lumpkin, G.T. (2010) "The Relationship of Personality to Entrepreneurial Intentions and Performance: A Meta-Analytical Review" *Journal of Management,* 36: 381–404.

Index

Printed and bound by CPI Group (UK) Ltd, Croydon, CR0 4YY